AF581039

PRAISE FOR
THE CALIFORNIA PIZZA KITCHEN STORY

"There's something profoundly human about leaping into the unknown, trusting your instincts when reason says to stay put. Rick Rosenfield's memoir captures that spirit. Leaving the familiar is never easy, but as Rick shows, the biggest successes often begin with the courage to chase an idea that simply feels right. This isn't just a story about pizza—it's about purpose, persistence, and the beauty of taking risks that can change everything."

—**THOMAS KELLER**, THE FRENCH LAUNDRY

"From the Supreme Court and mob trials to creating one of America's most iconic restaurant brands, this is storytelling at its best."

—**JACK CARR**, #1 *NEW YORK TIMES* BESTSELLING AUTHOR OF *THE TERMINAL LIST*

the california PIZZA KITCHEN story

HOW TWO FEDERAL PROSECUTORS CHANGED THE WAY AMERICA EATS PIZZA

RICK ROSENFIELD
CO-FOUNDER

www.amplifypublishinggroup.com

The California Pizza Kitchen Story: How Two Federal Prosecutors Changed the Way America Eats Pizza

The author has tried to recreate events, locales, and conversations from his memory of them. In order to maintain their anonymity in some instances, the author has changed the names of individuals and places, and may have changed some identifying characteristics and details such as physical properties, occupations, and places of residence.

For more information, please contact:
Amplify Publishing, an imprint of Amplify Publishing Group
620 Herndon Parkway, Suite 100
Herndon, VA 20170
info@amplifypublishing.com

Library of Congress Control Number: 2026907320

CPSIA Code: PRV0426A

ISBN-13: 979-8-90026-232-1

Printed in the United States

For Esther—
who had the faith to mortgage our home,
the grace to welcome our first guests,
and the love to carry us through it all

FOREWORD

I'VE SPENT MOST OF MY LIFE AROUND MEN WHO DO NOT flinch when the stakes are highest. In the SEAL Teams, that kind of calm in the storm was not optional—it was the difference between success and failure, life and death. Which is probably why, from the first time I sat down with Rick Rosenfield, I sensed that same fortitude in him.

Rick's first battlefield wasn't a foreign shore—it was a courtroom, where he stood toe-to-toe with mob bosses and aircraft hijackers. Later, he carried that same steel into the business world, where, with the odds stacked against him, he focused on what most considered a wild idea, a pipe dream. Though already at the top of the legal profession, instead of settling for comfort, Rick chose reinvention.

The story you are about to read is not just about pizza—though Rick and his partner, Larry Flax, did nothing less than change how America eats it. It's about vision, risk, loyalty, and the refusal to compromise values, even when the "right call" looked like certain failure. It's about the ROCK culture they built at California Pizza Kitchen, one that made ordinary employees into extraordinary teammates.

As you'll see in the pages that follow, Rick's journey is both improbable and inevitable—improbable that two federal prosecutors would become restaurateurs and inevitable because men who live with courage and conviction always seem to find new mountains to climb.

I have been honored to hunt beside Rick, to share stories of family and country over a fire, and to call him a brother. I know firsthand the values in this book are not nostalgia—they are lessons for us all.

The California Pizza Kitchen Story is more than a memoir. It's a blueprint for life, for the American dream, for defying the odds, for disruption, for revolutionizing an industry, for standing firm when compromise would be easier, and for finding purpose in the journey.

—JACK CARR

Former Navy SEAL sniper
#1 *New York Times* bestselling author

INTRODUCTION

PEOPLE THOUGHT WE'D LOST OUR MINDS WHEN LARRY Flax and I, two former federal prosecutors with zero restaurant experience, walked away from thriving legal careers to gamble on pizza. Who knew that leap of faith would lead to a successful international franchise called California Pizza Kitchen (CPK), with 265 restaurants worldwide and a frozen pizza line sold across more than twenty thousand retail locations?

By moving from the courtroom to the kitchen, we discovered valuable lessons that shaped not only our business but our lives. From the outside it might have looked easy. It wasn't.

Ours is a story of vision, trust, passion, friendship, and a rare partnership built on a unique *synergy*, the belief that one plus one can equal three. For nearly forty years, Larry and I shared a law practice, a business, and a deep friendship. We shared plenty of vigorous debates (trial lawyers can't help themselves), but we never let any disagreement turn into a grudge. Once a decision was made, we moved forward together.

Reporters often noted how we stepped on each other's lines and finished each other's sentences.

But it wasn't competition; it was flow. There was no jealousy, no "I told you so." Just trust. And we knew early on that trust had to extend beyond us. We needed people who not only worked with us but liked us.

I've always thought that Daddy Warbucks in the Broadway musical *Annie* had it wrong when he said, "I was ruthless to those I had to climb over to get to the top. Because I've always believed one thing: You don't have to be nice to the people you meet on the way up if you're not coming back down again." We believed the opposite. It's always better to have people rooting for you than waiting for you to fail.

The naysayers were relentless: "You'll never survive in the restaurant world." Once we left the law, though, there was no turning back.

Fear of failure was real, especially after mortgaging our homes, but fear became fuel. My wife, Esther, was there from the start as our third co-founder, our opening hostess, and later supporting us behind the scenes. Larry's wife, Joni, joined the journey a few years later, offering steady support.

If we'd known then what we know now, would we have done it? Honestly, I don't know. But we were driven by a shared dream, and we had plenty of encouragement from family and friends.

Somehow that was enough to pull off the improbable.

We weren't chasing a whim. From day one the vision was clear: Build a concept strong enough to grow into a chain—affordable but with quality and service that exceeded expectations. The catch? We had no operational experience.

So we put our faith in others, handing over responsibility to people who, in many cases, were learning on the fly right alongside us. Some became the backbone of CPK.

What we never willingly gave away, though, was control of the brand. We guarded it fiercely. Later, when we loosened our grip, the business faltered, as it always does when a company loses its compass. Success requires vigilance, someone at the top pushing for excellence. Every day. Nonstop.

Like all entrepreneurs, we believed failure wasn't an option. Over time we learned otherwise. Success isn't ever fully in your control. Timing, circumstance, and fate all play their parts. The pandemic drove that lesson home. But if timing is everything, resilience is what carries you through.

Through it all, skeptics never let us forget their favorite refrain: "California pizza isn't real pizza." To the faithful of New York, Chicago, Boston, and Detroit, ours was culinary heresy. We set out to prove them wrong and, in doing so, created a category all our own.

Passion and commitment won out. We found people who shared our vision and made the journey possible. This is their story as well as ours.

Our story is about more than pizza. It's about resilience, adaptability, and two friends who turned a crazy idea (barbecue chicken on pizza) into an American success story. We hope it will inspire others to chase their own dreams and maybe have a lot of fun along the way, as we did.

In our law practice, Larry left the briefs, motions, and letters to me. From the beginning of our relationship, I was always the writer. At CPK this pattern naturally continued. So when it came time to write this book, I offered to include Larry's personal journey as part of the story. But Larry wouldn't hear of it. "Rick," he told me, "this is your book. You've poured your heart and soul into it. I don't want to tell my story. I want to read yours and support it."

It was classic Larry—direct, gracious, and exactly why our partnership worked.

This book tells the CPK story in my voice. We built the business together, made decisions together, and collected more than a few unforgettable memories. While the first CPK opened its doors in Beverly Hills, the story truly began years earlier. It began in years shaped by experiences and relationships that set the stage long before we ever put a pizza in the oven.

That's why I've included what I call the "Prequel (and Then Some)" for readers who want to see how the road to CPK was paved and where it led. The prequel comes later in the book, after the main story. It's there if you're curious and want to read on.

The first part of the prequel covers my years as a federal prosecutor—first in Washington, DC, in the Appellate Section of the Criminal Division, handling cases before the United States Supreme Court and the courts of appeals, and then in Los Angeles, where I was drawn to the drama of trial work.

The second section covers twelve years of building a criminal defense practice with Larry, where we battled high-stakes cases and worked with unforgettable clients.

The third goes further back to my childhood on the South Side of Chicago, where family, friends, and mentors gave me the foundation that shaped my perspective. But it also reaches forward, tracing the friendships and pursuits that have enriched my life well beyond those early years.

I didn't set out to write a memoir. Honestly, it was the farthest thing from my mind. But through the years, whenever I shared stories from CPK or the courtroom, I kept hearing, "You really ought to write a book." What finally pushed me to do it was personal. Again and again, people told me how CPK had become part of their own lives—meals shared with parents, grandparents, and friends—and how much the restaurant had meant to them. That connection made me want to tell the full story of the fate, resolve, and unlikely turns that made it all possible.

So here it is. I hope you enjoy reading it as much as I've enjoyed writing it. It was truly a labor of love.

CHAPTER ONE

You chickenshit lawyers! Are you going to practice law your whole lives or do what you really want to do?

—BURTON GOLDBERG, FLORIDA HOTELIER AND RESTAURATEUR, TO RICK ROSENFIELD AND LARRY FLAX IN 1984

YOU MAY BE WONDERING WHAT MADE TWO LAWYERS walk away from the courtroom in the first place.

The truth is, there's no single answer.

I first met Larry in the summer of 1970, when I came to Los Angeles as a special prosecutor.

Larry was an assistant US attorney, and we hit it off immediately.

At the time I was on loan from the Department of Justice in Washington, DC, where I'd landed my dream job right out of law school through the DOJ Honors Program, writing briefs for the US Supreme Court and arguing cases in the federal courts of appeals.

That summer, with the court in recess, I arranged to come West to gain trial experience and sit for the California Bar exam—just in case I ever wanted to practice there. My plan was to return to Chicago, join my father and brother at Rosenfield and Rosenfield, and continue the family tradition. But California got under my skin.

Before I left, Robert "Bob" Meyer, the US attorney, offered me the chance to return and create the first Appellate Section in the Criminal Division. It took me a year to accept, but I'll admit the decision came a lot easier on a blustery DC day, with a windchill of minus forty degrees Fahrenheit, while Los Angeles basked in warm sunshine.

Two years later Larry and I took our first real plunge: We formed our own white-collar criminal defense firm. By then we'd both built solid reputations as prosecutors. I'd put away major organized crime figures, including the Detroit and St. Louis mob bosses who'd secretly owned Las Vegas's Frontier Hotel, and successfully prosecuted a hijacker who had diverted a commercial jet to Los Angeles to protest the treatment of Mexican Americans—an episode that led to the first metal detectors in the Los Angeles federal courthouse. Larry had been assistant chief of the Criminal Division and the very first chief of the Civil Rights Division.

We opened our Century City office in early 1973. Larry liked to call me the left-brained guy—logic and language—while he was the right-brained guy, wired for creativity. In truth our skills overlapped more than he ever admitted.

Together, with hard work and a willingness to take on the toughest cases, we earned reputations as fearless trial lawyers, first as prosecutors who wouldn't back down from mobsters or their high-powered attorneys and later as defenders in high-profile cases ourselves.

We'd found success, but at a heavy cost. When someone's freedom is on the line, the weight never really leaves you. The pressure was relentless, the stakes were unforgiving, and, truth be told, defending never carried the same sense of fulfillment. Over time it wore us down in ways we hadn't anticipated.

For me the writing was on the wall. As much as I loved the practice at times—and I truly did—I knew I couldn't keep doing it forever.

The tipping point came in 1980, when I was defending Rudy Tham, one of the most powerful Teamsters in the country. The Organized Crime Strike Force had indicted him for embezzling exactly $2,790 in union funds—money he'd supposedly spent on a Las Vegas trip to wine, dine, and provide prostitutes for Jimmy "the Weasel" Fratianno, the confessed head of the Los Angeles Mafia family and later the subject of *The Last Mafioso*. Yes, you read that right—less than $3,000.

This was Fratianno's first appearance after being granted immunity for, among other things, admitting to five murders. It was obvious Tham was collateral damage—a test run for Fratianno's credibility in bigger mob cases. I suspected I'd been chosen as Tham's lawyer precisely because of my background, first in prosecuting organized crime, then in defending prominent union officials. My cross-examination of Fratianno gained me some notoriety, and before long I had a role in defending Aniello Dellacroce—John Gotti's godfather and, in mob lore, the *capo di tutti capi*, the don of all dons.

But I wasn't looking for notoriety. I was in the heat of battle. As the trial dragged on, my frustration deepened. In my view the prosecutor wasn't just playing hardball. He was crossing the line by withholding exculpatory evidence, propping up a sleazy witness, and engaging in outright misconduct. Worse yet, the judge, the experienced and brilliant Hon. Stanley Weigel, seemed to know it and let it slide.

Motion after motion, objection after objection, every ruling went against me. I knew the judge understood the law. He was just refusing to act.

While waiting in the courtroom for the jury to return, I found myself watching another trial just to kill time. During a recess Judge Weigel, his clerk, and I were alone. He looked up and motioned me over to the sidebar—no court reporter, just the two of us—and said, "Mr. Rosenfield, I want you to know that in my eighteen years on the bench, no lawyer has ever tried a case in front of me better than you just did."

For about two seconds, I was flattered. But, still burning from his rulings, I took a breath and said, "Thank you, Your Honor. I appreciate that. But I just have to ask. Why, every time you knew I was right, did you rule against me?"

He offered only a shrug and a wry smile.

That told me everything. The unspoken message was clear: *Your client is a bad guy. He deserved to be convicted. So I overlooked the law. And I have the power to do that.*

It was a dagger—the straw that broke the camel's back. I had spent my career—on both sides—believing justice would win out. But in that moment, I felt betrayed, not by a client but by the system itself. If the rules could so easily be bent by the very people entrusted to uphold them, then what was the point?

When I returned to Los Angeles, I told my wife, Esther, “I can’t keep beating my head against the wall like this.” My days in the courtroom were numbered. I didn’t know when or how, but I knew my life was about to change.

Fortunately, the fickle finger of fate had already set the stage for our exit from law and our leap into something entirely different. It didn’t happen in a flash. There was no lightning bolt epiphany. But the Tham trial had marked a clear turning point for me, the moment when threads laid years earlier began to pull both Larry and me toward a new and unexpected chapter.

Back in 1974 Larry and I had met Burton Goldberg in Miami’s Coconut Grove. Burton was larger than life—a visionary developer who had transformed the Grove from a laid-back, bohemian enclave into a glittering playground. At the center of it all was the Mutiny at Sailboat Bay, Burton’s crown jewel—part restaurant, part private club, part stage for Miami’s elite.

The Mutiny was electric. It had the tropical ease of a beachside retreat but with a wild edge all its own. Hostesses and servers were glamorous, dressed as if for a party, each wearing a hat of her own choosing. It had a little of the Playboy Club’s allure—minus the bunny tails—but it wasn’t just for men. The place buzzed with women too: socialites, business leaders, entertainers.

Everyone wanted in.

And everyone was there. Judges, prosecutors, and defense attorneys rubbed elbows with real estate moguls, celebrities, and the occasional drug kingpin. At its peak the Mutiny had eleven thousand members and sold more Dom Pérignon than any place on Earth, much of it consumed in champagne towers by South American drug traffickers flush with cash. The atmosphere was so surreal that it inspired the Babylon Club in *Scarface*—and, years later, Netflix’s *Griselda*. But Hollywood never really captured the mix of glamour and sheer excess that defined the place.

Larry and I met Burton while representing Bernard “Bernie” Rubin, a powerful labor boss under investigation by the Justice Department's Organized Crime Strike Force. Bernie knew every major developer in Miami and counted Burton as a friend. Through Bernie, Burton took a liking to us—two young California attorneys who'd somehow been chosen over Miami's seasoned defense bar.

Our friendship deepened over time. At a pivotal meeting, we gave some blunt legal advice that blew up what would have been the biggest deal of his career—the Grove Isle development, a plan to build four luxury condo towers on a private island off Coconut Grove. At first he was furious and nicknamed us "the Sunshine Boys." But when the project later collapsed under environmental lawsuits, Burton realized the advice had spared him enormous trouble. The nickname that had started with irony became one of genuine affection.

From then on we became fixtures at the Mutiny, often staying as Burton's guests. When he came to Los Angeles, he stayed at my home. At the heart of it all was a shared love of food and wine. Larry and I weren't trained chefs, but we loved to cook and experiment. Burton encouraged it. Soon we were sampling dishes with him, offering feedback, and even developing recipes that found their way onto the menu. At the time we didn't think much of it. Looking back, those playful experiments in the Mutiny's kitchen were the first steps in a chain of events that would eventually change our lives.

By the early '80s, Burton had lost control of Grove Isle. Disillusioned, he sold the Mutiny, fled Miami, and began spending summers at a villa in Saint-Tropez. He often invited Larry, Esther, and me to join him there.

Those were glorious sun-soaked days with lunches at Le Club 55, long dinners at the villa, and family memories I still treasure. Our kids were welcomed as if they were his own.

Then came the summer of 1984. Burton had rented a villa in Saint-Tropez to celebrate the sale of the Mutiny and had invited us for an extended visit, but with a major trial in San Francisco looming, we simply couldn't go. That was when he dropped the words that would change everything.

"You chickenshit lawyers! Are you going to practice law your whole lives or do what you really want to do?"

It hit like a punch to the gut. The truth was undeniable: Neither Larry nor I could imagine grinding out another thirty years in courtrooms.

The weight was already closing in. My daughter Nicole was just two years old. My son, Ian, from my short first marriage, had recently made the bold decision—prompted by Esther's encouragement—to move in with us at fourteen and attend high school in Beverly Hills.

Soon after Burton's prophetic wake-up call, the San Francisco trial swallowed our days and nights. For months our lives blurred into a relentless cycle of airports and courtrooms—sleeping at Burton's San Francisco home during the week, flying home to Los Angeles on weekends, only to dive straight back into the grind. Layer on the constant demands of our practice and a string of high-stakes cases, and the pressure became suffocating.

Let's be clear: I'd rather have been hanging out with Burton and my family in Saint-Tropez. On the track we were on, that was never going to happen. Burton's challenge had stripped away any illusions. If we didn't take the leap now, we never would.

Larry and I were both proud to have built a successful law practice, but the truth was inescapable: As criminal defense attorneys, we essentially relied on criminals to support our lifestyles—and there weren't that many repeat customers in our line of work.

Looking back, we often joke, "It wasn't a great business model."

Both of us cherished our time as prosecutors. I loved my work before the US Supreme Court, and we both treasured our years at the US Attorney's Office. Stepping to the podium and announcing we were appearing "on behalf of the United States" was heady stuff—like wearing the proverbial "white hat"—with all the respect that came with it.

Switching to the other side was a whole new ball game. It was more lucrative, yes, but wearing the "black hat" wasn't much fun, especially for two guys who prided themselves on the highest professional ethics.

We finished that San Francisco trial on a high note—a major fraud case involving a currency scam that defrauded Californians out of millions. In our view our client was a scapegoat. The trial ended in a hung jury, and the government walked away, never to retry the case. It was the sweetest kind of win—the kind we could savor without a single what-if hanging over it.

And while that might sound like the end of it, stick around for the prequel where this trial makes a surprise encore, complete with a few courtroom moments you couldn't script if you tried.

CHAPTER TWO

ALMOST BY CHANCE, BUT AS IT TURNS OUT, CERTAINLY by good fortune, Larry and I had already gotten a taste of the restaurant business years earlier at Derrick's in the Beverly Comstock Hotel. Perched just on the border of Beverly Hills, Derrick's was a tiny thirty-five-seat spot owned by chef Derrick Schwartz and his wife, Judy, a talent agent with a big personality. Over time Derrick's became a gathering place for celebrities. Johnny Carson, Sidney Poitier, Henry Mancini, and Sally Struthers were regulars. Ed McMahon from *The Tonight Show* was a fixture. Joe Cocker lived upstairs in the hotel and often drifted into the piano bar to sing. And Richard Simmons—yes, that Richard Simmons—started there as a waiter before becoming the maître d'. He was infamous for outlandish nightly antics, which often included cutting guests' neckties, leaving them bewildered. Regulars learned to either wear their least favorite necktie or none at all.

Derrick was a terrific chef, but his ambitions exceeded the profits possible from this small space. He tried to buy the hotel and convert it into a private club. Unfortunately, the plan collapsed into bankruptcy, costing him both the hotel and his restaurant.

Undeterred, Derrick found an iconic site on the Sunset Strip at the northwest corner of Sunset Boulevard and Crescent Heights Boulevard. The space, once home to the famous Villa Frascati, was operating as the Chamonix restaurant. The owner wanted out, and the place didn't need much work.

We'd been doing some small legal work for Derrick and his wife and business partner, Judy. We'd become friends, so to help them launch the new location, we formed a limited partnership and raised $50,000 from friends and family. Larry and I were the general partners, which essentially meant we were the owners.

By maintaining the same name, the new Derrick's restaurant was an instant hit. Ed McMahon still came regularly, often with *The Tonight Show*'s guests and celebrities. Sally Struthers invested and sometimes waited tables for fun. Della Reese, as a friend of Derrick's, would occasionally sing in the piano bar.

Everything seemed set for success.

Then trouble walked in. Not only did the former owner want back in. But worse yet, he insisted on being the host at the front door, clad in a shiny polyester leisure suit—an image that clashed sharply with the atmosphere we were building.

The real problem, though, was that our partnership hadn't purchased the liquor license. That meant that he still had legal control. At the end of every evening, he'd fight with Derrick over the cash receipts. The tension became unbearable.

Despite what should have been a winning first foray into the restaurant business, we ended up in court, securing a receivership order to force the previous owner out. We won, but the victory felt hollow.

Lesson learned: If we ever reentered the restaurant business, we'd own the liquor license.

That experience might have scared us off for good, but instead, it only sharpened our appetites.

As chance would have it, during one of my frequent visits to Miami, Ed Smalley, the co-owner of the Miami Dolphins, invited me for a speedboat ride en route to a party at Stiltsville, a scattering of wooden houses on the edge of Biscayne Bay. There I met Tony Roma.

Larry and I were already fans of his Miami restaurant, famous for its tender ribs and basket of onion rings. Now that I had Tony in conversation, I just had to ask him about those onion rings.

Sure enough, he admitted he'd "borrowed" the recipe from Hackney's, a Chicago restaurant I knew well. By then Tony had sold his sole restaurant and rights to Clint Murchison Jr., the wealthy founder of the Dallas Cowboys.

Through a go-between, we pitched Murchison about the possibility of franchising. But we were told he didn't want lawyers as franchisees.

Years later, after CPK's success, I told this story at a national restaurant conference. A man introduced himself afterward as Murchison's son, now running the Roma Corporation. He shook my hand and said, "I think Dad made a mistake."

At the time, though, the rejection stung.

Larry and I briefly explored launching our own rib restaurant in Palm Desert, even negotiating for a location, but a big new legal case pulled us away. Still, the dream lingered. It was bubbling beneath the surface, and we both sensed it was only a matter of time.

CHAPTER THREE

THE FALL OF 1984 WAS A TUMULTUOUS TIME FOR MY family. My mother, who lived in Chicago, had just celebrated her seventy-fifth birthday. She had postponed a needed kidney surgery until after her party, but the complications and her declining health took their toll. She passed soon after.

It was a terrible blow. I'd lost my father to throat cancer twelve years earlier, and now, at age forty, I found myself parentless.

At the time I was an avid long-distance runner, having recently completed two marathons, including Chicago. While in town for her funeral, I ran ten miles a day along Lake Michigan, ignoring a painful hamstring tear. The grief was so consuming that I barely felt the physical pain.

Those daily runs became my time for soul-searching. Life was short. I knew I was ready to step away from practicing law.

While in Chicago, my brother, Neal, also a lawyer, introduced me to a new pasta cafeteria concept called Mama Mia. The design was fresh and modern, showcasing Italy's red, white, and green colors. A display case showed off an array of fresh pastas. Customers selected their pasta, sauce, and toppings and then moved down the line for a salad and a drink. By the time they reached the checkout counter, their dish was ready.

Back in Los Angeles, I told Larry about the discovery. He was intrigued, but we had a monthslong criminal fraud trial in San Francisco to get through first. Even so, the idea stuck in my head.

As soon as the trial ended, we called our friend Bob Mandler, a former attorney with whom we had previously shared a law office. Bob had recently left his law practice to open a China-meets-California restaurant, Chin

Chin, on the Sunset Strip. His sleek, modern restaurant was a sensation, thanks, in part, to its Chinese Chicken Salad. When we told him of our idea, he said he'd recently read about a similar pasta restaurant located in the nearby Glendale Galleria.

We jumped in the car and went to see it. Unlike Mama Mia, the Glendale restaurant offered pizza by the slice under heat lamps. The display didn't wow us, but we noticed how many people grabbed a slice to go with their pasta.

We drove back to our law office in Beverly Hills buzzing with ideas. As we fell into our usual brainstorming rhythm, finishing each other's sentences, the cafeteria concept quickly vanished, replaced by something far more exciting: pizza. We pictured an open kitchen anchored by a wood-burning oven, the kind of place where guests could see and smell their meal taking shape. Casual, comfortable, but with a fresh, modern edge. By day's end we had our blueprint: an Italian version of Chin Chin, built around the new and intriguing world of California-style pizza. That day our future found its fire.

At the time California-style pizza was in its infancy, pioneered by the legendary Alice Waters at the Chez Panisse Café in Berkeley. Waters was breaking all the rules, topping pizzas with fresh, farm-to-table ingredients and toppings that, in those days, felt downright exotic. Goat cheese. Seasonal vegetables. And most noteworthy to us, she used a wood-burning pizza oven. *And*, in an act of pure heresy at the time, sometimes no tomato sauce at all. Not a tomato in sight.

In 1982 Wolfgang Puck brought the idea south to Los Angeles, hiring Ed LaDou, a talented pizza chef who had been experimenting with unconventional toppings in the Bay Area. At Spago, in West Hollywood, LaDou turned out creations such as duck sausage and smoked salmon pizzas—dishes that were as much conversation pieces as meals.

We'd been to Spago a few times, but getting a reservation wasn't easy, unless you were famous, connected, or willing to discreetly grease the maître d's palm. Word was his "tips" alone could fund an early retirement.

That was the light bulb moment: Most people had never even heard of California-style pizza, let alone tasted it. By nightfall Larry and I had our rallying cry: "Let's create a Spago for the masses!" What we didn't know then was that our version—rooted in creativity, instinct, and a feel for what people wanted—would turn out to be something even more distinctive and beloved than we imagined.

Looking back, it's hard to believe. In a single day, we dreamed up a concept that would not only define our careers but change pizza forever: the ovens that baked it, the restaurants that served it, and even the frozen grocery aisle where our innovative pizzas inspired an industry.

Neither Larry nor I ever pictured a celebrity-oriented, chef-driven restaurant. We wanted something more approachable—a neighborhood gathering place that served the community. We drew inspiration from Hamburger Hamlet, a local chain that drew both families and singles. In our vision every upscale neighborhood in America could embrace a casual, full-service restaurant built around our unique style of pizza. That same day we decided that the menu would include pasta and salads for balance.

Atmosphere mattered. We wanted a space that felt comfortable for everyone, with counter seating that encouraged interaction but avoided turning into a bar scene. We especially wanted women, whether dining alone or with friends, to feel welcome.

Our intuition was right. As we later expanded into upscale shopping centers, naturally our most loyal customers were women. Whether shopping alone, meeting friends, or bringing the family, they embraced us wholeheartedly. Some would label our pizza as "chick pizza," perhaps condescendingly. Frankly, it didn't bother us in the slightest.

The open kitchen was essential to the concept. Larry and I shared a love of cooking and entertaining friends, and we were struck by how everyone naturally gravitates to the kitchen. By placing the pizza oven at the center—a warm, glowing anchor—everything around would need to be meticulous. That discipline, we knew, would earn customer trust.

We later recognized that there was another, albeit more subtle, benefit to an open kitchen. It was attractive to employees who appreciated being on stage, engaged with the room instead of confined to the back.

Now we had a clear vision—or at least what felt like one at the time—and boundless enthusiasm. Both of us were ready to leave the law practice, but while Larry was still single, I had to weigh how such a leap would affect my family. Looking back, I see now that our early vision was only the starting point. It would evolve in ways neither of us could have imagined.

When I told Esther I wanted to go into the restaurant business, her reaction was understandably mixed. She'd grown up in her family's diner in Birmingham, Alabama, and thought she'd left that life when she'd become a stewardess and married a successful young lawyer in California. But once she saw how much this dream meant to me—how determined I was—her support was instant. No hesitation. She was all in, simply because I was.

Later, as Larry often said, Esther was CPK's third founder, right there with us every step of the way.

By then Esther and I had been together ten years. We'd first met on my way back to Nevada from Miami, where I had been defending a top union official in a case launched by the Organized Crime Strike Force. I'd had plans to meet Larry and another client in Las Vegas, and my itinerary required a change of planes in Dallas. After boarding, I'd discovered I was the only passenger seated in first class.

Two flight attendants were working the cabin, and I couldn't help but notice Esther. She was stunning. I took every opportunity I could to chat with her, doing my best to not come across as too forward. More important than her obvious beauty, we had an easy and fun conversation. I was clearly taken by her "Southern charm."

As we approached our descent, she asked for recommendations for a good dinner spot in Vegas. I offered a few suggestions, then added, "How about joining me?" She smiled but politely declined, explaining that it was the crew's last night together, and all nine had plans to go out.

Not willing to let the opportunity pass, I said, "No problem. I'll take you all to dinner. My treat."

After conferring with her crew, Esther accepted. That evening I brought the entire group to the Oyster Bar at the Desert Inn Hotel. While I may have looked like a big spender, the truth was, I was fully comped—room, meals, drinks, the works.

When Larry arrived later with our client, Joe Hauser, a Beverly Hills businessman, they asked our casino host where I was. "Hosting a flight crew at the Oyster Bar," he replied. Larry and Joe walked in, took one look at the scene, and immediately understood my true motives.

After dinner, Esther left the crew and joined us at a craps table. Hauser was losing heavily; I was losing a little, but I was placing a few bets for her. By the time she had to leave, she'd won twenty dollars. She handed it to me with a smile and said, "Here. You need this more than I do." Then she slipped me a piece of paper with her phone number.

I was hooked.

As we got to know each other through nightly phone conversations, I found myself more smitten by the day. Esther was based in New Orleans, so I wasted no time arranging a return trip to Miami—this time with a layover in the Big Easy. Always up for an adventure, Larry, still happily single, decided to tag along.

Over the next couple of days, I wined and dined Esther at some of the city's most storied restaurants—Antoine's, Galatoire's, Arnaud's, and Felix's Restaurant & Oyster Bar. By the end of that visit, we had embarked upon a whirlwind romance that to this day has lasted fifty-one years—the last forty-eight of them as husband and wife.

We've been truly blessed beyond measure, not only by the life we've shared together but by the family we've built: our two wonderful daughters Nicole and Dana, my son Ian, Ian's children Largo and Laird, and Dana's husband, Ryan Jackson-Healy.

CHAPTER FOUR

THERE WE WERE, COMPLETELY IMMERSED IN DEVELOPING our new restaurant concept, which seemed to evolve by the hour. The next step was clear: Find the right spot for our first location. We knew the old adage by heart. Success in the restaurant business came down to three things: location, location, location.

During my morning jog, I spotted a small vacant retail space on South Beverly Drive, only half a mile from our family's home in Beverly Hills. The site came with a checkered past—four restaurants had tried and failed there. Adding to our cautionary chorus was David Orgell, a business client and friend and then-president of the Beverly Hills Chamber of Commerce. David was convinced South Beverly Drive was a restaurant graveyard. To him and many other knowledgeable people, the only chance of success in Beverly Hills lay in the "Golden Triangle," the high-rent, high-prestige zone north of Wilshire Boulevard.

(As a postscript, South Beverly Drive is now known as "Restaurant Row," and people tell us we were lucky to have found such a good location—but that's getting ahead of ourselves. Back then, in the fall of 1984, it was a gamble.)

At roughly eighteen hundred square feet, the space was smaller than our ideal footprint for the full-service restaurant we envisioned. Still, we were intrigued. For two apprehensive lawyers venturing into uncharted waters, smaller space meant lower rent—and lower rent meant fewer sleepless nights.

Despite the skeptics, I believed I knew the neighborhood better than most. Our home was just five blocks away, and I had a strong sense of the community's tastes. To me South Beverly Drive felt perfect. I was convinced that neighbors and friends would embrace the kind of restaurant we were dreaming up—and that previous failures had more to do with what was on the plate than where it was served. Larry knew Beverly Hills well and agreed.

With a promising location in sight, the next step was clear: Find a chef. That was when we learned that Ed LaDou, the man who'd launched Wolfgang Puck's pizzas at Spago, had just left and was looking for his next move.

We set up a meeting and laid out our vision for a family-friendly place with California-style pizzas, alongside pastas and salads.

Since we had no chef, no menu, and not even a name yet, hiring Spago's former pizza chef to create our menu felt like a no-brainer. To win him over, we offered an unusually generous deal: executive chef, a strong salary, and, most importantly, equity. When we offered 5 percent a year for five years, a quarter of the company if he stayed the course, Ed didn't hesitate. He said yes on the spot.

We could now focus on securing the lease. The space was in an iconic building near the intersection of South Beverly Drive and Charleville Boulevard. The owners were willing to take a chance on two lawyers-turned-restaurateurs, but there was a catch: They insisted on personal guarantees. If the business failed, we wouldn't just lose a restaurant; we'd be on the hook ourselves.

It was a gut punch. We spent days turning it over, weighing the risk, imagining the worst-case scenarios. (After all, we were lawyers.) But the vision had already taken hold, and the pull was stronger than the fear. After more deliberation—and more than a little hand-wringing—we agreed to do it.

We had everything lined up. The deal was ready, the lease sat waiting on my desk, and the only step left was Ed LaDou's signature on his employment agreement. With Larry overseas it fell to me to close it.

Ed walked into my office, and I was expecting a signature, a quick handshake, and a celebration. Instead, he dropped a bombshell. The night before, he said, he'd been back at Spago when he crossed paths with someone developing a restaurant strikingly similar to ours. According to Ed, this mystery backer had offered him the very same deal we had—plus an immediate 25 percent equity stake.

I didn't buy it for a second. Shocked? Absolutely—but I'd been thrown plenty of curveballs in trial work. My exact words to LaDou are burned into memory, though in the interest of propriety, I'll let the reader imagine them. Let's just say I suggested he attempt an anatomically impossible act.

Anger, disappointment, even panic surged through me, but instinct kicked in. Years in court had taught me to mask it, to project calm. So I stayed composed, showed him the door, and then tracked Larry down in Europe to break the news: LaDou had betrayed us.

Suddenly, we were back at square one. An unproven concept: no chef, no menu, no funding for construction, and no experienced management. And the clock was ticking. Moving forward meant signing a lease with personal guarantees—and then figuring out how to finance the restaurant, which would put us deep in debt.

It was terrifying. But I knew one thing: I had to move forward. This wasn't just a restaurant idea.

It was my escape from the practice of law.

Burton happened to be in Los Angeles, and he wouldn't let up. He was relentless—pushing, prodding, hammering, and never missing a chance to remind us how "chickenshitted" we were. In a quieter moment, he tried reassurance: "If you fall on your ass, I'm going to save you."

Comforting maybe, but he wasn't my father. I knew if the restaurant failed, the fallout would be mine to carry.

After talking it through with Esther, whose support never wavered, I made the decision. I was ready to risk it all.

Larry wasn't. He was getting cold feet. When I pressed him to sign the lease, he snapped, "You've got Burton to save you. Who's going to save me?"

That didn't land. I was past the point of hesitation. "Larry, Burton's promise only goes so far. Ultimately, this is *my* risk, and I'm willing to take it."

That line—*Who's going to save me?*—wasn't really about the lease. It was a glimpse into something deeper. Years earlier Larry's father, Bill Flax, had put money into our first restaurant venture, Derrick's—and lost it. For years afterward Bill needled Larry about it. That kind of experience leaves a scar.

Larry had no intention of asking his father for help. Yet I knew Bill well, and I'm certain he would have stepped in if things had gone sideways. Larry knew it too. He just didn't want to go there. Thankfully, that moment never came.

Still, for the first time in our relationship, I couldn't sway Larry on my own. I called Burton and asked for backup. He went full court press, phoning Larry constantly, urging him forward. We also enlisted our mutual friend, Dr. Richard "Dick" Bank, a Beverly Hills ob-gyn who had delivered both of Esther's and my daughters (and later became an investor), to help push Larry over the finish line.

It was an emotional touch-and-go for several days. Finally, Larry came around. We signed the lease. The die was cast. Our lives were about to change in ways we couldn't yet imagine.

CHAPTER FIVE

ONCE THE LEASE WAS SIGNED, THERE WAS NO TURNING back. We assumed we could finance the first restaurant ourselves, without outside investors. The truth was there was simply no way to create a budget since we only had the broad outline of our concept sketched in our heads. But ignorance was bliss. Had we known the true cost of what lay ahead, we might never have had the nerve to start.

Our first stop was our law firm's bank. The banker, quick to point out our lack of experience in the restaurant industry, immediately quipped the oft-cited statistic that 90 percent of restaurants fail in their first year. In truth about 20 to 30 percent of restaurants fail in their first year and roughly 60 percent within three years—about the same as other small businesses.

Despite his hesitancy, we secured a $250,000 loan, tied to the income from our law practice. The catch? The mortgages on our homes were to be used as collateral. Coupled with our personal guarantees on the lease, the risk was enormous. We were terrified.

We hired a recommended contractor who estimated construction at $250,000—roughly $725,000 in today's dollars. What he didn't mention, and what we were too green to ask, was that the figure didn't include kitchen equipment. That surprise came later, along with "soft costs." We hadn't considered a computer system, recruitment and training, insurance, accounting and legal fees, licenses and permits, smallwares, supplies, and opening inventory.

We learned the hard way just how fast the numbers add up. The truth was, we were flying blind, equal parts confidence and naivete, trusting we'd figure it out as we went.

Looking for guidance in creating a budget, we turned to our friend Bob Mandler, owner of Chin Chin. Bob graciously opened his books for us. His small restaurant was doing about $100,000 a month in sales (about $280,000 in today's dollars) and turning a profit. Using his numbers as a guide, we guessed we could match that after a year. In reality it was financial dart-throwing.

There we were, lease signed with personal guarantees, ready to mortgage our homes—and yet we had no chef, no menu, no design, and no money. To top it off, we still didn't even have a name. We'd tossed around a few "Spago-ish" Italian possibilities: Ciao, Primavera, and even Delari, a mash-up of our names—La from Larry, Ri from Rick, and De from Denise Domb, Burton's former significant other, whom he hoped might join us in the venture. But nothing clicked, including the idea of bringing Denise in as a partner.

Then early one morning, Larry called. He was unusually energized and wanted to meet for breakfast at Nate'n Al's, Beverly Hills' iconic Jewish deli. That alone was out of character. In all our years as partners, aside from mornings during trial, we had only met for breakfast once—the day I told him I'd decided to marry Esther. I wanted his blessing since it meant shaking up our long-standing bachelor routines. Of course, Larry immediately gave me his full approval.

As soon as I sat down, Larry was practically bursting. "I've got the name! California Pizza Kitchen!"

My initial response was less than enthusiastic. "That's really pedestrian for a pizza restaurant in Beverly Hills, Larry."

His face fell. The excitement drained away, replaced by a pout I knew all too well from our years together. "Fine. Call it anything you want, but you're going to be sick when someone opens a competing restaurant and calls it California Pizza Kitchen," he shot back.

That sent a jolt down my spine and left a hollow pit in my stomach. Larry was right. *California Pizza Kitchen* was the perfect name. "Touché." I grinned. "As a judge would say, call the next case." Done.

That evening, over dinner with friends from Rhode Island, we tested the name. Their verdict:

"Ciao and Primavera sound like every other Italian place in town. But *California Pizza Kitchen*? We'd go just to see what you fruits and nuts are up to."

We didn't really need the confirmation. The name was sealed at breakfast. That was the sum total of our market research.

When I've told this story over the years, people often marvel that I didn't immediately recognize the genius of the name. But my hesitation only makes sense in context. At that point there was no branding—no distinctive logo, no restaurant design. We had only a loose concept but no chef and menu.

Back then "California pizza" meant goat cheese, duck sausage, and smoked salmon. We were still thinking in Spago terms—Italian-ish with names to match. Compared to where we were headed, California pizza was still in the Stone Age.

Indeed, the name was pedestrian—and brilliant. Its power was in its simplicity and clarity, capturing the essence of a brand that would go on to become a global icon. Best of all, in trademarking the name, logo, and trade dress, we owned it!

How did Larry come up with the name California Pizza Kitchen? He'd recently returned from a trip to Monaco, where a glamorous hotel featured a "California Room." As a native Californian, he'd been struck by how the word resonated around the world, evoking a vivid blend of imagery: sunshine, palm trees, Hollywood glamour, and a laid-back, coastal vibe.

From that morning at Nate'n Al's, I was all in. California was more than a place. It was a mindset that invited innovation. In the ensuing years, we'd lean heavily on what we called the *California halo effect*, the built-in credibility that gave us freedom to experiment boldly.

Now we had a lease and a name. But the bank demanded a business plan. Sitting in the quiet of my law office, I began typing—not a technical spreadsheet filled with business jargon but a dream, outlining a new style of pizza: fresh ingredients, innovative toppings, a distinct California style. We boldly declared California-style pizza would stand alongside New York and Chicago as one of the top three pizza styles in the United States and, in time, become important internationally.

The boldest prediction of all was that California-style pizza would be defined by one name: California Pizza Kitchen.

Looking back, those claims were pure chutzpah—that perfect blend of confidence and audacity.

In truth it bordered on pure hubris. Yet we wrote without blinking that we would redefine California-style pizza. Within six months we would debut our Barbecue Chicken Pizza—a single menu item that would redefine California-style pizza and change the face of pizza forever.

CHAPTER SIX

When we signed the lease for our Beverly Hills restaurant—backed by personal guarantees, our homes mortgaged to the bank to finance it—we were sailing into uncharted water. Passion, we had in spades; restaurant experience, none.

I stopped taking cases to throw myself fully into the restaurant. Larry focused on keeping the law practice afloat. Then luck struck: A ground floor suite opened next to our future CPK. We jumped to move our law office there—law on one side, dream on the other.

That was when the fallout hit. The moment word got out we were opening a restaurant, the referrals stopped. Our practice thrived on cases from other lawyers who didn't want to tangle with federal court. That was our niche. Now, in their eyes, we weren't focused. And honestly, I got it. Would you hire a brain surgeon who spent most of his waking hours at his restaurant?

Worse, we were maxed out financially. We'd bet the house—literally. To use a baseball analogy, it felt like stepping off first base without knowing whether we could steal second—and knowing there was no turning back.

With no Restaurant 101 guidebook to help us, one thing became clear: We needed outside investors.

Enter our mutual friend Bob Kahan, a well-respected lawyer with whom we'd shared our first office suite when we'd gone into private practice twelve years earlier. Bob suggested raising funds from friends and family. We were concerned about whether people would invest in two criminal defense attorneys with no restaurant experience. Additionally, we didn't want to dilute a significant portion of our future equity to secure funding for the first restaurant.

Bob proposed forming a limited partnership. Larry and I would be the general partners, earning a 5 percent management fee and maintaining the brand rights. We'd offer investors 80 percent of the cash flow until they received 125 percent of their money—then split profits fifty-fifty.

We asked Bob if he thought we'd be able to attract investors on those terms. Without hesitation Bob said, "I would—and I will."

Buoyed by his confidence, we set out to raise an additional $250,000—on top of the $250,000 we'd already spent. I started with my regular Beverly Hills High School running group. The first check, for $20,000, came from my friend Dr. Phil Yalowitz—followed by Dr. Robert Carroll, immigration lawyer Ralph Ehrenpreis, legendary DC attorney Plato Cacheris, my cousin Ronald Guttman (a successful actor and producer), his brother, Michael (a world-famous violinist and conductor), and Alexandre de Lesseps, a French entrepreneur and descendant of Ferdinand de Lesseps, who'd built the Suez and Panama Canals.

Our lawyer, Bob Kahan, and his law partner, Larry Stein, also came in, along with Larry's friend Christine Morton (who later married Beverly Center developer Sheldon Gordon), and our mutual friends Cindy and Michael Flagg and Jude Turner Green. And while Larry never asked his father to invest, his sister Linda and her husband, Bob Lytle, jumped in without hesitation.

Remarkably, we made twenty-three phone calls in one afternoon and received twenty-two commitments, ranging from $5,000 to $40,000, the largest investor being our mentor, Burton Goldberg.

Another was the actress Jane Seymour, whom Esther met by pure chance in the recovery room at Cedars-Sinai. Esther had just delivered our daughter Nicole, and Jane had delivered her daughter, Katie, just twenty minutes earlier. That meeting sparked a lifelong friendship. Over the years Jane has often recalled how she convinced her then-husband and business manager David Flynn to ignore his own standard advice to clients: "Don't invest in restaurants."

Looking back, it was extraordinary to receive that level of support, given our complete lack of restaurant experience. Of course, our investors believed in the concept. But more than that, they believed in us—and that faith paired with patience would later pay off handsomely.

Still without a chef but with our Beverly Hills location secured, our next step was to hire a restaurant designer. We turned to our friend Gene Adcock, a noted interior designer on the verge of retirement. Gene agreed, on one condition: "Keep it fun."

Fresh back from Milan, he told us that bright yellow was the "hot" color. Building on that spark, he designed our entire look—crisp white-and-black tiles accented with a bold-yellow band, topped off with a yellow ceiling. The first time the contractors started painting that ceiling, we heard what would become a running joke: "California Banana Kitchen."

Soon after the paint went up, Larry's father came in to see our progress. Larry, holding his breath, asked, "What do you think?" His father looked up at the yellow ceiling and, in that blunt way only a father can, said it looked a little green. I saw it register—a quick flinch—and for an instant, I thought our bold element, which would later become such a strong visual signature of our brand, might not survive the moment. But Larry didn't waver. Esther, Larry, and I loved the unapologetic use of yellow. It felt fresh, energetic, different. We saw it instantly as part of our brand's identity. Larry's mantra later became "We want to own yellow!"

We couldn't have known then that one day CPK's yellow pizza boxes would be instantly recognizable in frozen pizza cases nationwide.

Keeping our color palette in mind, we met with a Los Angeles–based graphic designer, Rod Dyer, famous for creating iconic logos in the restaurant and entertainment industries. From the outset we were driven to create a brand that was instantly recognizable.

Brainstorming the logo with Rod turned out to be both fascinating and time-consuming. We went through countless iterations in a series of meetings, tweaking every detail. Finally, we landed on the design that would become our visual signature: a distinctive white-diamond backdrop with a bold-yellow-checkered diamond at its center. Most importantly a black silhouette of a palm tree stood proudly in the middle—a clear nod to our California roots. While the logo has evolved over the years, the yellow diamond and palm tree have endured, remaining the unmistakable symbol of the CPK brand to this day.

We learned later that the palm tree that became our iconic logo was originally conceived by Clive Piercy, then a designer with Rod Dyer's firm and later a professor at ArtCenter College of Design.

Years later the circle came full: Clive would mentor my daughter, who had grown up around CPK and worked as a hostess and server before pursuing design. Midway through her studies, CPK's marketing team asked her to take a year off school to redesign our entire visual system—menus, packaging, takeout materials. I encouraged her to go for it, and she delivered a fresh, modern identity that carried CPK into its next chapter. Dana later returned to finish her degree, and today she's thriving in her own career as a freelance graphic designer. Please indulge me in a proud fatherly moment. Her work can be seen at www.drosi.co.

At one of our early design meetings, we wrestled with how to capture the essence of our centerpiece: our wood-burning oven. "How about wood-fired?" I suggested. Heads nodded instantly. At the time the term was almost unheard of. Our trademark lawyer told us we couldn't protect it, but we didn't need to—we simply made it ours. We stamped *wood-fired* across the logo, a banner that helped push the term into the mainstream. It stayed there until the late '90s, when we introduced a new kind of oven that would change not just our logo but the industry.

Larry added another spark. Inspired by a long-gone neighborhood ice cream parlor that everyone knew by its initials, he proposed adding *CPK* into the logo. California Pizza Kitchen was, admittedly, a mouthful, and we hoped the shorthand might stick. It did more than stick—it became *the* name. Before long no one bothered with the full version. And yet in those earliest days, Beverly Hills locals had their own nickname. They simply called us the Pizza Kitchen.

At that stage our focus was on the visual positioning of the brand. We knew that when we opened the restaurant, the pizzas would be the hook—after all, we were calling ourselves California Pizza Kitchen—but we believed it needed to be more than that. The full package mattered: restaurant design, bold branding, consistent food quality, and a culture of training and service. We didn't know it then, but we were laying the groundwork for what the industry would later call *polished casual dining*. To us it was just common sense.

Next step? Find a wood-burning oven!

From day one we knew the wood-burning oven wasn't just a piece of equipment—it was the heart of CPK. The hearth would be the visual and emotional center of the restaurant, the thing customers gravitated toward. But in the early '80s, options were scarce. Chez Panisse and Spago had theirs—hand-built brick fireplaces by a Bay Area craftsman—but that route was slow and costly.

We heard that in the parking lot of Il Giardino, a Beverly Hills Italian spot, an imported wood-burning oven from Italy was sitting idle—twenty-five hundred pounds of volcanic-ash-floored beauty, reduced to anchoring a party tent because the city had refused its use in the residential neighborhood. We checked with the building department to make sure our site wouldn't face the same problem.

Once they cleared us, we wrote the check. $2,500. *Ecco!* We had our oven.

The Italian oven worked great, and for our first ten restaurants, we imported the same model. But this process proved to be slow, expensive, and buried in red tape. That was when we discovered Wood Stone, a small start-up in Bellingham, Washington, just beginning to build wood-burning pizza ovens.

Intrigued, Larry and I flew north to meet founder Keith Carpenter and his son, Keith R. The ovens impressed us, but what won us over was the company itself: a family business rooted in community and supported by local employees. Larry felt an immediate connection—his mother had grown up in Seattle, and he himself was a proud University of Washington alum.

Switching from imports to Wood Stone turned out to be a defining decision—not just for CPK but for the pizza oven industry worldwide. From that point on, every new CPK showcased a Wood Stone oven front and center, its logo proudly displayed. Our visibility helped catapult them from a scrappy local start-up to the world's largest manufacturer of wood-burning ovens.

Neither of us could have guessed it then, but that relationship was the spark that would later transform not just our restaurants but the pizza industry itself.

In addition to juggling so many moving parts, Larry and I still faced three daunting tasks: finding the right chef, creating a menu from scratch, and forming a management team.

At the time we were eating regularly at a new Beverly Hills spot called DDL Foodshow, owned by legendary Italian movie producer Dino De Laurentiis. The ground floor housed an Italian deli, while the upstairs restaurant, which featured Beverly Hills' first wood-burning pizza oven, served unapologetically Italian fare. No California influence whatsoever.

The young pizza chef, Michele, had recently arrived from Italy. His English was limited, but his cooking spoke volumes—especially a potato-pesto pizza that fell perfectly in step with the vision we were shaping for CPK. After several visits (and sampling plenty of pizzas and pastas), we offered him the job as our first chef—never imagining how many surprises would come with him.

CHAPTER SEVEN

IN JANUARY 1985, EVEN BEFORE WE HAD A CHEF, LARRY and I were enjoying lunch at Cutters, an upscale spot in Santa Monica. Our server that day was a twenty-three-year-old aspiring actress named Julie Carruthers. She wasn't just good; she was unforgettable. Professional, poised, and warm in a way that felt completely genuine. By the end of the meal, Larry and I looked at each other and knew the same thing: This was exactly the kind of service we wanted to build into CPK.

So we told her—probably with more confidence than we had any right to—that we were starting a *restaurant chain*. Not just one restaurant but something bigger. And we wanted her to be part of it. Julie didn't laugh us off, which says a lot. Instead, she agreed to meet us the next day at our law office. Calling it an "interview" would be a stretch. We didn't ask questions. We sold the vision. And she bought in. By the time she walked out of that office, Julie was our first hire.

It wasn't just luck. It was a blessing. On her very first day, Julie started drafting what became our company training manual. As opening day drew closer, she took charge of hiring and training our front-of-house team. And as CPK grew, so did Julie. She became our vice president of human resources and training and ultimately a nationally recognized leader in hospitality training.

Then life delivered her a cruel blow. Julie was diagnosed with a rare form of cancer that led to the catastrophic amputation of her leg at the hip. Most people would have become crushed. Julie refused. She reinvented herself, becoming a mentor to other amputees, working with the Amputee Coalition of America, and fundraising for the AmpSurf foundation for veterans. She poured her heart into helping others until a freak accident ended her life far too soon.

Julie's story is woven into the fabric of CPK. She didn't just train servers—she helped shape our culture, raised the bar of service, and touched countless lives well beyond our restaurants. To this day I carry a deep pride that she chose to believe in us that afternoon at Cutters. Her mark on CPK—and on all of us—will never fade.

With the flagship restaurant's opening slated for March 1985, we still lacked restaurant managers. A friend recommended his son, Bret Goldberg (no relation to Burton Goldberg), who was managing a restaurant in Denver. After interviewing the affable and seemingly capable young man, we decided to hire him as our first manager.

As opening day approached, everything seemed on track—until we discovered we'd blown past our ever-elusive budget by $50,000. After a quick (and painful) discussion, Larry and I agreed on one thing: We were too embarrassed to go back to our investors. So as uncomfortable as it was, we did what any proud, overextended entrepreneurs would do—we ponied up the money ourselves.

Now in the final stretch, our new manager, Bret, along with Esther and our chef, Michele, headed to a restaurant-supply store in downtown Los Angeles. The mission was simple: Pick up smallware—pots, pans, and assorted kitchen essentials.

While they browsed, Michele pulled Bret aside and, as casually as if he were asking for the time, told him to keep the salesman distracted while he "loaded the truck."

Bret froze. There was no mistaking it—Michele intended to steal the supplies.

When Bret and Esther told us what had happened later that day, neither Larry nor I was surprised. Michele had been setting off alarms from the start, especially with his insistence on controlling every vendor and supplier "to get the best prices." We weren't that naive. Bret's story didn't soothe our suspicions; it confirmed them.

There were no deliberations, no second chances. Michele was gone.

CHAPTER EIGHT

OUR PRELAUNCH JITTERS QUICKLY SPIKED INTO FULL-blown panic. We were just weeks from opening, and once again, we had no chef.

And then—an unexpected twist.

Despite the fiasco at my law office, when I'd flatly rejected Chef Ed LaDou's take-it-or-leave-it ultimatum, he now resurfaced, asking for another meeting. We agreed to hear what he had to say, so we met at the Breadwinner, a casual bakery-café across the street from our soon-to-open CPK.

LaDou's tone was different now. He blamed his earlier posturing on bad legal advice, confessing that he and his lawyer had gotten drunk at Spago and cooked up a phony story about a phantom partner ready to launch a competing concept—all just to squeeze us for more.

Then came the kicker: He said he was now ready to sign on as chef on the original terms, but he had one new demand. He wanted the restaurant named *LaDou's California Pizza Kitchen.*

We were stunned. But only for a beat. I steadied myself, looked him squarely in the eye, and gave him my answer, loud and clear: "Fuck you, Ed."

However, we had recently spotted Ed LaDou pressed against the front window of our restaurant, peering in at the construction like a kid outside a candy store. It didn't take a genius to figure out he wanted another shot.

With the clock ticking and no better options, hoping that the third time would be the charm, we sat down with him. In early March 1985, just weeks before opening, we struck a deal: a flat $15,000 consultation fee to create the original menu and help launch the restaurant. Beyond that we kept it deliberately vague. If he proved himself, we'd talk about something more permanent.

But trust would have to be earned.

Still, in the back of my mind, I couldn't shake the feeling: A snake may shed its skin, but it's still a snake.

By then Larry and I had the menu categories sketched out: pizzas, pastas, salads, and a short dessert list. The bigger challenge was the price–value equation—that little bit of mental math every customer does, usually before the check even hits the table. Nail it, and they'll be back next week. Miss it, and you'll never see them again, whether you're selling dollar tacos or a hundred-dollar steak.

To make it a nonissue, we decided to price every item under $10.

Another decision on the table was whether we'd stick to beer and wine or spring for a full liquor license (which came with a hefty price tag). That one was easy. We didn't have the money, we didn't have the space, and serving cocktails didn't really match the menu we were building.

I'd been collecting wine for years, though my cellar leaned heavily French. For CPK the choice seemed obvious: Our wine list should match our California vibe and feature only California wines. At the time, though, we had too many balls in the air to focus on the wine list. Later, when we caught a breather, true to our value-driven DNA, we stocked recognizable, crowd-pleasing labels—but at prices that would make people do a double take. Our motto became "familiar wines at unfamiliar prices."

With opening day racing toward us, we had to create a menu at breakneck speed. LaDou, however, wasn't exactly open to input from two lawyers, and he made sure everyone knew it. The friction was constant, sharp enough to cut, but the clock was ticking. We bit our tongues, at least outwardly, while quietly keeping our own creative instincts in reserve.

Then came the reveal. LaDou slid his proposed pizza menu across the desk, and we stared at it in disbelief. It was bold, daring—maybe too daring. Just twelve pizzas, each more unconventional than the last: rabbit sausage, marinated grape leaves, lamb with Madeira mustard sauce, spicy shrimp with mint and lime.

Larry and I were stunned. Most of Ed's pizzas were too exotic, too far out for what we knew our guests would embrace. Rabbit sausage? Grape leaves? Lamb with Madeira mustard? Interesting, sure—but not the kind of thing that would keep people coming back for more.

We put our foot down. The menu needed some traditional anchors: pepperoni, mushroom, sausage, and at least one simple cheese pizza. We also lobbied hard for a Margherita, but the closest Ed would come was a pie topped with fresh sliced tomatoes.

We didn't have the term for it then, but we instinctively understood the "veto factor"—the idea that in a group, one person's hesitation could send everyone looking for another restaurant.

Anchors mattered.

Still, amid all the oddities, one idea leaped off the page: the Barbecue Chicken Pizza. We'd worked with Ed on tasting different sauces, and when we tried Gayle's Sweet 'N' Sassy BBQ Sauce—sweet, tangy, and just smoky enough—everyone lit up. Paired with smoked gouda and mozzarella cheeses, red onion, and fresh cilantro, it created a combination no one had ever tasted on a pizza before: fresh, approachable, and flat-out delicious. In that moment we knew we had something special. We couldn't wait to introduce it.

We always knew salads would play a big part of our menu, but in the rush, we didn't have time to develop them—and we were completely in Ed's hands. He had no interest in salads. After all, he was the pizza guru. The result was a bare-bones selection: a Caesar for $4.75 and a trio of pasta salads. One, a cold chicken and pasta with a spicy peanut-ginger sauce, would later inspire our Thai Chicken Pizza, still a favorite to this day. There was also a salmon-and-scallop ceviche—though in hindsight, why it landed under "salads" is still a mystery.

Beyond that came three calzones, two deep fried and one oven-baked with Brie and spinach. And in a particularly adventurous twist, Ed pushed a category of cheeseless pizzas: one with Japanese eggplant, radicchio, sun-dried tomatoes, and cilantro; another with duck, onions, pancetta, spinach, and mushrooms—served with sour cream.

Daring? Absolutely. Interesting to our customers? Doubtful. With opening day barreling toward us, the menu was set. The case was made. Now it was out of our hands. The jury would be the people of Beverly Hills—and their verdict would decide the fate of CPK.

CHAPTER NINE

WHILE INTRODUCING A NEW STYLE OF PIZZA WAS the spark that drew Larry and me into the restaurant business, our vision went well beyond the pies. We wanted an upscale yet approachable place—relaxed enough for families, polished enough for date night, and welcoming to anyone who just loved good food.

Here's the truth: The only one of us with any hands-on restaurant experience was Esther, and that came from helping out in her family's diner while growing up. That was a far cry from operating a full-service casual-dining restaurant in Beverly Hills. The reality was, none of us had ever managed a kitchen or run a restaurant.

But we carried a quiet confidence. What we lacked in résumés, we believed we made up for with something just as valuable: the instincts and expectations of customers. We weren't seeing things through the lens of industry pros; we were seeing them as people who loved to eat out, who valued great service, and who knew exactly how it felt to be on the other side of the table. That perspective was our compass.

We knew the stakes. If we didn't meet customer expectations right out of the gate, our concept would be dead in the water and could sink without a trace. We dreamed of CPK becoming a global brand, but no matter how innovative or delicious our food was, if the experience fell flat, we'd be toast. One and done.

Larry and I also drew inspiration from Ray Kroc, the founder of McDonald's. In his 1977 autobiography, *Grinding It Out*, Kroc boiled the business down to three core principles: quality, service, and cleanliness. Later, he added a fourth—value—creating the philosophy known as

QSCV. We saw these attributes not just as relevant but as essential goals for CPK. In our minds they weren't just McDonald's principles; they were the foundation for any successful restaurant or chain.

It felt like all the stars were aligning perfectly, starting with a unique pizza concept, enhanced by the allure of California's sun-kissed lifestyle and reinforced by our early unwavering commitment to QSCV.

Yet there was one more essential ingredient in that formula for success: *people*.

From the very beginning, we understood that everything depended on having the right people on our team. We didn't talk about *culture* back then, but we knew this much: For CPK to thrive, our employees had to like and trust us, and we had to feel the same about them.

This recognition underpinned our core goals. We had created a unique platform, and we aimed to create a fun and respectful working environment. We also wanted to ensure that our guests enjoyed their visits, and we aimed to use our success to give back to the local community.

Achieving this ambitious vision required aligning many moving parts to bring it all together. As we approached opening day, Julie and Esther took the lead in interviewing and hiring our front-of-house (FOH) staff. Among our original servers was Shawn Holley, then a law student. She later built a distinguished legal career—first as a member of O. J. Simpson's famed "Dream Team" defense and then as the managing partner of the Cochran Law Firm, representing numerous high-profile clients.

With Bret, Julie, and Esther overseeing the FOH operations, we managed to build a team of talented, committed individuals—both on the floor and in the kitchen. There were others on that opening crew whose names escape me now, but their contribution was no less essential.

Looking back, it's remarkable that we were able to assemble such a strong and dedicated team for a start-up with no industry track record.

With the benefit of hindsight, I see now that this team helped set the stage for something that's hard to define or measure. It went beyond service. What we created—what they delivered—was *hospitality*.

True hospitality. It's a higher bar, and it comes from something within. CPK had it from day one. And it all started at the front door, with the woman who set the tone, led by example, and brought warmth and grace to everything and everyone she touched: the third founder, Esther.

CHAPTER TEN

AS OPENING DAY DREW NEAR, WE WERE JUGGLING more tasks than we could count—just pedaling as fast as we could to get the restaurant open on schedule. Advertising never even crossed our minds. For one thing it wasn't in the budget. But even if it had been, it went against our instincts. We didn't go to restaurants that advertised, and we didn't want to be one that did.

We believed—maybe stubbornly—that if CPK was going to succeed, it had to be on its own merits. The food, the service, the energy of the place—that's what would get people talking. If it wasn't good enough for word of mouth, it wasn't good enough. Period.

Later, we summed it up with a mantra that stuck: "We don't want *to* advertise. We want to *be* advertised."

So our entire "advertising budget" came down to one thing: a small handwritten sign taped to the front door. It read simply, **OPENING MARCH 27TH AT 5PM.**

That was it. No fanfare, no press releases, no grand opening campaign. Just a date, a time, and the belief that if we built something special, people would come—and tell their friends.

On the appointed day, at exactly 5:00 p.m., we stood frozen in place, holding our breath as the first customer pushed through the door. And who was it? None other than Shirley MacLaine. For a moment we thought fate itself had blessed our opening. Then came the order: a single cup of coffee before heading upstairs to see her agent. No pizza. Just coffee.

It felt like the air had gone out of the room. Was this the grand beginning of our dream? A Hollywood star . . . sipping coffee? Hardly the launch we had imagined.

But within the hour, the tide shifted. Customers began to trickle in—less glamorous, perhaps, but actually hungry. And by night's end, the moment of truth arrived. The Barbecue Chicken Pizza was flying out of the kitchen. Reactions echoed through the dining room: "I don't even like pizza, but I love this."

That weekend sealed it. Our friend-turned-investor, Jane Seymour, hosted her *The French Revolution* cast and crew, who devoured ten Barbecue Chicken Pizzas with unanimous approval. The restaurant pulsed with discovery, laughter, and the sense that something entirely new was happening.

In the days that followed, customers didn't just return—they came back with urgency. One man set the record: lunch, dinner, and a late-night encore with his daughter so she could try it too.

We'd believed in the Barbecue Chicken Pizza from the first taste. But what opening week confirmed was something larger: This was no gimmick.

We were onto something big.

At first we debated whether to take reservations—a difficult proposition for a place with only sixty-seven seats. Still, we gave it a shot and booked a birthday gathering for the son of the owner of the Beverly Hills Hotel.

It was a disaster. The group of fifteen diners trickled in late, forcing us to hold empty tables while a crowd of impatient customers stared through the windows. Watching empty seats while you're stuck outside. Not a good look.

That night we made a monumental decision: no reservations. From then on it was first come, first served.

The policy didn't make Esther's life any easier as hostess, especially when the inevitable *resquilleurs* (French for "line-jumpers") tried to charm, name-drop, or muscle their way past the crowd spilling onto the sidewalk.

I recently learned that another hostess handled the crush a bit differently. Suzanne Goin, now a James Beard Award–winning Los Angeles chef, worked as a hostess at CPK that first summer while she was still in college. She later recalled, "We didn't take reservations. I remember I would basically gauge, by looking at the person, how angry they'd be if I told them how long the wait really was, then give them a glass of wine and have them drink on the sidewalk."

Yet since Larry and I were always at the restaurant—and excited to be eating there—we made sure that any waiting customer was seated before us. The last thing we wanted to do was to be escorted to an empty table while real guests stood in line. Optics mattered. We wanted our behavior to reflect the culture we were building: respectful, humble, and always customer first.

But there was something more. From the very beginning—even in our earliest conversations about the restaurant business—Larry and I knew this wasn't about celebrity or creating a place to hang out.

It was also my promise to Esther. When I first told her I wanted to open a restaurant, it stirred memories of her father working night and day at the family diner. I pledged this would be different—that we'd build something strong enough to thrive without us living in the restaurants.

We weren't building a restaurant for us—we were building one that didn't need us.

A few years later, an investor cut the line at our Brentwood location and announced he wanted to be seated immediately. The host didn't miss a beat. "I'll put you in the same place as I would Rick and Larry," he said, escorting the investor straight to the end of the line. Fortunately, the man had a sense of humor.

On a less savory note, from that same restaurant, one host quietly accepted a folded bill in a stealthy handshake to let a customer leapfrog the line. His fatal flaw? Bragging about it to a server, who promptly sang like a canary to the manager. Let's just say that his career at CPK ended as quickly as that handshake began.

Word of our success spread quickly, and since our little restaurant didn't take reservations, there was often a crowd outside. Seeing a line turned out to be the best possible advertisement we could have asked for. We discovered the advantage of a small restaurant with a wait over a large one that could feel empty.

We learned that lesson the hard way later, when we built some bigger locations that lacked the energy and buzz of the small, packed space. Finding the right balance is always a challenge, and there is no simple formula.

For Esther and me, CPK was a family affair. My son, Ian, got an early introduction to the restaurant business at fifteen. Living with us and attending Beverly Hills High School, he spent his spare time helping at the takeout counter.

In our first days of business, while Ian was working, our manager took a call from an irate customer who claimed she'd picked up her order, only to discover a pizza missing when she got home. She even suggested the solution was to fire the kid at the takeout counter. The manager calmly replied, "That might be a problem."

Naturally, Ian was shaken, but I learned that he'd stayed courteous and apologetic throughout. I told him that if he had done his best to defuse the situation, then he could be proud—that grace under pressure was more important than getting every order perfect. When I saw the ticket and noticed that she'd received the Barbecue Chicken Pizza, I told him not to worry—she'd be back.

Sure enough, the next day Ian came running up to me, grinning ear to ear, with the pure satisfaction only a fifteen-year-old could feel. The angry customer from the night before had been the first through the door—not to complain but to get another Barbecue Chicken Pizza. In that moment I saw my son stand a little taller.

Now my mornings took on a new ritual. Instead of jogging the mile straight to the Beverly Hills High School track, I'd detour a block to our tiny CPK office to grab the computer printout of the previous day's sales. Every sheet felt like a report card. The results were striking. Barbecue Chicken Pizza was off the charts—hundreds sold daily. The more exotic pies? Maybe two or three apiece. As we'd predicted, the classics—mushroom, pepperoni, and sausage—and the fresh tomato pizzas sold steadily.

The numbers told a clear story, but Ed LaDou wouldn't hear it. When I showed him the sales printouts, he waved them off. In his mind the chef always knew better than the customer. For me, as a trial lawyer who had built a career on evidence, it was maddening.

Larry and I, though, had no doubts. We could see exactly where the menu needed to go: rooted in familiar flavors, elevated with fresh twists, anchored by the Barbecue Chicken Pizza that was already stealing the show.

Ed liked to say his creations were "ahead of their time." Maybe so. But the jury had already spoken—and we weren't about to ignore the verdict.

The pastas told the same story. Undeniably creative. Rarely ordered. Our personal favorite, maltagliati with duck sausage, roasted shallots, sun-dried tomatoes, and thyme, was brilliant. If anyone besides us had ordered it, it might have survived.

The fettuccine with a saddle of rabbit and mushrooms in a tomato-sage sauce was flavorful, but the few who tried it swore it tasted like chicken. Eventually, we swapped the rabbit for chicken, and sales took off.

The spinach-brie calzone was another near miss. Customers loved the idea, but fresh from the oven, it was volcanic, taking forever to cool. Plus, it had an unfortunate tendency to balloon, then burst, sending molten spinach and brie splattering across the kitchen like culinary shrapnel.

But none of that mattered. Word was spreading like wildfire.

The Barbecue Chicken Pizza was destined to make history.

One of our early fans, Bruce Enderwood, a former executive of Baskin-Robbins, gave us an interesting insight. He told us our experience mirrored theirs: Baskin-Robbins's top seller was Jamoca Almond Fudge—but right behind it were the classics: vanilla, chocolate, and strawberry.

For Larry and me, it was a light bulb moment. Until then California-style pizza meant goat cheese at Chez Panisse or smoked salmon at Spago. But once CPK opened its doors, California-style pizza would forever be defined by Barbecue Chicken Pizza.

We'd grabbed the tiger by the tail, and we weren't letting go.

Our original dream of "Spago for the masses" evaporated overnight. Based on what we were seeing in real time, the market for overly sophisticated pizzas didn't exist—and judging by our sales, Beverly Hills had zero interest in rabbit sausage or gorgonzola with radicchio and pine nuts. We didn't need to spend a dime on market research to know: If the high-end crowd in Beverly Hills wouldn't touch it, the rest of the world never would.

So our vision shifted—quickly, boldly, and permanently—to flavors people instantly recognized but had never imagined on a pizza. That was the magic. Not gimmicks, not shock value, but reimagining what pizza could be.

Over time we came to define CPK's approach as one of infinite possibilities. We even adopted a slogan that captured it perfectly: Pizza is a canvas you can paint on.

But in that moment, we understood. Pizza might be our canvas, but we weren't interested in abstract art. From then on every flavor had to be craveable. It couldn't just sound good; it had to deliver.

Larry and I were through the moon with excitement. At every opportunity Larry began to call CPK the Baskin-Robbins thirty-one flavors of pizza. I always quickly added, "Just not in a pink ice cream parlor." Personally, I preferred the Ben & Jerry's analogy—partly because it rhymed with Rick & Larry's. But either way the idea stuck—endless possibilities, grounded in comfort and familiarity, with one more element that soon emerged: playfulness.

Larry believed the secret to our success was on the menu. I nicknamed him "the Pied Piper of Pizza," and he wore it like a badge of honor. But from the start, I sensed something more at play. The pizzas were the sizzle—but the steak was everything around them: the buzz, the energy of our staff, the way guests felt the moment they walked in and were greeted with genuine warmth. It was hospitality at every level. And beyond that there was something harder to define—a spark, a sense of discovery. We had tapped into something. Our guests didn't just enjoy the food—they felt part of something new.

For the first time, the weight lifted. The dream we'd been chasing no longer felt like a fantasy. It felt possible, tangible—close enough to touch. And the rush that came with that was unlike anything I'd ever felt.

The dream wasn't just a dream anymore—it was becoming real.

Still, beneath all the excitement, I carried a sobering concern: If we didn't deliver on service, none of it would matter. No matter how inventive or delicious our food, if the experience fell flat, the concept would die after one location. One and done.

In the end we were both right. Larry zeroed in on *flavor.* I obsessed over *feeling.* That contrast wasn't a weakness—it was our advantage. We didn't always see things the same way, but together we saw the whole. And that synergy became the bedrock of CPK.

What we didn't expect was that the pizzas would eventually outgrow the restaurants. But maybe we shouldn't have been surprised. From day one the vision had always been about the pizza—California style, bold and original. It was right there in our name. And just as we hoped, we came to own it.

Still, for all our dreams, we were rooted in the restaurants—in the rhythm of the kitchen, the energy of the dining room, and above all, the fire. That hearth wasn't just a cooking tool—it was the soul of the experience.

Years later, when we launched our frozen line, CPK pizzas would reach more than twenty thousand stores nationwide and outsell what we served in-house. Some customers never even realized we had restaurants. But what they were buying, whether they knew it or not, was born of that fire. That culture. That *feeling.*

But in the meantime, one major obstacle stood in the way of turning our vision into reality: LaDou. The temperamental chef got along with us like oil and water. In his mind he was the pizza guru, and we were just two lawyers who should bankroll his operation and stay out of his kitchen. He made that opinion loud and clear. Needless to say it didn't sit well with us, but at that stage, we were at his mercy.

And while he escalated by flat-out telling us to stay out of the restaurant altogether, the demand had the opposite effect. What LaDou failed to understand was that Larry and I were all in—financially, physically, emotionally. We had poured ourselves into getting CPK off the ground, and we weren't about to step aside. This was our vision coming to life, and we intended to protect it.

Still, it was a stormy mix. Exhilaration from CPK's early success collided with a volatile partnership that couldn't possibly hold.

After his cat and mouse game, leading up to the opening, LaDou had signed on as a consultant for three months. But as soon as the doors opened, he demanded a partnership, threatening to quit otherwise. Reluctantly, and with no viable alternative, we granted him a small ownership stake, though strictly as a limited partner.

That said, LaDou's attitude cost him dearly. We admired LaDou's talent. Had he shown even a shred of balance, we would have bent over backward to make it work. Instead, his stubbornness pushed us to create a quiet vow: We would not remain at his mercy any longer than necessary.

LaDou thrived in front of the pizza oven and especially enjoyed preparing pizza for old Spago regulars or chatting with friends perched at the counter. But he couldn't tolerate criticism. When a manager once returned a burned pizza to him, Ed exploded, slamming the peel down, storming out the back door, leaving the oven unattended mid-service.

He wasn't alone in volatility. Our first pasta cook, Angelo, was talented but combustible. Upset, he'd shout and fling pans, sending a crashing echo throughout the dining room. Angelo didn't last long, and when we let him go, the staff breathed a sigh of relief.

Those moments taught us that an open kitchen—a feature we'd seen only as an asset—could also be a liability. The flame-fired hearth, the fresh ingredients on display, the spotless white-tiled walls—they built trust and energy. But they also left us exposed. Any tantrum, any misstep was on display. Still, we believed the benefits outweighed the risks.

And the customers agreed. Later, when we asked guests to describe CPK in a single word, we expected "innovative" or "creative." Instead, the overwhelming answer was "clean." It wasn't the word we had in mind, but in the restaurant business (especially with the women customers we most hoped to attract), it was music to our ears.

Yet the real challenge remained LaDou. His ownership stake had done nothing to temper his volatility. Just weeks after opening, we were already searching for a solution. Fortunately, one was emerging right in front of us.

LaDou had convinced a former colleague at Spago, Gary Beauregard, to join us. At CPK, Gary started as a line cook and assistant kitchen manager but quickly proved to be far more. A UC Berkeley grad with a background in social work, Gary had spent time helping people manage stress—experience that became priceless in our high-pressure kitchen. Calm, steady, unflappable, he often kept the place from boiling over.

As we got to know him, our respect grew. He mastered the recipes, managed the crew, and showed the capacity to run the kitchen himself. It became increasingly clear that Gary was emerging as the answer to our LaDou problem.

The breaking point with LaDou came faster than we expected. His simmering disdain for our service staff had boiled over too many times, but one night it crossed a line we couldn't ignore. Larry and I were in our office next door when a young server—Julie Carruthers's roommate—burst in, sobbing uncontrollably. It took several minutes to calm her enough to speak. When she did, her words came out in ragged bursts: In front of a dining room full of customers, LaDou had loudly accused her of being on drugs. She swore it wasn't true.

We called Julie in to corroborate, and she didn't hesitate. Her roommate never used drugs. This was pure humiliation.

That was it. We summoned Gary to confirm he could step in, then called LaDou to our office. He admitted to the outburst but, unbelievably, insisted it was our duty to back him. We told him in no uncertain terms that our restaurant would be built on respect—for customers, for staff, for the truth. And in that moment, we fired him.

It was barely two months after opening. Our futures were on the line. As the door closed behind him, Larry, Esther, and I sank to the floor in my office. The adrenaline that had carried us through the confrontation evaporated, replaced by an almost crushing weight. Spontaneously, we all broke into unabashed crying—all three of us. There's no other way to describe it. We were terrified. With our financial lives on the line, we'd just let go of our chef in the middle of our launch.

But as we sat there, raw and shaken, we also knew we had done the only thing we could do. If we sacrificed our values now, there would be nothing worth saving later. It was the hardest decision we had faced up to that point, and the fear was palpable. But beneath that fear was something stronger: resolve. Whatever came next—success or failure—we would face it together.

Most importantly it would be on our terms.

LaDou went on to open his own restaurant, Caioti Pizza Café, but as CPK grew nationwide and beyond, he regularly reappeared—granting interviews and firing off letters to editors after any flattering press we received—insisting that two lawyers with no restaurant experience owed their success to him. We didn't respond. We stayed focused on building the company.

We always acknowledged his contribution. His Barbecue Chicken Pizza, created at our inception, was a lightbulb moment that opened our eyes to the endless possibilities that would define CPK.

He died in 2007 after a long fight with cancer. We spoke before the end and made peace; we're glad it ended on that note.

CHAPTER ELEVEN

FOLLOWING LADOU'S DEPARTURE, OUR HEADS SPUN with ideas we could finally bring to life. At the top of the list was one inspired by chicken satay skewers with peanut-ginger dipping sauce, a staple at Indian restaurants. Since we always dipped naan in the leftover sauce, it felt like a natural fit for our expanding vision.

That pizza, our now-famous Thai Chicken Pizza, didn't just introduce a new pizza flavor to the world—it coined a term. To our knowledge "Thai chicken" wasn't widely used before we popularized it. We later learned we might have been able to trademark it, but at the time, we had bigger priorities. Now it's part of the foodie lexicon.

Fueled by our newfound vision for innovation and Larry's love of mayonnaise, he came up with the BLT Pizza: tomatoes, cheese, and bacon that's baked on the crust, then topped with chilled lettuce tossed in mayo just before serving. (Years later we would serve slices to the audience at *The Oprah Winfrey Show*.) It was a hit. Today a tweaked version lives on as our California Club Pizza.

Esther and I created the Sante Fe Chicken Pizza, inspired by a quesadilla at Bistro Gardens in Beverly Hills. It featured grilled chicken, cheese, and generous dollops of guacamole, sour cream, and pico de gallo—toppings customers could spread over each slice. The Sante Fe Chicken Pizza paved the way for future hits such as the Carne Asada, Spicy Chipotle Chicken, and Tostada Pizzas.

With LaDou out of the picture, we could finally do what we'd wanted from day one—serve salads worth coming back for. Until then our lone green option was a Caesar. Now we set out to build an entire lineup of fresh, inventive salads tailored to the women who were fast becoming our core customers.

With salads underway we also turned to developing our California-centric wine list. Since collecting wine was my hobby, this was my province. For the opening we'd kept it concise, with every bottle under $20.00 and house wines at $2.25 a glass and $8.95 a bottle. Once we had a little breathing room, we rolled out our "familiar wines at unfamiliar prices" strategy. One of my favorite examples was the Jordan Cabernet Sauvignon. A prestige bottle selling for around $60.00 at Spago and the Grill on the Alley cost us $12.00 a bottle. We priced it at $20.00. Other restaurants were furious—which only proved we were on the right track.

Those exhilarating early days reinforced our instincts: Our branding would be a powerful magnet for customers. The clean, sleek decor, the unapologetic splash of yellow, and the iconic palm tree all drew attention. But the real showstopper was the wood-fired oven, blazing at the heart of the restaurant.

Larry and I were so proud that we'd sometimes cross the street just to admire its flame from a distance. Seriously, we did that. Decades later it's undeniable: CPK didn't just define California-style pizza—it made the whole world rethink what pizza could be.

Our confidence got another boost when we met Morris "Morrie" Hazan, the founder of the Original Cookie Company. Morrie had built his brand on an irresistible sensory hook—shipping cookie dough to stores nationwide and having them baked with doors open so the aroma drifted through the malls. He was intrigued by our open-flame oven and immediately saw its potential as a mall centerpiece. His encouragement was fuel to the fire propelling us forward.

* * *

With LaDou gone and Larry and me fully in control, our first priority was reassuring the staff. We'd earned their trust by being present, but we still needed to make sure the sudden change hadn't shaken morale. Just as our different personalities had balanced our law practice, they now helped us manage our employees.

Our first move was to station Larry as food expeditor, posted at the point-of-sale printer in front of the massive prep table—affectionately nicknamed the Queen Mary. His job was to coordinate orders, eyeball each dish for quality, and prevent mix-ups when servers grabbed whatever pizza was closet.

The only problem? Larry is a large man, and the space was so tight that servers struggled to squeeze past. Our solution: Whenever they needed through, they'd tap a key to print a ticket that read, "Excuse me, Larry."

But that wasn't our only challenge. We quickly learned a hard truth: There was a palpable tension between our front-of-house (FOH) and back-of-house (BOH) teams. On paper the FOH included hosts, servers, and bussers, but in practice, many of the bussers—though technically FOH—were culturally and socially aligned with the kitchen crew. The BOH included our line cooks, prep cooks, and dishwashers. We were told this wasn't unique to CPK; in fact it was practically baked into the restaurant business. But that didn't make it acceptable.

We could clearly see the stark reality. Most of our BOH employees were Hispanic men, many working multiple jobs to support families—sometimes across borders. Our FOH team, by contrast, was made up largely of Caucasian men and women, many working part-time while pursuing other careers. The split, along racial and cultural lines, fed the tension.

We knew CPK couldn't succeed without bridging that gap. We started holding full-staff meetings to remind everyone that we were interdependent—success in the dining room depended on the kitchen and vice versa. We encouraged FOH to recognize the dedication of BOH teammates and BOH to understand that happy customers kept all of us employed. Over time this emphasis on mutual respect became a cornerstone of our culture.

Looking around that first crew, we also realized something else: CPK was diverse—not because we had set out to make a statement but because that's what the restaurant business looked like. We didn't need a policy memo to tell us what was fair. From day one our rule was simple: Hire great people, period. Color, gender, sexual orientation, religion, education—none of it mattered if you could do the job and bring the right attitude.

On a much lighter note, while we were working hard to balance FOH and BOH dynamics, we hadn't fully agreed on the restaurant's ambience. Esther and I, having a young daughter at home, liked it bright and welcoming, with conversation-level music. Larry, working nights, would arrive for the evening shift, dim the lights, and cue up *Blade Runner* on the sound system—a moody, synth-heavy soundtrack that made the restaurant feel more like a nightclub than a family restaurant.

As we got our feet wet with hands-on operations, the day-to-day issues of running a restaurant started to surface. One that loomed from the beginning was theft. Everyone asked about it, and frankly, it was one of the scariest thoughts we had when we first considered getting into the business.

To stay ahead I researched the problem and installed what was then a state-of-the-art Remanco point-of-sale system. No cash registers, no slipping a twenty out of the till. Each server had a key, every order was printed in the kitchen, and at the end of the shift, cash and credit card vouchers had to balance. Clean, tight, foolproof.

Or so we thought.

One counter server found a flaw—and couldn't resist. Unfortunately for him, he also couldn't resist bragging about it to another server, who went straight to the manager. What he didn't realize was that every keystroke could be traced. We pulled the records and discovered he'd skimmed about $8,000 over a few months.

His father, a prominent Beverly Hills dentist, was mortified. After one very frank conversation, he wrote us a check for $15,000 for our troubles.

Then there was the human relations side. One of the perennial challenges in restaurants is keeping "fraternization" within legal limits. It's a notoriously high-pressure business, and when people work long hours with little time outside, they're naturally drawn to coworkers. But the law draws a line: It's improper for a manager to be involved with a subordinate. Naturally, as lawyers, we enforced a zero-tolerance policy.

So we were very disappointed when we learned that a popular assistant manager had violated the rule—not just with one server but with several. We called him into the office to confront him.

He admitted it immediately.

“Why?” we asked.

He shrugged. “Well, once I started with one, I knew you guys would catch me and fire me. So I figured I might as well keep going—in for a nickel, in for a dime.” It wasn’t romance. It was an all-you-can-eat buffet. Case closed.

While we all agreed in principle that CPK was family-friendly, Larry didn’t fully embrace it—until the moment of epiphany years later at our Oakbrook Mall location in suburban Chicago. Walking in, we saw a virtual sea of strollers parked outside. Larry commented that it looked like a stroller parking lot. Inside, the manager greeted us with a smile and a plea: “What we really need are more high chairs.”

That sealed it. From then on Larry was all in. Coloring books, crayons, booster seats—whatever it took to keep our youngest guests (and their parents) happy.

Later, we capped our commitment to families with the release of our fourth cookbook—*The California Pizza Kitchen Family Cookbook*—with every penny of proceeds donated to charity. By then CPK had become more than a place to eat. It was where three generations could sit around the same table, share a meal, and all leave happy. For us there was no greater compliment.

CHAPTER TWELVE

THROUGH THE YEARS I'VE OFTEN THOUGHT ABOUT THE wisdom of former heavyweight champ Mike Tyson, who said, "Everyone has a plan until they get punched in the face."

Looking back, we had a plan for CPK. What we didn't have was a guarantee it would work. Our first glimmer of relief came with $103,000 in sales during our very first month. We were thrilled—until we remembered that sales aren't the same as profits. With food and labor costs out of control and so many moving parts, we weren't there yet. Not even close.

That was when Norman "Norm" Habermann, CEO of W. R. Grace Restaurants (with more than one thousand restaurants at the time) and a big CPK fan, dropped a pearl of wisdom that stuck with me forever: "Sales cure everything." If you can get customers in the door, you can fix inefficiencies. But if you can't get them in the door, there's no easy fix.

We had the customers—more than we ever expected. And that was the problem. Our kitchen wasn't designed for such high demand. Instead of a walk-in refrigerator, we had what I called a "reach-in." Storage space was a joke. The wood for the pizza oven? We stacked it in my yard six blocks away.

To help reduce these inefficiencies, we scrambled, renting a refrigerated van for weekends, adding a small refrigeration unit out back, then even installing extra fridges and freezers into the courtyard of our law office next door.

A few years later, when the video store next door closed, we grabbed the space—not for more seats but for more efficiency. We expanded the kitchen, added refrigeration, relocated the front door, and created a proper takeout area. That decision turned out to be a masterstroke. Forty years later that same layout is still in use.

Meanwhile, our sales kept climbing, and we reached $130,000 by the end of August. But our banker still called it a honeymoon period and assured us we'd already peaked. By September we'd had enough of his doom and gloom. We changed banks.

Just as we were feeling unstoppable, reality smacked us. After Labor Day, sales dropped from $130,000 monthly to about $100,000 as families went back to school and parents back to their kitchens.

We panicked. But then our neighbors, Paul Fleming (Ruth's Chris) and Bob Spivak (the Grill on the Alley), explained this was an annual ritual in the business. Sure enough, the customers returned, and we learned a rookie's lesson: This wasn't just our problem; it was everyone's.

CHAPTER THIRTEEN

DESPITE THOSE EARLY HURDLES, CPK ENDED ITS FIRST year with $1.3 million in sales—roughly $4 million by today's measure after adjusting for inflation. That was well above our initial projections and enough to achieve modest four-walls profitability, meaning the restaurant was in the black if you looked only at direct operating costs.

With all the excitement surrounding our early success, our investors were thrilled. From the day we opened, we could feel it. The energy was electric, the lines were constant, and we were itching to grow.

It didn't take long.

One of our regulars was Sheldon Gordon, a prominent developer who had codeveloped the upscale Beverly Center shopping center with Alfred Taubman and E. Phillip Lyon. Sheldon suggested we look at a street-level space in the center. The location was tempting—prime real estate—but it was less than two miles from our original CPK. We worried it might cannibalize sales.

After some debate, we reasoned that Beverly Hills' sixty-seven seats were already stretched to capacity (or so we thought then), so adding another one hundred seats at Beverly Center felt like a natural step. The market was dense, affluent, and seemed ready for more.

The catch? We were already drowning in debt. The bank had cut us off, and income from our law practice had all but vanished. Expansion made perfect sense—except for the small detail of how to pay for it.

Needing a solution, we turned once again to our friend and fellow lawyer, Bob Kahan.

We'd been hearing regularly from investors that instead of receiving distributions from a single location, they'd rather roll their money into a larger play—betting on CPK's long-term future.

Bob came up with a creative fix: Create a new corporate entity, California Pizza Kitchen, Inc.; transfer all Larry's and my rights and intellectual property into it; and then convert our limited partners into shareholders of the parent company. That way, everyone would own a piece of the potentially larger pie (pun intended).

For Larry and me, there was another advantage: We could set salaries for ourselves, easing the personal financial pressures we'd been facing.

We still needed a valuation—never an exact science but especially difficult for a company only a few months old, with one restaurant and a lot of ambition. Truth be told, it felt more like throwing darts than doing finance. After much hand-wringing, we settled on $5 million. That number wasn't the product of spreadsheets or bankers. It was our attempt to balance two instincts: (1) to guard our precious shares from needless dilution, and (2) to keep things fair enough to bring everyone along.

The math worked out neatly. The original $300,000 investment translated to 6 percent of the company. To be fair we offered to buy out anyone who wanted to cash out—sweetening it with a 20 percent premium. Only two accepted the buyout: one with $10,000 invested, the other with $5,000. Both happily pocketed their quick profit.

However, years later, after CPK took off, each called with the same regret: They wished they'd stayed in. Larry and I couldn't help but grin. At the time they'd celebrated their win—but in hindsight it might have been the most expensive $3,000 they ever made.

Not long after, we faced the next hurdle: raising $600,000 to bring the Beverly Center location to life. This time the math was more deliberate, but the principle was the same. We nudged our share price from $5 to $6 and issued one hundred thousand new shares, pegging the company's value at $6.6 million. In a letter to our original investors, we explained the move and offered them the chance to buy more. Many did—and for those who took us up on it, it turned out to be one of the best bets they ever made.

Then came the kind of break you can't plan for. At the time Larry was dating Elaine Okamura, former wife of Las Vegas headliner Wayne Newton. One day they found themselves flying home from Vegas aboard casino owner Verna Harrah's private jet. Also on board was Steve Wynn, the man behind the Golden Nugget.

Larry and Steve got to talking. Before long, Larry was giving him the full CPK pitch—Beverly Hills, wood-fired ovens, Barbecue Chicken Pizza. Steve was intrigued enough to make the trip to our flagship, meet with us, and see for himself. He loved it. Within days he invested $250,000—by far our largest single investment to date.

Steve's money helped, but the bigger win was his blessing to drop his name when talking to other investors. In Las Vegas terms, it was like having the house back your hand. And this was before Steve had even dreamed up the Mirage. His own next act was still in the wings—and eventually, it would cross paths with ours in ways we couldn't yet imagine.

Larry and I were such neophytes that we didn't know the term *start-up*, but that's exactly what we were. We understood one thing clearly: It would take time before CPK turned a profit, and raising more capital was essential to get there.

Our path forward sounded simple enough—open one successful restaurant after another, each proving the concept and justifying more investment. Profitability would come with scale, we told our investors. "We're building a money machine," we liked to say. "It just isn't plugged in yet." Now that the original limited partners had converted into shareholders of California Pizza Kitchen, Inc., we returned to our friends-and-family fundraising playbook. This time it was far easier. Investors now saw CPK as an exciting brand with momentum and real growth potential. When our first group received a letter offering them a bigger slice of the pie, many reinvested and sent new prospects our way. Parents, cousins, friends—and friends of friends—joined in.

Our publicist, Joan Luther, also introduced us to three more who became both investors and friends: Fred Hayman, the impeccably dressed founder of Giorgio on Rodeo Drive, known as "Mr. Beverly Hills"; Don Tronstein, a quiet man who owned much of Rodeo Drive's prime real estate; and Herb Fink, the savvy owner of the fashion retailer Theodore's.

It was an exhilarating time. Our fear of failure—though never entirely gone—was fading. Momentum was building. And truth be told, we were suddenly a lot more popular as CPK founders than we'd ever been as criminal defense lawyers.

Then came the light bulb moment. After our early Beverly Hills experience in a residential neighborhood, we were offered something entirely different: a prime space in an upscale shopping center. We saw it instantly—this was the future. We weren't just opening another restaurant; we were stepping into a whole new category. One that didn't even exist yet.

At the time mall dining meant Hot Dog on a Stick or Orange Julius. We saw the chance to flip that script—to bring restaurant-quality food into a modern, inviting setting, right where people shopped. Upscale shopping centers became the perfect stage for our vision. With Beverly Center we weren't just expanding—we were pioneering what the industry would later call "polished casual dining."

To keep pace our financing had to grow with us. After raising the capital for Beverly Center, we secured another $1 million—enough for a third restaurant and a cushion of working capital. Each round meant revaluing the company, and this time we pegged it at $8.5 million. Arbitrary? Yes.

Aggressive? Definitely. Especially since we weren't yet profitable.

We met often with prospective investors, always candid. "You're not profitable yet," some pointed out. Our response never wavered: "Our goal is to deliver a great return for all investors. But if you don't believe in the company, don't invest."

Most did. Some didn't. And yes, over time, more than a few wished they had.

CHAPTER FOURTEEN

WE'D WORRIED THAT A SECOND LOCATION LESS than two miles away from our Beverly Hills restaurant might cannibalize sales. The opposite happened. The day Beverly Center opened, the Beverly Hills restaurant set a new record. Both restaurants thrived, and the added exposure only strengthened the CPK brand.

Almost immediately, we were in deep talks for our third location—Topanga Plaza Mall, in the San Fernando Valley's Woodland Hills area. The spot couldn't have been better—right at the mall entrance, directly next to a Nordstrom.

Those first locations set the template for what became our corporate strategy: Put CPK in the country's top retail center, ideally anchored by Nordstrom, Neiman Marcus, or Saks Fifth Avenue. It wasn't just about foot traffic (although that mattered)—it was about signaling that CPK belonged in the same orbit as America's best shopping experiences.

While negotiating the Topanga Plaza lease, the leasing agent asked how much "build-out allowance" we expected. At the time I had never heard the term, so I played it cool.

"I don't know. What do you think is reasonable?"

He suggested $50 per foot. That was when I instantly grasped the concept—tenant improvement allowance ("TI"). At five thousand square feet, he was offering $250,000 toward construction.

Wow! That was an eye-opener. And since it was obvious they wanted us, I decided to swing for the fences.

"We'd want $100 per foot," I said. (That was the equivalent of $500,000!)

"Done," he said, without hesitation.

In that moment I realized I had stumbled upon a crucial concept in lease negotiations: tenant improvement allowance (often referred to as "TI").

When I hung up, I told Larry, "I just discovered something that could change everything." Upscale shopping centers weren't just our target—they could actually help finance our growth.

Win-win.

Now emboldened, I called Beverly Center's leasing agent, part of the Taubman Company, based in Michigan, and said we'd require TIs.

His answer was curt. "We're the Taubman Company. We don't give tenant improvement allowances. You're lucky we're offering you such a prime space."

I didn't miss a beat. "If that's the case, there's no reason to continue our conversations. TIs are a common industry practice, and we're not coming there without them."

The call ended right there.

A short time later, the agent called back. Bobby Taubman, son of founder Al Taubman, a top executive of the company, wanted to meet at our Beverly Hills location. Sitting at the counter, Bobby restated Taubman's position: no TIs. We held firm. After some back-and-forth, he finally offered $150,000, roughly $50 per square foot, while claiming it wouldn't even cost us that much to build. He went so far as to suggest we were just trying to put money in our pockets.

Hyperbole, of course, and he knew it—better than we did. The build-out ended up closer to $600,000. From that point on, our relationship with Bobby was . . . let's just say "strained."

The truth is, TIs aren't free money. Developers have their own cost of capital and rent targets, and if they give you an allowance, they expect to make it back—often by raising the rent.

Sometimes we took the TI deal; other times we passed if we thought the long-term rent hit would be too steep. Over time we got smarter about lease economics, learning how to balance base rent and percentage rent to unlock meaningful TI funding without overpaying in the long run.

And before anyone's eyes glaze over—I promise I'll save the lease math for later.

Over the years many have assumed that the rents in high-end shopping centers were prohibitive. In reality the foot traffic in these prime locations more than justified the cost—these were our most profitable restaurants.

Still, our relationship with the Taubman Company soured after Beverly Center. At the time Westfield was building the Westside Pavilion in West Los Angeles, and both sides wanted CPK there. But Beverly Center's lease had a four-mile-radius restriction. Westside Pavilion fell just inside that zone, and under the clause, any sales there would count as Beverly Center sales—meaning we'd owe Taubman 7 percent of them.

Initially, Taubman told us they'd approve a waiver. Relying on that, we finalized terms with Westfield—only for Billy Taubman to reverse himself at the last minute.

Larry and I flew to Taubman's Michigan office to plead our case. The timing was bad—Bobby was in the middle of a divorce and wearing a neck brace. He told us exclusivity was nonnegotiable. I replied, "Beverly Center will still be exclusive. It'll be the only Taubman mall in America with a CPK."

My reasoning didn't move him.

Westfield's president, Richard Green—a friend—believed Taubman wouldn't actually sue and offered to indemnify us. But as former litigators, we avoided lawsuits unless necessary, so we walked away.

Our distrust deepened when we learned Hard Rock Cafe was paying 6 percent rent at Beverly Center, despite being told they paid 7 percent—the rate we'd agreed to match. We never forgot the misrepresentation, and when our lease came up for renewal ten years later, we dropped to 6 percent.

For the next decade, we refused every Taubman proposal, no matter how attractive the location.

Eventually, we relented and agreed to open a CPK at Willow Bend Mall in Plano, Texas.

A couple of weeks before the opening, Sarah Goldsmith Grover, our senior vice president of marketing, shared a troubling call from a new Neiman Marcus marketing manager in Dallas. Historically, we'd had a great relationship with Neiman Marcus—joint promotions, participation in their InCircle loyalty program, and so on. But this newcomer flatly said that Neiman Marcus no longer wished to partner with us, adding insult to injury by flatly declaring, "A Neiman shopper is not a CPK customer."

It was a ridiculous claim, and I asked Sarah for longtime CEO Burt Tansky's contact info so I could address it directly.

Before I had chance to write, I was on a plane to Dallas for the grand opening of Willow Bend. The mall was beautiful, anchored by Neiman, which made the slight even more absurd.

As I strolled through the mall, I ran into Bobby Taubman, Billy's brother and also a top Taubman Company executive. Despite our history with Billy, I'd always gotten along with Bobby. He told me that while he knew CPK didn't take reservations, he'd appreciate an exception that day so he and Burt Tansky could come for lunch. I assured him that I'd be there and would be happy to welcome them.

When Bobby introduced me to Burt, I said, "This must be your first time at a CPK."

"Not so." He smiled warmly. "We eat at California Pizza Kitchen all the time. It's my wife's favorite restaurant."

I couldn't resist. "Her favorite restaurant? Well, she must not be a Neiman shopper!"

Burt looked confused, so I related the Neiman marketing manager's comment. His face went pale. "I apologize," he said. "I'll take care of it."

The very next day, Sarah received a call from a *new* marketing manager at Neiman, eager to tell her how much they valued our partnership—and to ask how they could better support us going forward.

Apparently, Mrs. Tansky was still a CPK customer.

CHAPTER FIFTEEN

WITH TOPANGA PLAZA OPEN, WE NOW HAD THREE successful CPKs under our belt. But it was the fourth that would prove to be a game changer. The buzz from Beverly Hills got a boost when food critic John Mariani named us one of *Esquire's* Outstanding Bars and Restaurants in 1985.

That kind of press naturally caught the attention of major developers, among them Al Barr, head of leasing at Lenox Square in Atlanta, the premier shopping center in the Southeast.

Al wanted us in the heart of Lenox's soaring atrium, where two levels of shoppers would look down at the action below. From day one we had envisioned CPK as a national, even international, brand. We also feared competitors wouldn't be far behind. The more noise we could make early as little guys, the better.

The clincher came when Esther's brother Louis Graffeo, a Birmingham-based restaurateur and caterer, offered to move to Atlanta to run it. Esther and I decided to relocate there for a couple of months to help launch. With our daughters, Nicole, aged five, and Dana, just three months, Esther dove in, serving as daily hostess, greeting guests with her trademark Southern hospitality and warmth (and an accent that grew more noticeable each shift).

The restaurant was "slammed" from day one—two hundred seats with lines snaking out into the wide-open atrium space (no door to slow them down) and weekly sales volumes of more than $100,000—about $270,000 today. Thirty-eight years later, it's still going strong. When people asked why we opted to expand to Atlanta so early, we'd say it was like getting CPK center court at Wimbledon.

Next came Honolulu. Phil Lyon—one of the developers of Beverly Center and owner of the Kahala Mall in Hawaii's upscale neighborhood—offered us a space occupied by a small local department store. Though the mall wasn't in a tourist area, the community was affluent and tight-knit.

Intrigued, partly by the business opportunity and partly by the idea of spending time in Hawaii, we negotiated a lease. Fortuitously, we were introduced to local celebrity, Carole Kai. Born and raised in Hawaii, Carole had made a name for herself as a singer, even successfully performing in Las Vegas. By the time we met her, she had ostensibly retired from entertaining (at least temporarily, as she later became executive producer and co-host of *Hawaii Stars*, a popular, locally produced, televised karaoke/talent show) and was dedicated to philanthropy.

Not only was Carole charming—she was also deeply passionate about the people of Hawaii. We were so impressed by her charisma and dedication that we asked if she would consider representing us as our public relations liaison in Hawaii.

Carole worried that she didn't have the right experience in public relations. We weren't the least bit concerned. It was like tossing a duck into the water and saying, "Let's see if you can swim." She accepted, and over time she chose to represent only one other client, Mauna Loa nuts, a beloved local company.

Meeting Carole was an extremely fortunate twist of fate. While it's challenging to quantify the exact impact she made for CPK, we're certain that she played a vital role in the success of our Hawaii locations. Once again this experience taught us a valuable lesson and reaffirmed our commitment to working with kind people who care deeply about their community. When working with the right people, anything is possible.

* * *

To celebrate the Hawaii opening, we held a preopening fundraiser for Carole's favorite charity, the Variety Club. We expected a full house—but not this full. Somehow 150 tickets had been sold for a restaurant with only 105 seats.

What could have been a disaster turned into a perfect example of the Aloha spirit. Knowing we'd oversold, we scrapped regular service and set up a buffet along the counter. By the time the doors opened, every seat was filled, a line snaked into the parking lot, and we were moving through the crowd apologizing—only to be met with smiles and comments such as "No problem! Thank you for bringing CPK to Hawaii."

The room buzzed like a neighborhood block party. Everyone seemed to know each other, no one wanted to give up their seat, and somehow it all worked out perfectly. That night confirmed we'd chosen the right spot. Even though we weren't in a tourist district, Kahala became our highest-grossing CPK in the United States.

Whenever Larry and I visited Honolulu, we were treated like celebrities—invited onto local TV, mentioned in the newspapers, and welcomed as honored guests. On television we quickly learned that what we had once dismissed as *tourist* shirts—bright Hawaiian floral shirts—were local attire. The hosts would greet us warmly, saying, "I see you've gone local." It was a lesson in embracing the culture that so generously had embraced us.

Kahala's success brought an unexpected but welcome problem: Demand for Jordan Cabernet, the cult wine of the era, far exceeded the state's entire allocation. Our solution? Quietly ship cases from the mainland in CPK supply containers. The winery knew but graciously looked the other way.

Soon after, we opened another hit in Hawaii, this one at Phil Lyon's Pearlridge Shopping Center—again, well outside the tourist area. Then came Ala Moana Center, one of the most successful malls in America and another blockbuster CPK location. Beyond that we continued to build successful restaurants in the area, including franchised locations in the Honolulu and Maui airports.

Carole's connections also led to one of our lifetimes' most memorable experiences: meeting Adm. Steve Chadwick, commander of Pearl Harbor. For his retirement we hosted a glamorous send-off at our Waikiki restaurant. The night before, he took us—along with Esther's visiting mother—on a private, after-hours tour of the USS *Arizona* Memorial aboard the admiral's barge. Standing there with the admiral in the quiet of the night, reflecting on the history and sacrifice it represented, was a deeply profound and unforgettable moment.

The next day's ceremony, complete with visits to Schofield Barracks and a battleship, was unforgettable.

Steve later became commandant of the Naval Academy. Years later his son Rob followed in his father's footsteps, making them the first father-son duo to hold the position. He later went on to become the lead admiral at Pearl Harbor, a true testament to this extraordinary family legacy.

CHAPTER SIXTEEN

AROUND THE SAME TIME THAT WE WERE DEVELOPING the Kahala location, our largest investor—and by then our friend—Steve Wynn called. He was in the middle of building something that would change Las Vegas forever: the Mirage, the most expensive hotel in the world.

He told us he'd planned to put a hot dog stand next to the massive Sports Book, but he was having second thoughts. "How about a CPK instead? I'll be the franchisee."

Normally, the answer would have been a hard no. Larry and I were adamantly against domestic franchising—too much risk of losing control, diluting quality, and damaging the brand.

International franchising was one thing; at home we wanted to keep a firm hand on the wheel.

But this wasn't just anyone. This was Steve Wynn—an extraordinary visionary and our largest investor—who had backed us when we had one restaurant. We didn't hesitate for a second.

Steve mentioned one little twist: The design wouldn't follow our signature black, white, and yellow. It would blend into the Mirage's tropical theme. We shrugged that off too. If Steve wanted tropical decor, we were all in.

Two weeks before the grand opening in November 1989, though, our advance team called in a panic: "You're going to hate it. You may want to pull the plug." Larry and I caught the next flight to Vegas.

Steve met us to escort us through the hotel. The Mirage itself was jaw-droppingly lush, over the top, every inch designed to wow. When we finally reached the restaurant, we braced ourselves. What we saw were multicolored booths, a full-on tropical theme. Nothing like CPK's signature look. We glanced at each other and burst out laughing. It was stunning. Even better, the location was next to Siegfried & Roy's famous white tigers.

We would have preferred black-and-yellow tigers, of course, but we turned to Steve and said, "Looks great to us."

The Mirage opened like an adult Disneyland. The CPK was a smash from day one—$5.5 million in first-year sales (1989 dollars), turning tables an average of sixteen times in thirteen hours.

There were often two lines—one for regulars, one for VIPs—each over an hour long.

Best of all, the location became our ultimate marketing tool. Every May the International Council of Shopping Centers Convention brought the nation's biggest mall developers to Las Vegas. They all stayed on the Strip, they all toured the Mirage, and sooner or later they all wandered past our restaurant, right there next to the white tigers.

For CPK it was priceless exposure. We had a living, breathing showcase—packed with customers, buzzing with energy. I started calling it "a billboard that pays us." But the truth was—behind the joke—it really was.

One of those visitors was Mel Simon, founder of Simon Properties—the largest mall developer in the world and eventually our biggest landlord. When he called asking for a table for his team and himself, we happily made an exception for our usual "no reservations" rule.

Steve Wynn didn't just change our business; he opened doors we never could have imagined. While the Mirage brought us invaluable connections with developers and investors, it also came with an extraordinary perk: Shadow Creek. Designed by Tom Fazio and built at a staggering $40 million, Shadow Creek wasn't just a golf course—it was a hidden kingdom, tucked away in the Nevada desert, shrouded in secrecy, accessible only to a chosen few.

From the moment I stepped onto it, I knew Shadow Creek was unlike anything else. Thousands of trees, waterfalls, streams—and, to my astonishment, wildlife you'd expect in a dream rather than a golf round.

Snow-white swans glided across ponds. Exotic birds darted through the trees. Wallabies and wild turkeys roamed the fairways. It was surreal, as if Steve had conjured a nature preserve in the middle of Las Vegas.

As a lifelong golfer, I was awestruck. When Steve asked what I thought, I borrowed a line from playwright George Kaufman: "It's what God would have done if he had the money." I've only used that line twice—once for Shadow Creek and years later on the Hawaiian island of Lanai, when my lifelong friend Larry Ellison showed me his lush, luxurious Four Seasons Sensei Resort.

Shadow Creek's early days were pure fantasy. No tee times, no green fees. Steve personally decided who played, and most days fewer than ten people were allowed through the gates. The clubhouse kitchen served a full menu, with everything comped, and guests were told not to tip the caddies. Larry and I not only got to play, but we were also given engraved lockers. Mine sat right next to my golf hero, Arnold Palmer's.

The club manager, a CPK fan, extended us a privilege: We could bring guests. Steve knew and never objected. Among those we hosted were Steve Garvey, the baseball legend, and Bruce Jenner—now Caitlyn—the Olympic decathlon champion.

From countless rounds with Garvey, I learned one ironclad rule: Never needle him before a shot. All it did was sharpen his focus—and then you'd be sorry. Jenner, on the other hand, was the opposite. A well-timed jab and you could watch the double bogey form in real time.

One afternoon Steve was on the driving range, holding court with a few guests—including Jerry Weintraub, the legendary Hollywood producer—when he stopped mid-conversation and surprised us. "You know who I owe a debt of gratitude to? When the Mirage first opened, it was sheer chaos—five thousand chickens running around with their heads cut off. Except for CPK. They were the calm in the storm."

The truth was, that calm didn't happen by chance. Before we'd ever served a pizza, we'd sent in a handpicked training team and set the tone. One of them—Brian Sullivan, a sharp young manager from our Beverly Center restaurant—moved his family to Las Vegas and took the reins as general manager. Under Brian's leadership, the restaurant didn't just survive the opening frenzy—it thrived.

Brian stayed on for several years before returning to the company in Los Angeles, where he became our senior vice president, leading our culinary team, safeguarding quality control, and working side by side with Larry and me on menu development. To this day I believe Brian was one of the biggest contributors to CPK's long-term success.

Our business and personal relationship with Steve Wynn didn't just create great memories—it proved highly profitable for CPK and Steve. The company itself collected substantial royalties on the Mirage sales. CPK clipped coupons while, on Steve's side of the ledger, his $250,000 investment ultimately delivered a return of roughly 2,000 percent. Not a bad deal for anyone involved.

But there's more. Not long after the Mirage opened, Steve's longtime personal assistant, Joyce Luman, called to say Steve wanted to fly in to meet with us at our office the next day.

When he arrived, he got straight to the point. He owned a parcel of land just north of the Mirage and was planning a new family-oriented resort—more affordable than the Mirage but still spectacular. The trouble: He was struggling to come up with the right name.

"You guys are creative. I need your help," he said.

That night I turned ideas around, but nothing clicked. The next morning, as Larry was heading out of town, he called me. "Call Steve when you can and tell him I've named his hotel: Treasure Island."

I phoned Joyce right away, but she said Steve was en route to Australia. "Tell him to call me," I said, "because Larry's named his hotel."

Minutes later my phone rang. It was Steve, calling from his private jet. "Hi, Ricky, I heard Larry named my hotel."

"He sure did," I said. "Treasure Island."

"That's it!" Steve roared with glee. "Give him a kiss for me!"

Days later Steve returned to Las Vegas and staged one of the great unveilings, in true Steve Wynn fashion. Dressed in full pirate regalia, he stepped off his plane, onto the airport tarmac, and announced his new resort: "Treasure Island."

When a CNN reporter asked him how he'd come up with the name, Steve didn't miss a beat.

“I didn’t,” he said. “A friend of mine, chairman of California Pizza Kitchen, did.” And just like that, Larry’s reputation as “the name guy” was sealed.

A few weeks later, at Steve’s fiftieth birthday party, he pulled us—along with Chris Hemmeter, the pioneer of Hawaiian megaresorts and a loyal customer at our Honolulu CPK—into a private conference room. Since returning from Australia, Steve had already poured $1 million into a working model of the now-famous pirate ship battle that would play out nightly in front of Treasure Island. Larry took one look at the massive display and, without missing a beat, deadpanned, “Just as I intended.”

CHAPTER SEVENTEEN

WE DIDN'T SET OUT WITH SOME GRAND MASTER plan around company "culture." It wasn't a buzzword we tossed around. Truthfully, we didn't even know any. What grew at CPK came naturally out of one simple instinct Larry and I shared: Do the right thing. From day one we knew we were working with real people—people with personalities, emotions, and lives outside of work—and treating them with respect became our North Star.

We used to tell our team that CPK was a "work with" company, not a "work for" company. It wasn't just a line—it was how we led. Later, when we picked up some business vocabulary, we called it a "reverse pyramid." The people on the front lines—hosts, servers, cooks, bussers, dishwashers—sat at the top, while leadership, including the CEOs, belonged at the bottom. Our job as leaders was to support the people doing the real work. That wasn't a slogan. We meant it.

We believed that if we empowered our team and gave them real ownership, they'd take better care of our guests—and of each other. That's why our corporate office wasn't called "headquarters." We named it the Restaurant Support Center—because that's exactly what it was.

Training was at our core before we ever served a customer. As customers ourselves, we knew how frustrating it was to have a server who couldn't answer basic menu questions. At CPK our servers had to know every ingredient in every dish—and prove it by passing written tests before they could hit the floor. In the early days, a father whose son worked for us told me his son claimed he'd studied harder for his finals at CPK than for his finals at Harvard! I can't vouch for the accuracy, but it said something about the standard we set.

Over the years, when friends asked me to help get their kids a job at CPK, I was always happy to. But I had one condition: I could help them get the job. I couldn't keep it for them.

At the core our training was built on one word: *hospitality*. It wasn't something we said—it was who we were. In those earliest days, Esther worked as hostess, greeting guests with genuine warmth and the meticulous eye for the details that made a visit memorable. Our very first employee, Julie Carruthers, carried that torch—creating our first training manuals, waiting tables in Beverly Hills, and setting a tone of professionalism that became the CPK standard.

By sheer luck, when the *Los Angeles Times* restaurant reviewer came in, Julie happened to be her server. The review was glowing. Sometimes luck matters!

In those early days, Esther worked nights at the restaurant while I often stayed home with our three-year-old daughter Nicole, watching *Star Search*. She says those nights set her on a path to music. Please excuse another moment of fatherly pride, but today she has built a career as a singer-songwriter under the name *Claude Fontaine*, performing world music and touring internationally. She has opened for renowned artists and played the iconic Blue Note in Tokyo. Her songs have been featured by global brands, including Ralph Lauren and Starbucks, both of which have showcased her music as part of their curated music programs.

As the company grew, Esther—true to her nature—stepped back from the spotlight. But her influence never faded. She remained my most trusted sounding board. Her support—steady, honest, and unwavering—helped quietly shape so many of the decisions Larry and I made along the way.

A few years later, Joni entered the picture when she married Larry. She never had an out-front role, but I have no doubt she became for Larry what Esther was for me. We were both lucky.

Through all the highs and lows, Esther and Joni were our constant foundation as we built CPK.

With the business running relatively smoothly, we borrowed a playful touch from Steve Wynn's Mirage: Servers wore name tags with their hometowns. It personalized the experience and gave guests an easy icebreaker. Some servers had fun with it, listing far flung or even fictional hometowns just to spark conversation. The side effect? Built-in accountability. Guests knew exactly who to praise—or, on the rare occasion, whom to call out.

Hospitality was our heart, but quality and safety were our backbone. Every manager, front and back of house, was expected to know how to make every item on the menu, and each shift, they were required to taste each ingredient on the line to guarantee quality and freshness.

Our first quality assurance team was built by my son, Ian, and Larry's stepson, Peter Gillette. Both put in long hours in CPK's kitchens, learning the food from the ground up. Ian eventually launched his own wealth management firm, Elevon Wealth in San Francisco, while Peter earned his MBA and returned to CPK as senior vice president of international and franchise operations. They carried the same pride in CPK that Larry and I did—and represented us well.

Quality wasn't just a slogan—it was the standard. Not long after Beverly Hills opened, a young manager brought me a pizza with a burned crust.

"Should I serve it?" he asked.

"If you have to ask," I told him, "the answer is no."

He looked puzzled. "I've never worked for a company that didn't care about the bottom line."

"I care about our bottom line," I assured him. "But the cost of tossing out one pizza is nothing compared to the damage of serving it."

As we expanded into new markets, we created traveling training teams made up of our very best employees. They weren't just there to open doors. They stayed on, side by side with the new crews, until everyone felt confident running on their own. For those who traveled and those being trained, it was more than just instruction; it was an energizing experience that forged friendships and deepened loyalty across the company. These bonds became the living proof of the culture we were building—pride in the work, trust in one another, and a shared commitment to excellence.

* * *

By the early '90s, CPK had become a nationally recognized brand with a loyal and growing customer base. That was when some of our more corporate-minded friends began encouraging us to formalize our vision by drafting a mission statement. A few even tossed out suggestions such as "Sell more pizzas than anyone in the world," "Be number one," or "Out-profit other pizza chains."

But none of those slogans resonated with us. We knew that CPK would never rival market heavyweights such as Pizza Hut, Domino's, or Papa John's, and we were perfectly fine with that. Our aspiration was to build a company we could be proud of—a place that was respected in the community, that served great food, and that offered a work environment people genuinely enjoyed. The rest would take care of itself.

At its heart what we were really after was something harder to define—a sense of quality. Not just in the food or the service but in the overall experience.

And that extended to our team. A phrase that kept coming up in interviews and conversations was "quality of life." Larry and I met it head-on. To us quality of life meant waking up in the morning actually wanting to come to work, feeling challenged, and working alongside like-minded people toward a common goal. Just as important, it meant being proud of where you worked.

In these conversations Larry would inevitably chime in with "As Confucius said, 'Choose a job you love, and you'll never work a day in your life.'"

In researching this memoir, I discovered that Confucius probably never said that. But it certainly *sounds* like something he *should* have said—and Larry and I subscribed to this point of view.

From those earliest days in Beverly Hills, we'd learned a truth that mattered more than any menu item: Without the right people to share our vision, we'd be dead in the water. Barbecue Chicken Pizza might have gotten the headlines, but it was our team that kept us afloat. So when it came time to define our company's purpose, we skipped the flashy slogans and grandiose mission statements. Instead, in the little conference room between our offices, we talked not about our business plan but about the people who made it possible. In just a few minutes, we landed on an acronym that said it all: ROCK—Respect, Opportunity, Communication, and Kindness. These four words became the foundation of our culture, the bedrock we built on from that day forward.

Respect ensured that all employees, regardless of their role, were treated with dignity. However, we emphasized that respect is a two-way street. "We all have the right to be respected, but we can't demand respect," we said. "It has to be earned."

Opportunity provided real avenues for personal and professional growth. We welcomed and promoted great people without regard for color, gender, sexual orientation, religion, education level—none of that mattered. While we knew that some employees would only be with us part-time or for a short time, we encouraged them to think beyond themselves and help others benefit from the same opportunities.

Communication encouraged open dialogue, breaking down barriers between FOH and BOH staff. But it also meant management had to truly listen—and act—when the best ideas or concerns surfaced. However, like respect, it was a two-way street. Speaking up mattered, but listening often mattered more.

Kindness was the glue that held it all together. We needed kind people in every position. We pointed out that if one person came to work in a bad mood, it could drag down the entire team. A chain is only as strong as its weakest link. Kindness was also the most essential element for being recognized as a "ROCKstar," the name we gave to people who embodied the culture that defined CPK's success.

Whenever Larry and I evaluated people for a job or promotion, we'd start by asking ourselves, "Is this person a ROCKstar?" It became our rudder, and it never steered us wrong.

While our ROCK principles fostered a strong bond and inspired our team, we faced a practical management challenge: Not everyone was suited for our organization. In his autobiography Ray Kroc had warned that every business encounters employees who are detrimental and need to be terminated—and that managers must act promptly because if they don't, it will come back to bite you worse than you imagined.

We sometimes wrestled with how to merge that reality with our ROCK values. Termination seemed inherently unkind, but we came to see it as aligning with "Opportunity." Our success depended on having the right people in the right roles. Letting someone go could be the kindest thing—giving them the chance to succeed elsewhere—while keeping them could harm our committed team members and poison the culture we worked so hard to protect.

In later years employees would nominate peers for "ROCKstar of the Month" awards, honoring those who truly embodied our values. At a national level, we celebrated our finest ROCKstars each year at an annual conference.

The *C* for Communication assured that everyone would be open to accepting feedback—even the co-founders. We regularly heard and implemented good ideas suggested by any of our team members. Perhaps the most notable example came in 1991, at a managers' conference near our Restaurant Support Center by LAX. During the open forum, a manager stood up and said, "Why does CPK allow smoking? We're having trouble finding staff to work the smoking section."

At the time smoking was permitted in restaurants, though movements to restrict it were gaining momentum. Some localities, such as Beverly Hills, had begun implementing requirements for designated smoking sections and advanced ventilation systems to prevent drift. Many restaurateurs, especially those with bars, feared the financial impact.

Larry and I paused the meeting, stepped into the hall, and asked ourselves, "Knowing what we now know about the dangers of secondhand smoke, how can we ask anyone to work in a smoking section?"

When we returned, we told the team to call their restaurants. Effective immediately, CPK would no longer allow smoking inside the restaurant. When asked about patios, we initially allowed smoking to continue—until the next day, when we got calls from our restaurant managers pointing out the new complaints from customers dining downwind of the smokers. We amended the policy on the spot. No smoking on patios either.

With that CPK became the first national restaurant chain to ban smoking. Years later, when we mentioned this to a *Los Angeles Times* reporter, she confirmed it with *Nation's Restaurant News*, the industry's top journal. The decision didn't please every guest, but it fit our mantra: *Do the right thing*. No regrets.

While we were immensely proud of the culture we'd built at CPK, and we felt confident that it had already left a lasting mark on the industry, there was a deeper truth about the restaurant business in America—one we understood from the very beginning: It runs on the strength, resilience, and dedication of immigrants.

That was true when we opened our first restaurant in Beverly Hills in 1985, and it's just as true today. Roughly a third of all restaurant workers in the United States are foreign-born. In California and much of the country, the largest group by far is Hispanic. Anyone who's ever spent time in a restaurant kitchen knows these workers are the quiet engine that keeps the place running. Many hold down two full-time jobs to support their families and send money back home. Their work ethic is extraordinary.

At CPK they became much more than employees—they became the heart of our company. Over time we had entire families—parents, siblings, cousins—all working with us, often across multiple locations. Many of them rose through the ranks, not just because they worked hard but because they brought leadership, loyalty, and heart. Rudy Sugueti's story—from a nineteen-year-old pizza cook to senior vice president of franchising and global operations—is one we often told with pride. But Rudy was just one of many. Our kitchens, our culture, and our growth were all built on the shoulders of these quiet leaders, our ROCKstars—dedicated team members whose names may never have made headlines but whose impact was felt every single day.

When we expanded into new cities, we quickly learned that until we connected with the local Hispanic community, we lacked the stability and spirit that made our restaurants thrive. Building that connection often took grassroots efforts—going into neighborhoods, sharing who we were and what we stood for. But the real trust was built in the restaurants—not on what we said but in what we did. Once those bridges were built, everything changed.

CHAPTER EIGHTEEN

THERE WAS ANOTHER ELEMENT THAT WENT HAND IN hand with ROCK that we never had to formalize or write down, yet it was part of our DNA from the start: our ability to delegate and empower. It was one of the most critical reasons for our success.

I was reminded of it recently while watching an interview with the owner of a successful pizza restaurant on Long Island. He lamented that he'd love to expand but couldn't—because he could never find employees who had his passion or cared as much as he did. I wanted to reach through the screen and tell him, "Of course, you can't—and you shouldn't." Why? If you're waiting to find someone who cares as much as the owner, you won't. What you really need is the ability to delegate—to inspire people to be at their best for the sake of the team. The restaurant business is a team sport, and if your players aren't performing, you're not unlucky. You're a bad coach.

Even before we opened our first restaurant, we knew we'd need to depend on people. And if we were going to hit our lofty goals, we'd need to rely on a lot of them. No one was ever going to care *quite* as much as we did, but that didn't mean they wouldn't care. CPK was built on people who deeply cared. That was our linchpin to success.

We succeeded because we created an environment where people wanted to come to work. They wanted to be surrounded by others who shared their enthusiasm, and their workplace became part of their quality of life. Maybe most of all, they were proud. It was fun to be part of CPK—the same way it's fun to be part of a winning team. I always loved hearing employees say that when they told someone where they worked, the response was immediate: "It must be fun to work there."

Of course, fun alone doesn't cut it. People also have to feel valued, financially and otherwise. If they go to work feeling underappreciated, the whole thing falls apart.

Larry and I never felt the need to micromanage. First of all, at the beginning, we didn't know anything about running a restaurant—we were flying on instincts. From the moment our first employee, Julie Carruthers, wrote the first training manuals, we delegated and empowered her to take the lead in that area. Our philosophy was simple: Find the right people, give them space to do their jobs, reward them when they succeed, give them leeway—but hold them accountable if standards slip. And we were always there for support.

But there was one thing we never delegated. Ever. *The brand.* Larry and I—with Esther's input—fiercely controlled, yes, *controlled*, every aspect of it. That wasn't about meddling; it was about safeguarding the essence of who we were.

Sure, we had a marketing department, and yes, we delegated certain campaigns and collateral matters. But brand positioning? That was our terrain. The way the guest experienced CPK from the moment they walked in. The tone of our messaging. The style of the logo. The colors. The menu language. We were not about to release those crucial decisions to anyone else.

That was why when Larry declared, "We want to own yellow!" during the design process, it wasn't just a color choice—it was a brand statement. The unapologetic yellow band, ceiling, and most importantly the logo became as much a part of CPK's identity as the food itself. We carried it into all our branding materials, reinforcing it everywhere the CPK name appeared. Okay, maybe it wasn't as important an identity feature as Barbecue Chicken Pizza, but in its own way, that bold-yellow color became iconic. After all, that yellow would one day light up twenty thousand frozen pizza cases across the country.

And here's another truth about our brand: No matter how much we wanted the focus to be on the food, the press couldn't resist focusing on us: the two lawyers—two former federal prosecutors.

Over time our identities and the CPK brand became so intertwined that when the company went public, the connection was spelled out in black and white. Larry and I weren't just the founders—or even just part of the company's DNA—we were listed as a bona fide "competitive advantage." Not many restaurants can say their brand equity includes the people who started it.

Admittedly, we were all in on the strategy. The two lawyers plus Barbecue Chicken Pizza made for a fun, memorable hook—and we leaned into it. The food was always the star, but the story of who we were gave people one more reason to connect with the brand.

CHAPTER NINETEEN

JUST AS OUR CULTURE EVOLVED OVER TIME, SO DID our menu. Hard as it is to believe today, our original vision was simple: pizza, pasta, and salads—all under $10.00. Back then that was entirely doable. A fresh tomato pizza was $5.50. A glass of house wine? $2.95.

As I mentioned earlier, Ed LaDou deserves full credit for creating the Barbecue Chicken Pizza and opening Larry's and my eyes to what was possible. But Ed was with us for only a couple of months. When he left, we seized the opportunity we'd always wanted: to be deeply involved in creating the menu ourselves.

From our days brainstorming dishes for our friend Burton Goldberg's Mutiny Hotel in Coconut Grove, we'd never pretended to be professional chefs, but we trusted our taste buds and our sense for what customers wanted to eat.

We never hired another company chef. Instead, Larry and I rolled up our sleeves and got to work. Every time that I reviewed the sales reports, it was glaring: Barbecue Chicken Pizza was a runaway hit. The takeaway was obvious: Create flavors people already loved but had never seen on pizza.

Some things needed fixing immediately. Rabbit sausage pizza? Radicchio and pine nuts? Rabbit in tomato sauce on pasta? All curiosities but none of them selling.

One of LaDou's few pasta contributions that stuck was spinach fettuccine with sautéed chicken and multicolored bell peppers in a jalapeño tequila-lime cream sauce. It looked great, sounded great, and even sold well—but too often we heard the same complaint: bland. We agreed.

Unfortunately, LaDou wasn't exactly the "take feedback well" type, so we had to grit our teeth every time someone ordered it.

The minute he was gone, we made one tiny change that transformed the dish: a splash of soy sauce to caramelize the chicken. That little tweak turned it into a signature CPK pasta that's still on the menu today. It also gave me one of my own favorite mantras: "Salt cures blandness."

From the start we insisted on a few comfort-zone classics: the mushroom, pepperoni, and sausage pizza—christened the "MUPSA" by our servers before the first week was out—and what was supposed to be a plain cheese pizza for the kids. That last one became a small battle of wills. We wanted simple cheese and tomato sauce; LaDou would only budge as far as fresh tomato and basil. The moment he left, we quietly swapped it for the classic cheese. Sales didn't just improve—they soared. Sometimes the kids really do know best. Their parents seemed to think so too—they rarely let the kids have the last slice.

We intuitively understood what we called the "veto factor"—the one person in a group who isn't interested in a restaurant and, by default, decides where the whole group ends up instead. That early insight led to an interesting conversation with our neighbor and friend Paul Fleming, who'd opened his Ruth's Chris Steak House franchise across the street a couple of months before we launched. We always thought of ourselves as "joined at the hip" in revitalizing (or perhaps "vitalizing") South Beverly Drive, since it had a reputation as a restaurant graveyard.

Paul, then a thirty-five-year-old oilman from Baton Rouge, Louisiana, had persuaded Ruth Fertel, owner of the lone Ruth's Chris Steak House, to let him be her first franchisee—despite having no previous restaurant experience. When he opened, his menu was all about steaks. Not a single chicken dish. We suggested that not everyone in Beverly Hills wanted steak all the time and that he might consider a chicken option.

Paul's reply was quick: "The day that four people come in and order chicken, I'm in trouble."

Our counterpoint was just as quick: "The day four people fill an otherwise empty table and order *anything*, it's a good day."

Paul took our advice and soon added a boneless chicken breast, and it turned out to be a hit. It also became our regular choice when we dropped in—though we certainly also enjoyed one of his great steaks now and then.

Paul's success certainly didn't surprise us. He went on to open several more Ruth's Chris Steak House restaurants, before he sold them back to the company and founded P. F. Chang's China Bistro, Pei Wei Asian Diner, Fleming's Prime Steakhouse and Wine Bar, and Paul Martin's American Grill. Quite the entrepreneur—and a terrific guy.

And here's a bit of restaurant trivia: By sheer coincidence, three future success stories all launched within a three-block stretch on Beverly Drive. Paul opened his Ruth's Chris. Larry and I opened CPK. And back in 1978 David Overton opened the first Cheesecake Factory just a few blocks away—which at that time was a modest sandwich and salad shop with a one-page menu and ten cheesecakes.

What are those odds?

As Larry and I gained confidence in menu development, we formed a strong partnership with our kitchen manager, Gary Beauregard, a former line cook with real culinary talent and a calm, unflappable demeanor. We'd pitch ideas, and Gary would craft recipes—often adding unexpected modifications we called the "Beauregard twist." From there we would taste and tweak as needed until we hit the mark.

That process worked for years, leading to the publication of *The California Pizza Kitchen Cookbook*, which Larry and I coauthored in 1996, with all proceeds going to charity. In it we summed up our philosophy: top our pizzas with the food Americans love most—no matter the cuisine. "We realized we could put the entire world on a pizza," we wrote. And we did. Unabashedly.

The menu became a reflection of popular tastes and trends as they surfaced. Cajun cooking was all the rage in the mid-'80s, and customers craved anything blackened. The trend eventually faded, but we constantly adapted to meet clients' interests and to match whatever was resonating.

Some ideas were particularly clever, such as the Eggs Benedict Pizza, crafted by twisting pizza dough into a figure eight and then baking it with an egg at the center. Not only was it creative, but it also reinforced our motto that anything that's delicious on bread can be exceptional on a pizza.

Larry's enthusiasm for mayonnaise gave birth to the Egg Salad

Pizza—warm cheese pizza topped with cold egg salad. A handful of egg salad fans loved it; the rest of our customers . . . not so much. It flopped but became one of our favorite running jokes. For years, when asked about our biggest failure, Larry would point to the Egg Salad Pizza. I'd always add, "If tossing out two quarts of egg salad is the worst thing that happens in your career, you've done all right."

Another creation of Larry's that didn't make it past the drawing board was his early experimentation with a Cheeseburger Pizza—cheese, ground beef, and ketchup. He asked what I thought after my first bite. I candidly told him, "It makes me want a *real* cheeseburger."

He was disappointed, but it sparked an important conversation that led to one of our core principles in our menu development: Every menu item had to more than *sound* good—it had to *deliver* the taste people expected.

Over time we added bold new pizzas—Jamaican Jerk, Buffalo Chicken, Greek, Carne Asada, Shrimp Scampi, and Chipotle Chicken. Some, such as our Peking Duck Pizza, didn't sell well but generated enough buzz and press attention to justify keeping them around.

We also expanded the traditional side with favorites such as our Five Cheese and created a new category of thin-crust Neapolitan pizzas, including the Margherita and the Sicilian. With my Chicago roots and Esther's Sicilian heritage, that one was a sentimental favorite in our house—though if you asked my favorite, I'd still grin and say, "Barbecue Chicken Pizza has always been good to me."

From day one we saw salads as more than just a supporting act—they could be a signature part of CPK's identity. Our original menu offered only a Caesar, but we were already looking ahead, eager to add chopped salads. The concept was still a novelty in much of the country, but in Los Angeles, it had deep roots, tracing back to the Brown Derby's legendary Cobb salad of the '30s.

Before we introduced our version on the Cobb, though, we had our sights on an Italian chopped. In the '50s Beverly Hills restaurateur Jean Leon created one at La Scala—finely chopped lettuce, salami, mozzarella, garbanzo beans, and a red-wine vinaigrette—that became the city's gold standard. In the '70s Larry, Esther, and I often lunched at La Scala Boutique. We always ordered it with turkey, though the upcharge pushed it into splurge territory.

At CPK we built our own version with turkey included in the price—under $10. It's been my personal go-to for forty years. La Scala may have invented it, but CPK helped take it nationwide.

In a classic chicken-or-the-egg dilemma, we knew from the start that our target was families. And because women drove dining decisions, families followed. Either way the answer led us to the same place—upscale shopping centers where our audience naturally gathered.

As we expanded our salad offerings, we took inspiration from our friend and fellow attorney, Bob Mandler, whose Chinese Chicken Salad at Chin Chin was a runaway hit. We created our own version, originally called the Oriental Chicken Salad, which we later appropriately renamed the Chinese Chicken Salad as cultural awareness evolved.

Then Larry's boundless creativity delivered the blockbuster we'd always been chasing: the Barbecue Chicken Chopped Salad. Chopped lettuce, black beans, sweet corn, jicama, cilantro, basil, corn tortilla chips, and Monterey Jack cheese, all tossed in homemade ranch, topped with chopped barbecued chicken breast and tomatoes, and finished with a drizzle of barbecue sauce. It became such a sensation that on some days, it outsold the Barbecue Chicken Pizza. And like its pizza counterpart, it inspired countless imitators.

Larry scored again with the Thai Crunch Salad: grilled chicken, cabbage, edamame, crispy wonton sticks, and roasted peanuts in a tangy Thai peanut dressing. Another instant classic. We followed the same formula with pasta. After the smash success of the Chicken-Tequila Fettuccine, we pushed the envelope with creations such as Kung Pao Spaghetti and Jambalaya Linguini while keeping traditional favorites such as Angel Hair with fresh tomatoes and basil, Spaghetti Bolognese, and Garlic Cream Fettuccine—all steady crowd-pleasers.

While we started with a limited dessert menu, with the opening of our fourth restaurant at Atlanta's Lenox Square in 1987, we introduced a key lime pie from a local bakery, Kenny's Great Pies. It became such a hit that as we grew—and as word spread—Kenny's business flourished alongside ours. It was just one of many examples where our vendors' success went hand in hand with ours.

For years we kept our menu tightly focused: pizza, pasta, salads, and dessert. Larry was devoted to that approach, and I, for a long time, went along. But I saw it as self-imposed limitation that risked playing into our old nemesis, the "veto factor."

I consistently pushed for menu expansion. While "pizza was our middle name," I believed the "California halo effect" gave us permission to venture into unique, innovative dishes beyond our traditional categories. Eventually, Larry agreed—and, as usual, when he bought in, he was all in.

That was when another of our running jokes would kick in: Once Larry was all in, he regularly adopted the idea as if it had been his all along. Within minutes—or a few days at most—he'd be explaining it to someone, finishing with "And I think Rick agrees with me." Which, of course, I did. He just didn't always agree with me at first.

We rolled out a soup category that took off immediately, led by the hearty Dakota Smashed Pea and Barley and the zesty Sedona Tortilla. And then came a fun one—almost like a culinary magic trick—that defied simple explanation: the Two in a Bowl. Guests would get both soups at once, poured side by side in the same bowl, somehow staying perfectly separated until they dipped in their spoon. No divider, no sorcery—just a careful pour and the right consistency. People loved the flavor contrast, but they also loved the little gasp of surprise when it arrived at the table. More than once we saw guests smile and ask, "How do they do that?"

We also branched out with sandwiches on freshly baked focaccia—standouts such as the Grilled Chicken Dijon and the Grilled Chicken Caesar—and launched an appetizer category that quickly became a guest favorite. The Spinach Artichoke Dip led the charge, followed closely by Chicken or Shrimp Lettuce Wraps, Avocado Club Egg Rolls, and Tortilla Spring Rolls.

Menu creation was always our shared passion, though Larry took it to another level. I had plenty of hobbies. Larry essentially had just one—creating new CPK menu items. He tried golf but always drifted back to his comfort zone: the kitchen. Over the years we worked first with Gary Beauregard, then for many years with Brian Sullivan and his Culinary Creation Team, tossing out ideas, letting them work their magic, and taste-testing every iteration until we had something worthy of the menu.

In the early days, we could get into lively debates over which dishes would succeed. But as we grew, we realized that our expanding network of restaurants was a built-in R and D lab. Our philosophy became simple: "Everything is testable!" We launched new items at our Redondo Beach location—home to a dedicated R and D kitchen—and selected about a half dozen locations around the country as test markets.

We'd flag new items on the menu and often used colorful table placards to attract attention, knowing it gave sales an artificial bump.

That's why we relied on more than numbers—we wanted guest feedback, not just on whether they liked it but whether they'd order it again. If a dish scored well on sales, satisfaction, and "intent to reorder," it earned a permanent spot on the national menu. But even then we had one final rule: It had to survive without the "new" label or any special promotion. Only the truly loved dishes made the cut.

Even as our menu grew, we kept a watchful eye on our SKUs—those unglamorous stock-keeping units that quietly kept our kitchens sane. Whenever we dreamed up something new, we tried to build it from ingredients we already stocked, not a laundry list of exotic one-offs. And we had one hard-and-fast rule: For every dish that came in, one had to leave. If it wasn't pulling its weight, it was out.

Much later in our history, our menu grew to include Baja Fish Tacos, Chicken Milanese, Pan-Sautéed or Ginger Salmon, Chicken Piccata, and Chicken Marsala. We were proud of the variety, but a small voice in the back of my mind wondered if the pendulum might be swinging a bit far from our original identity. At the time it seemed like harmless experimentation—after all, pizza was still front and center—but looking back, I can see the first hints of a challenge we'd face later.

CHAPTER TWENTY

WHILE CREATING NEW MENU ITEMS WAS GREAT fun, we had big dreams, and expansion was in the cards, it didn't change the reality that we still had to figure out how to pay for it.

One of the most memorable answers strolled in early on, when a gentleman literally walked in off the street and said, "I want to invest."

He was Dean Pitchford, the Oscar- and Grammy-winning songwriter behind *Fame* and the producer of *Footloose*. Dean told us he had worked as a server in his youth, frequently ate at our Beverly Hills CPK next door, and was impressed by what he saw.

A short while later, Dean came back with his well-known business manager, who—after analyzing the deal—flatly told him not to invest. Dean didn't bat an eye. He ignored him and wrote a $40,000 check. Each time we went back to investors, Dean unhesitatingly invested another $40,000. Later, when our investors were rewarded with the generous buyout offer from PepsiCo, Dean had the last laugh. We had a chuckle too.

In the investment world, "friends and family" money is often dismissed as "dumb money," in contrast to the supposedly "smart money" from institutional and professional investors. In our case it was the "dumb money" that turned out to be brilliant.

Over the years plenty of would-be investors came knocking, eager to get in on CPK's growth.

Larry and I were always willing to hear them out—talk was cheap, and we were always open to learning. Yet when it came to the bigger offers, after listening to the proposals, we often walked away shaking our heads. They called themselves venture capitalists; we had our own term: *vulture capitalists*.

One encounter stands out as a cautionary tale. We met several times with a man we believed to be wealthy and well respected, representing what he claimed would be a large investment from the Middle East. As his proposal became clearer, our former federal prosecutorial instincts kicked in. It was a classic "advanced fee scheme": the promise of a large, guaranteed, favorable loan—if we first paid several hundred thousand dollars up front. Once we were on to his plot, we cut off the meetings for good.

Through the years we've surprisingly heard plenty of names floated as supposed major investors in CPK who, in reality, had no stake in the company. Just as often we've heard of people claiming to be founders or mentioned as founders. Our response has always been the same. Unless they were Larry, Esther, or me, they were most certainly not founders of CPK.

One persistent rumor is that Wolfgang Puck was somehow involved. While we admire Wolfgang and credit him with providing some early inspiration, he never had any ownership in—or connection to—California Pizza Kitchen whatsoever. In fact his former wife and partner, Barbara Lazaroff, made no secret they were aiming at us with their Wolfgang Puck Cafes. The effort fizzled, but in our view, competition just came with the territory.

As we expanded nationally, our capital needs grew—especially since we avoided domestic franchising and, with the exception of the Mirage, were developing only company-owned restaurants. Fortunately, we were able to go back to our growing investor base with nothing more than a letter announcing we were raising funds. With each offering we increased the stock price based on our own belief in CPK's value—and each time we had willing investors. Starting at a $5 million valuation, we moved to $8.5 million, $15 million, $22 million, and $35 million, raising a total of about $6.5 million along the way.

While these private placements were our primary funding source, traditional bank financing played a role. Still, it took a leap of faith by the banks because, despite the exponential revenue growth, we were only marginally profitable.

With our early success and rising profile, we were invited to join Hillcrest Country Club—a storied, primarily Jewish enclave of Hollywood power brokers and legends, including the Marx Brothers, George Burns, Sidney Poitier, and Sammy Davis Jr., among others. (More recently it's been in the spotlight as home to Doug Emhoff, the former Second Gentleman of the United States.)

It was there we met Bram Goldsmith, founder and chairman of City National Bank, who took a personal interest in us and extended CPK a $500,000 loan.

An opportunity came up to lease a prime ground floor space at the Wells Fargo Center, a premier downtown Los Angeles high-rise. The landlord, Robert Maguire, a prominent Los Angeles developer, sought us out and offered favorable terms. Confident in the location, we signed.

Not long after, Bram Goldsmith summoned us to his office. He got straight to the point. "I want you to leave the bank."

We were stunned—and admittedly, more than a little uncomfortable. He explained we had violated our loan covenant by signing a lease without the bank's approval. He added he would never have approved the Wells Fargo location, insisting, "No restaurant can make it downtown."

I recovered quickly. "Bram, we didn't know about the covenant, and if we had, I assure you we would have discussed it with you. But if you wouldn't have approved the lease, we'd have left the bank anyway. We're not going to let you decide our locations."

With that we found another bank. The Wells Fargo location was a hit from day one. On a personal note, we later made amends with Bram and his son, Russell, a golfing friend who went on to lead the bank's phenomenal success. All's well that ends well.

As our borrowing power grew, we secured a $5 million loan from the Bank of California. What began with just twenty-two investors had expanded to nearly three hundred.

By 1992—about seven years in—despite our growth and apparent success, neither our investors nor Larry nor I had received a dividend or any liquidity. While almost all our investors remained extremely patient, we began to hear the first faint squeak from a potentially squeaky wheel.

Occasionally, an investor wanted out, and we were able to accommodate them by arranging private transactions, simply finding new investors to buy their shares. The earliest to bail was our first chef, Ed LaDou, who sold his shares shortly after being terminated. We were happy to swiftly arrange the sale. As the saying goes and as history would show, he left a lot of money on the table.

CHAPTER TWENTY-ONE

FROM OUR EARLIEST DAYS OF EXPANSION, LARRY AND I saw an opportunity others didn't. We started from a single storefront in Beverly Hills, then opened our second restaurant at the upscale Beverly Center, followed by Topanga Plaza, Lenox Square, and Kahala Mall. In each case we saw how placing CPK in an upscale shopping center brought in a steady stream of customers.

Traditionally, developers relied on department stores as "anchors" to drive foot traffic. But we believed that, in time, upscale restaurants could play that same role—acting as "mini-anchors" that attracted high-income shoppers and kept them in the center longer.

Not everyone agreed. Early in our expansion, in a tense meeting at the Taubman Company's offices in Bloomfield Hills, Michigan, CEO Billy Taubman dismissed our idea with a laugh: "That'll be the day when Laura Ashley wants a California Pizza Kitchen next to them."

His skepticism stuck with us and motivated us to prove him wrong. And we did.

CPK became a pioneer in the concept of the restaurant anchor. We weren't alone for long. The Cheesecake Factory, P. F. Chang's, and others followed the trail we'd blazed. Sometimes we'd open locations near each other, but instead of feeling competitive, it often felt collaborative—even synergistic.

One of the most serendipitous boosts to our expansion came at a golf club, not a mall. In the early '90s, Esther and I were building a vacation home at the Vintage Club, a private golf and social club near Palm Springs. One morning I spotted a fellow member in the locker room and introduced myself: "You don't know me, but you do my demographic studies."

That fellow member was Jim Nordstrom, president of the family-run Nordstrom department store chain. Jim was warm, engaging, and—lucky for us—married to a CPK fan. Turns out, CPK was his wife's favorite restaurant.

He invited Larry and me to Nordstrom's Seattle headquarters, where he explained that they were struggling to perfect their Nordstrom cafés. Then he made an intriguing offer: License CPK to operate inside Nordstrom stores.

It was flattering, but I had to be honest. "Jim, if we put CPK inside Nordstrom, where are we going to grow?" I suggested an alternative: "When Nordstrom opens a new store, tell the developer you want a CPK right next door."

Jim liked the idea, and true to his word, he helped make it happen—landing us prime sites in some of the most successful retail centers in the country.

We formed strong relationships with the best developers in the business—Simon, General Growth Properties, Westfield, Macerich, Forbes/Cohen—and were soon fielding offers from local developers eager to have us in their projects. We planted our iconic palm tree in marquee centers from Ala Moana in Honolulu to Lenox Square in Atlanta, from the Prudential Center in Boston to Tysons Corner in Virginia, from Chicago's Water Tower Place to Boca Town Center in Florida.

Our real estate strategy was purely opportunistic: Take the best site available, then build a cluster of nearby locations to strengthen brand recognition and improve operational efficiency. We never set a target number for restaurants. Whenever someone asked, we'd smile and think, "As Adam said to Eve, 'Stand back, honey, I don't know how big this thing is going to get!'"

Looking back, the vision we pitched in those early days—that restaurants could anchor a shopping center—proved correct. Many of our original locations are still thriving decades later.

And to anyone who doubted us back then, well, we can say it now: We told you so.

CHAPTER TWENTY-TWO

BY 1992, SEVEN YEARS AFTER OPENING OUR FIRST restaurant in Beverly Hills, CPK had expanded to twenty-five restaurants in seven states and was in the process of expanding internationally. Our investors had placed immense trust in us, often reinvesting even when the company was not yet profitable. We felt the weight of that trust, and while our focus remained on growth, we also knew it was prudent to start thinking about liquidity. Truthfully, Larry and I had doubled down ourselves, and at some point, even founders deserve to take a little off the table.

Our lawyer, Bob Kahan, reminded us of a looming threshold: Once we reached five hundred investors, we'd be required to register with the SEC and become a public company. With three hundred investors already, the possibility of going public was no longer abstract—it was inevitable if we kept raising money the same way.

Individually, each of the CPK restaurants was highly profitable, but at the company level, we were reinvesting every available dollar into new restaurants, infrastructure, people, and systems. We were in a "damn the torpedoes—full speed ahead" phase.

Still, the pressure to take some chips off the table for our investors and ourselves was building. Private equity firms had been circling for a while. We were a hot concept, and there was no shortage of people looking to grab a piece of the action. But we never found their pitches appealing. Too much about control, too much about short-term exits.

At that point we still had complete control of the fate of the company. Thanks to our lawyer, Bob Kahan's, foresight, all outside shareholders owned nonvoting stock. Even though our ownership had been diluted from 94 percent to 60 percent, Larry and I still held 100 percent of the votes. The company's destiny remained in our hands—for the time being.

Yet we were realists. To outsiders I'm sure it looked like arrogance—our insistence on holding tight to the reins, speaking with conviction, never flinching. Deep down we knew the truth: Whichever path we chose, control would eventually slip from our hands. It was the inevitable cost of creating liquidity for our investors and ourselves. Still, as we weighed our options, we were hell-bent on delaying that moment. For as long as we could, we were determined to steer the ship and control our destiny.

While we rejected the private equity path at that stage, there was no shortage of investment banks approaching us, eager to lead us through a public offering.

As part of the selection process, we interviewed numerous investment banks in what's commonly referred to as a beauty contest. Larry and I often joked, as we screened multiple suitors, that it was nice to be the prettiest girl in the bar. While it was flattering to have options, our decision came down to chemistry and trust. For us there was a clear winner. A friend, Aaron Eshman, who was affiliated with Wertheim Schroder, introduced us to Dan Levitan, an investment banker at his firm. Wertheim Schroder had a strong Wall Street legacy, and we'd instantly connected with Dan. At Bob Kahan's recommendation, we brought in the prestigious law firm of Skadden, Arps, Slate, Meagher & Flom to handle the legal work.

Ironically, at the same moment, another fast-growing concept was making the same choice: Starbucks. In his memoir, *Pour Your Heart into It*, Howard Schultz noted that his bankers were Dan and Wertheim Schroder—the same team we had used. Howard called Dan a mensch—that wonderful Yiddish word for a person of honor and integrity. We couldn't have said it better ourselves.

With bankers and lawyers in place, our IPO preparations were underway. Drafts of the S-1 were already circulating when—out of nowhere—we received a call from Richard Frank, chairman of Lawry's Restaurants. He wasn't calling on his own behalf. He'd been asked to deliver a message: A Fortune 100 company was interested in us. Would we be willing to talk?

We lived by the rule that talk is cheap, so we agreed to a call.

Soon after, the phone rang. It was Ken Stevens, senior vice president of strategic planning for PepsiCo. At the time PepsiCo was not only one of the world's largest companies but also a powerhouse in consumer brands. In addition to its global beverage business, it owned Frito-Lay (the world's leading snack company) and three major restaurant brands: Pizza Hut, Taco Bell, and Kentucky Fried Chicken.

With its restaurant portfolio alone, PepsiCo owned more restaurant units than any company in the world. This caught our attention. We knew it could be a game changer for CPK.

We scheduled a meeting. By then we had long since moved out of the cramped Beverly Hills law office that once doubled as headquarters. Our new digs were full-floor offices on Sepulveda Boulevard in West Los Angeles, with a shared conference room between Larry's and my corner offices. Our doors were always open—by design. This made collaboration easy, and it reflected the way we had always worked: close, constant, and within shouting distance.

Ken was instantly likable. He was already a fan of CPK, which made breaking the ice easy. The truth is, Larry and I enjoyed the attention—we were easily flattered. But make no mistake, we weren't an easy sell.

After the small talk, Ken got right to the point and explained that, while PepsiCo owned only quick-service restaurants at the time, they were interested in expanding into the casual-dining category. They admired CPK's innovative menu, food quality, and (even more so) our consistent level of customer service. Over the course of several discussions, it became clear they viewed us as sort of a laboratory experiment—a chance to study our training practices and service methods with the hope of applying them to their other brands.

One thing struck us as odd. They told us this would be PepsiCo's first entry into full-service dining. That puzzled us. To our eyes thousands of Pizza Hut "red roof" restaurants, with their full menus, servers, and sit-down dining rooms, already fit that category. But PepsiCo didn't see it that way.

As we later spent time with PepsiCo and Pizza Hut executives, the reason became clear. They explained Pizza Hut's service by saying, "We get a different quality of employees—young kids who haven't worked before."

We were stunned. And blunt.

"*That's* your problem," we told them. "You don't set the proper goals and expectations for these kids. Worse yet, you don't train them. What do you expect?"

Our philosophy was the opposite. No one starts their first job wanting to perform poorly. When a company sets low standards and fails to train or support its people, it usually gets exactly what it deserves—poor attitudes, bad service, and disappointing performance.

For us the formula was simple: Hire kind, curious people with a willingness to learn. Then through training and culture, give them the tools to succeed. That's where service excellence came from—not experience, not credentials. Just the right kind of people, supported in the right way.

Once we settled in and the conversation was flowing, Ken dropped the bombshell. PepsiCo wanted us to shelve our plans for a public offering and let them purchase a majority stake in CPK. But then came the real hook—the part that made us sit up a little straighter. If Larry and I were looking to cash out and walk away, they weren't interested. What they wanted wasn't just the restaurants or the brand—it was us. They wanted us to stay, to keep building, and to lead to the next chapter.

It was a breathtaking proposition and a lot to take in. On the outside we kept our cool. On the inside my heart was pounding. No numbers had even been mentioned, but I could already sense we were heading toward the proverbial offer we couldn't refuse.

Ken then suggested that we visit PepsiCo's offices in Purchase, New York, to explore the partnership further.

It was a seminal moment. Of course, we were going to explore the opportunity. How could we not? Within a week or so, we found ourselves in Manhattan, climbing into a limo they had sent for us, and headed north toward their corporate campus.

When the security guard directed the driver toward the front entrance, we noticed something odd. The road ahead wasn't really a road at all. It looked more like a cobblestone walking path, clearly not designed for cars. It was a small detail, but it spoke volumes. Larry and I exchanged a look. We both felt it instinctively; this wasn't just a meeting. We were about to be seduced.

Even if I didn't say it out loud at the time, something clicked in the back of my mind. It was just a sense—a feeling I couldn't name then but recognize now. PepsiCo had *deal heat*. They wanted this. A lot.

And that realization triggered an immediate shift in my thinking. We needed to stay cool, keep our footing, and make sure the deal worked on *our* terms—not just theirs.

Ken greeted us warmly at the front door and personally escorted us on a tour of the PepsiCo's impressive headquarters. The property was breathtaking, with 168 acres of manicured grounds named after former Chairman Donald M. Kendall. A massive three-story building rose at the center, surrounded by towering trees, gardens, ponds, fountains, and world-class sculptures by artists Rodin, Moore, Calder, Giacometti, Dubuffet, and Oldenburg.

Inside, Ken introduced us to several senior executives, including Don Nickerson Smith, a former Burger King CEO and PepsiCo's senior restaurant guru. The moment we sat in his office, we felt at ease. Don had the calm authority of a father figure—someone we instinctively felt we could trust.

Eventually, we moved from small talk to business discussions. Ken said that PepsiCo wanted to buy all the outstanding shares in CPK, except the ones that Larry and I personally owned. We would retain our shares and continue to run the company as co-CEOs.

Then came the moment that we had been waiting for: valuation. Everything else had been foreplay.

Larry and I were full of big ideas and pie-in-the-sky possibilities. But this was the part when things got real. A number that was too low could pop our bubble in an instant.

Then *poof*—it became clear. We were miles apart in how we valued the company.

It wasn't entirely surprising. Larry and I had always been unapologetically aggressive in our valuation. And when a prospective investor pushed back, we never wavered. Our answer was simple and direct: "Fine—don't invest. We've got plenty of people who believe in us."

At the time CPK boasted twenty-five company-owned restaurants, spread across seven states, with projected 1992 sales to be about $50 million. On paper the company looked barely profitable. But looking below the surface showed a different picture. Our operating restaurants generated strong cash flows, delivering impressive returns on investment. The overall profitability was dragged down by corporate overhead—the people, systems, and infrastructure we were building to support further growth. It was a classic challenge of an early-stage growth company: Invest ahead of the curve, and your books look weaker than your reality.

Ken delivered PepsiCo's number: an enterprise valuation of $60 million, based on all outstanding shares of CPK. He explained that this formula was based on 120 percent of projected annual sales—a formula he assured us business appraisers swore by.

Maybe so. But we had no interest in letting number crunchers playing by someone else's rules define our value. We hadn't done that in the past, and we weren't going to start now.

We quickly countered. As we saw it, PepsiCo was lucky to have the chance to buy into something with so much upside, still in its early innings. We told them bluntly that they should be paying a premium just for the privilege.

True to form, we stuck to our time-tested method of valuation: throwing darts and trusting our gut. We floated a wild number: $200 million—roughly 400 percent of annual sales. Fair? Not exactly. Aggressive? Absolutely. But in our view, it reflected the potential PepsiCo would be buying into.

And then, with a touch of chutzpah, I dropped a line I'd used before—half grin, half dead serious: "I think it's the low side of reasonable."

I knew this. If a deal was going to happen, it was going to be at a number closer to our opening bid than his.

Beyond valuation, we also discussed the implications for our outside shareholders. While Larry and I initially owned 94 percent after converting our limited partners in the Beverly Hills restaurant into parent company shareholders, the series of private placements had gradually diluted our ownership to 60 percent. Still, we had 100 percent of the voting shares.

PepsiCo floated the idea of us executing a legal maneuver, called a "cramdown," that would force minority shareholders to sell their stakes. For us that was a nonstarter. Our position was firm.

These were people who believed in us—who had trusted us, stood by us, and in many cases waited patiently for years to see their returns. There was no way Larry and I were going to tell them that they had to sell, while we stayed on with the company—positioned to benefit from PepsiCo's backing and future growth. That wasn't how we did business. In fact one of the reasons we were taking this opportunity so seriously was because we wanted to be heroes to our investors and see them receive great rewards for daring to bet on our dream.

The first day was actually fun. There was a bit of cat and mouse to the financial haggling, a smooth give-and-take with just the right amount of tension. Yet Larry and I sensed an air of inevitability. Candidly, it was hard not to be impressed. We were treated like royalty. Every detail seemed designed to impress us. To be honest the strategy worked.

That evening we were invited to dinner at the home of Wayne Calloway, PepsiCo's former chairman and CEO. Wayne and his wife, Janice, were gracious and engaging, and the evening felt effortless.

Life was good.

But the next day told a different story.

When we returned to PepsiCo's offices, we were informed that Ken Stevens had been called away on an unscheduled trip to Chicago. Instead of continuing with him, we were ushered into a meeting with one of PepsiCo's lawyers—a man Larry and I quickly dubbed *the Liquidator*.

From the moment he opened his briefcase, the tone shifted. The Liquidator played hardball, systematically downplaying CPK's value, insisting we'd be lucky to have PepsiCo's backing, and laying out a laundry list of rules we'd have to follow if we struck a deal.

The contrast was jarring. Day one felt like a royal welcome. Day two felt like an ambush. It didn't take us long to figure out what was happening.

With Ken unexpectedly out of the picture, our instincts kicked in. This was classic good cop, bad cop. While this tactic might work in law enforcement, it wouldn't work on us.

That popped the balloon. We were back down to Earth. The ride back to New York City was quiet, heavy. Larry and I had been best friends, law partners, and business partners for twenty years—we didn't need to say much. We both knew the feeling in the pit of our stomachs. At the same time, this was familiar territory—we'd suffered plenty of mood swings in courtrooms and in business.

By dinner we'd picked ourselves up and were steeled to move forward. We both knew it: If PepsiCo wasn't going to work out, going public was back on the table.

Still, neither of us slept much that night. On the drive back upstate the next morning, we were convinced the deal was dead. We weren't just miles apart on valuation—we were light-years apart. And even if that gap could be closed, there were land mines everywhere: control issues, investor treatment, and a dozen other details waiting to blow up the deal. Worst of all, if they were going to send the Liquidator to negotiate, we weren't sure either of us had the patience to stick it out.

Over dinner the night before, we'd discussed something that one of Larry's longtime friends, Dick Ziman, a successful real estate investor, once told him: "To be considered financially successful, you need to have $10 million in the bank."

By that standard we were woefully short.

Over the past seven years, we'd worked tirelessly to build CPK's value. While we had taken reasonable salaries, we had never cashed out a dime of equity.

One of the biggest motivations in even sitting at PepsiCo's table was the chance to create a "liquidity event"—both for us and our investors. Going public would give our investors the liquidity they deserved (which mattered deeply to us), but as founders, Larry and I would be locked out from selling our shares for a long stretch.

When we got back to Purchase that morning, we asked for a private meeting with Don Nickerson Smith, their restaurant guru. Don hadn't been part of the previous day's theatrics. To us he felt like a steadying presence and someone whose perspective we could trust.

By the time the car pulled up, we'd worked ourselves into a frenzy. I didn't waste a second.

"Don," I said, "this is no longer fun. We've packed our bags, and we're ready to fly home to California."

We weren't bluffing. We had unwavering confidence in CPK's future and truly enjoyed running it independently. If PepsiCo thought they could bully us into a corner, they were sorely mistaken.

Then we laid it out straight. We told him about our friend's comment about the $10 million benchmark. I got right to the point. "For this deal to happen," I said, "Larry and I each need to walk away with $10 million in the bank—*after* taxes. That's the number that lets us sleep at night. If things don't work out, at least we'll know that we're secure."

And then I put it in even plainer language: "Don, what we need is *fuck-you* money."

If they weren't willing to meet that threshold, we were out. That's how Larry and I had operated for nearly twenty years—draw a line, stick to it, and let the chips fall where they may. At that point it was up to the fates.

Don listened carefully. He didn't push back. He just said, "Be patient. Let me work on a solution."

And so the PepsiCo number crunchers got to work.

At the time CPK's historical numbers spoke volumes. On average, sales at each restaurant grew 30 percent in its second year and another 27 percent in the third. Same store sales growth like that was gold—proof of a scalable concept.

After hours of waiting, the finance team came back with a new proposal. They had run the math. If CPK built fifteen new restaurants in 1993 and twenty-eight per year after that, all performing like our existing locations, they could justify a $140 million valuation.

It was a jolt. I could barely contain myself as they walked us through the deal structure. On the surface I stayed composed, listening intently, but inside I was already imagining the headline—"From Beverly Hills to the Big Leagues"—and the welcome home accolades from our investors.

Here's how they proposed structuring the deal:

PepsiCo would purchase half of CPK's shares for $70 million. CPK would then issue a $50 million dividend to existing shareholders. That dividend would result in $17 million payouts to Larry and me, individually.

After paying taxes, each of us would clear $10 million in liquidity, achieving the financial target we'd set as a condition.

In the end PepsiCo hadn't made us an offer that we couldn't refuse; we had *negotiated* a deal that we couldn't refuse. We left PepsiCo's offices on a high. There were still plenty of deal terms to be hammered out, but it was clear that PepsiCo was going to stretch to make a deal. At that point we were feeling gleeful.

Over dinner that night, dollar signs danced in our heads. We had the framework of a deal that would greatly benefit our shareholders, and it wasn't just a home run—it was a grand slam.

* * *

Returning home to Los Angeles with the broad strokes of a deal in place, it was time to bring in the nuts-and-bolts guy—our lawyer, Bob Kahan. While Larry and I considered ourselves capable litigators, we knew our limitations. Transactional law wasn't our lane. From the beginning Bob had structured every aspect of CPK, and now we were ready to place the biggest financial deal of our lives—and his biggest transaction—squarely in his hands.

Eager to keep the momentum, we returned to PepsiCo's offices, this time with Bob at our side. Ken Stevens was there, and—an encouraging sign—the Liquidator was nowhere to be seen.

Instead, PepsiCo sent in their in-house counsel, Kathleen Luke. From the moment she walked in, the tone felt different. Kathleen was smart, approachable, and friendly. It was clear: PepsiCo wasn't posturing anymore.

They were bent on making this deal happen.

PepsiCo proposed a tender offer to buy out all the other shareholders, except for Larry and me. But we stuck to our guns: no cramdown. Every investor would be fully informed, and the choice to sell or stay would be theirs.

Still, the offer revealed the elephant in the room. When we had left New York, our impression was that PepsiCo would be satisfied with 50 percent. Now it was obvious they wanted more than equity—they wanted control. That was a redrawing of the power map.

And that caught us completely off guard. Perhaps naively, we hadn't seriously contemplated losing control—at least not at this point. But suddenly, we were staring at the first real deal killer since agreeing on valuation.

Yet on its face, PepsiCo's position made sense. If, after the tender offer to our other shareholders, PepsiCo ended up owning two-thirds of the stock, they'd expect two-thirds of the voting power. But for us that was a nonstarter. We dug in. No way. We were even ready to pack our bags again.

It's hard to fully capture what I was feeling in that moment. Yes, PepsiCo had deal heat—but if I'm being honest, so did I. I wanted this deal—for Larry, for myself, and for our investors who had backed us from the beginning. But not at any cost. We weren't emotionally ready to give up control. Not yet.

Then Bob Kahan stepped in—calm, deliberate, and creative as always. This was his wheelhouse. While Larry and I had spent our careers in courtrooms, Bob thrived in the world of complex transactions, and this was his moment to shine.

"What if," he suggested, "Rick and Larry retain the right to vote on any shares PepsiCo acquires from the other shareholders?"

It was an audacious idea but brilliantly simple. If PepsiCo agreed, Larry and I would keep equal voting power with them, no matter how much stock they bought in the tender offer.

It was a complete Hail Mary. A structure so unconventional it bordered on unheard of. But Bob laid it out with such clarity and confidence that it stuck. PepsiCo agreed.

With that single stroke, Bob had protected our voting control and kept the deal alive. It was a master class in creative lawyering—quiet, deft, and exactly what the moment required.

From there everything shifted. We settled on a split board of directors: Larry and me representing CPK and two members appointed by PepsiCo—Ken Stevens and CFO Bob Dettmer (who would later be replaced by John

Martin, the former CEO of Taco Bell and a strong advocate for the deal). Just as astonishing, Bob convinced them to leave out any mechanism to break a deadlock. No tiebreakers, no arbitrators, no mediators. If a conflict arose, we'd simply have to work it out together. It was pure trust—or maybe bold optimism. But either way it was extraordinary.

Larry and I played our part too—sitting steady, not flinching, and weighing in with a firm stance when it mattered. There was an organic rhythm between the three of us, and together we made the perfect tag team.

The reality, of course, was that as much as we wanted the deal, PepsiCo wanted it more. These executives were playing with OPM (other people's money)—a lot of it. We knew it. And we kept pressing.

Once the control question was resolved, attention turned to financing future growth. Here again, PepsiCo came through. They agreed to provide unlimited loans to the company at just 2 percent interest—when the going rate was three to five times higher. And even more extraordinary, there would be no payments—no principal, no interest—for fifteen years. The entire balance, along with accumulated interest, would come due in a single balloon payment in 2007.

What PepsiCo gave us was unheard of—unlimited capital at a fraction of the going rate, with no payments due for a decade and a half.

Got that? Unlimited loans—a blank check, 2 percent interest, and no payments for fifteen years.

It was surreal.

The assumption was that if things went according to plan, in fifteen years, PepsiCo would buy out the remaining shares, simply deducting the balloon balance from the purchase price. That gave us fifteen years to make the company wildly successful—for ourselves, for PepsiCo, and for the investors who chose to stay in. Then we'd cash out and ride off into the sunset, leaving the rest of life to figure itself out.

At the time it seemed brilliant. The structure gave us the kind of patient, low-cost capital only a company such as PepsiCo could provide. More importantly, it confirmed what we already knew: PepsiCo wanted this deal badly, and we had managed to hold our ground without giving up what mattered most—control.

As we sat and worked through the day, I could barely contain myself. Naturally, I was excited about the personal financial benefit to my family and me, but just as much for our investors. The deal was truly remarkable.

An investor who had originally put in $20,000 would receive a $189,000 dividend, while still having the choice whether to accept PepsiCo's tender offer. If that investor chose to sell, then including the dividend, they'd walk away with $424,000, a staggering 2,020 percent return. In other words they made more than twenty times their money in seven years.

Many of our original investors had continued to make additional investments over time, and we had attracted hundreds of new ones. Even someone who invested only a year earlier would see at least a 400 percent return.

Closing the deal wasn't just a financial milestone. It was personal. For us it meant rewarding the people who had believed in us from the beginning—and proving their trust had been well placed. And deeper still, though unspoken between Larry and me, this was the moment that would silence every doubter.

In hindsight it was pie-in-the-sky thinking—on both sides. But it marked the beginning of a learning curve for us. Still, we and our investors were the clear beneficiaries of PepsiCo's largesse. They were the ones putting up the capital. We were more than happy to use it.

Walking out of PepsiCo's offices with a deal that was, by any measure, mind-bogglingly favorable, I expected high fives all around—Larry, Bob, and I should have been riding high. Instead, Bob and I were blindsided. There was one last hurdle.

Larry wasn't convinced.

Despite everything we'd negotiated, he still had deep reservations. Even a partial loss of control didn't sit right with him. Going public, he argued, might still be the better path.

Bob and I were stunned. This wasn't posturing. Larry was dead serious. He was getting worked up in a way I had seen many times in our years together.

Larry wanted complete autonomy, free of outside oversight. But that was a fantasy. While I didn't yet have firsthand experience with public company boards—that would come soon—I knew this much: If we went public, our stake would be diluted, and even with a sizable share, a board's loyalty would only last as long as results did. If things turned, their support would vanish overnight.

Better, I reasoned, to cast our lot with PepsiCo—especially with the extraordinary governance structure we had just negotiated.

While in New York, Bob and I had developed a morning routine, jogging in Central Park and talking through details as we ran. Suddenly, the runs weren't about the deal points—they were about how to bring Larry around.

Back at the hotel, tensions escalated. Larry continued to dig in, emotional and stubborn. The conversations got heated. Larry had always trusted my judgment, but this time it took every ounce of Bob's calm, steady finesse to finally bring him along.

Finally, Larry relented.

Of course, once the deal closed, the press lauded it, and our investors erupted with joy, Larry was elated. Later, when I reminded him of his initial reluctance, he brushed it off. He'd only been playing the devil's advocate, he insisted.

Thanks to Bob's creativity, calm demeanor, and legal skills, the deal never went off the rails. And thanks to PepsiCo's willingness to bend, Larry and I emerged with something priceless: the assurance that PepsiCo could never dictate CPK's future without our agreement.

Bob had proven once again that he was worth his weight in gold.

I could barely contain myself. This was our moment to prove the skeptics wrong—the ones who'd insisted from the start that our valuation was overblown. I waited with bated breath for the deal to close, knowing we were about to deliver a huge win for our investors—those who had backed us from day one and those who had come aboard later but shared the same confidence.

It felt good to reward our backers and to prove the doubters wrong. In the end the so-called "dumb money" had the last laugh.

With the major terms resolved, we set the closing date for May 19, 1992, at PepsiCo's offices.

Coincidentally, Larry and I had already planned a golf trip to Ireland with our friend Steve Garvey, the former Los Angeles Dodger and San Diego Padres All-Star first baseman. The timing worked perfectly; we could fly directly from Ireland to New York for the closing.

While Bob Kahan worked on finalizing the contractual details with PepsiCo's lawyer Kathleen Luke, we headed off with our wives to Ireland. It was a remarkable trip, until we were thrown another unexpected curveball: Aer Lingus, the Irish airline, had gone on strike, grounding our return trip to New York.

Still riding high from the excitement of the PepsiCo deal, we improvised. Instead of scrambling for an alternative flight, Larry, Joni, Esther, and I flew to Paris, spent the night at the Ritz, and took the Concorde the following morning back to New York. We arrived in style for what we anticipated to be one of CPK's biggest moments.

Anyone who's had the privilege of flying the Concorde will tell you it's an unforgettable experience. The buzz in the cabin, seeing the curvature of the earth, a sip or two of Dom Pérignon, the thrill of crossing the Atlantic in less than four hours, and arriving earlier than you left. It was pure magic. By comparison a regular commercial flight would have taken more than eight hours.

The next morning we walked into PepsiCo's offices, ready to sign. Ken Stevens greeted us warmly but quicky dampened the mood. The lawyers were still fine-tuning the details; the deal wouldn't close for a couple of weeks.

Larry and I were stunned. Our faces must have said it all because Ken picked up on it immediately. Sensing something was wrong, he asked, "What's the problem?"

We were honest, telling him that we'd expected the deal to close that day and to have the funds wired immediately.

Ken excused himself to confer with senior PepsiCo executives. After what felt like an eternity, he returned with the words we'd been hoping to hear: "We trust you, guys. We'll wire the money."

On nothing more than a handshake, PepsiCo agreed to wire $70 million to us in good faith, trusting the documents would catch up in the weeks ahead.

That very day the money hit our bank in a series of $20 million increments—so unusual that our bank thought the wires were a mistake. It was understandable. Outside our CFO, Philip Gay, our inner circle and families, no one knew about the deal. We had kept it completely under wraps.

As expected, over the next couple of weeks, Bob and Kathleen hammered out the final details. The way it all unfolded was a testament not only to PepsiCo's confidence in our integrity but also a reflection of their trust for Bob, known in legal and business circles as a "dealmaker" rather than a "deal-breaker."

This trust was further reinforced when shortly after closing our deal, PepsiCo approached us with an unusual request. They were in the process of acquiring Chevys (a Mexican restaurant chain) for $100 million. Because they'd been so impressed with Bob's negotiation skills, they wanted him to represent them in the acquisition.

Out of respect they asked if we would waive any potential conflict of interest so Bob could take on the role. Of course, we agreed.

To this day Bob has remained our trusted lawyer and friend—a personal and professional relationship that's lasted more than fifty years.

We were elated to notify our investors, who had patiently entrusted us and were now about to see their faith handsomely rewarded. In the letter we sent, we explained that PepsiCo would be making a tender offer to purchase their shares. We emphasized that if they chose not to sell, they would remain minority shareholders alongside Larry and me. We were candid: There was no guarantee if, or when, another opportunity for liquidity would come.

When the dust settled, PepsiCo had paid about $100 million for 67.5 percent of CPK. Larry and I retained 30 percent, equally as always. The remaining 2.5 percent stayed in the hands of the outside shareholders.

Back in Los Angeles, our investors—already friends and supporters—were ecstatic. Larry and I held our heads high. This wasn't just about financial success. It was about fulfilling the trust that our investors had placed in us.

As monumental as this was for us (and for our investor group), it was merely a drop in the bucket for PepsiCo. That reality hit home shortly after the deal closed, when we were invited to a PepsiCo senior retreat in the Lake Champlain region of upstate New York. It was a remarkable multiday event where senior leaders from around the world gathered. Naively, we assumed that CPK would get a spotlight.

We were warmly welcomed, but presentation after presentation went by with no mention of us.

Finally, in his closing remarks, Wayne Calloway summed up the year's activity and added, almost as an afterthought, "We've made a number of strategic investments this year, even investing in a gourmet pizza chain."

It was humbling. But in the end we didn't need a spotlight to feel proud. The deal had given us what we set out to achieve: fantastic returns for our investors and a new chapter for CPK. Our egos might have taken a gentle bump—but the future looked bright.

We had taken some chips off the table. From here on out, we'd be playing with a bit more freedom and a lot less pressure. Best of all, we'd be playing with house money.

That sense of relative insignificance was reinforced later when I scoured the company's annual report. CPK wasn't mentioned anywhere except for a tiny footnote in their financial statements.

CHAPTER TWENTY-THREE

AFTER CLOSING THE DEAL WITH PEPSICO, IT WAS TIME to get to work. The valuation assumed we could open fifteen restaurants the following year and twenty-eight annually after that. It was a staggering target, given that our record to date was just seven in a single year.

We didn't have the infrastructure in place to support that level of hypergrowth. So the first order of business was building a real estate pipeline. From day one our strategy had been to target the most upscale neighborhoods and the most prestigious retail centers in the country.

Developers saw the same future we did: upscale casual dining as a cornerstone of their success. CPK had become a highly sought-after tenant, and we were determined to leverage those relationships to secure the very best locations as we grew at an aggressive rate.

Soon after PepsiCo invested, they placed John Martin, chairman and CEO of Taco Bell, on our board. John was a visionary in fast food, credited with value pricing and assembly-line systems that transformed Taco Bell.

From the outset he challenged us to think bigger. Indeed, he taunted us and our senior team as wimps! "Why build twenty-eight restaurants per year when you have a blank check from PepsiCo?" he goaded. "You should be building one hundred!"

Tempting as it sounded, Larry and I knew it wasn't realistic. John was a fast-food visionary entering a full-service world.

We were challenged enough to meet the goals already established. To urge us on, John told us to be experimental. He wanted us to try all types of sites across all different demographics to see what worked and what didn't. It was apparent to us that John had spent a lot of years using other people's money.

Yet building and operating a Taco Bell is far different from a full-service restaurant such as CPK, which was dependent not only on maintaining consistent food quality but on extensive training and hospitality in service. Also, the demographics of our core customers were dramatically different.

At the first meeting with our senior team, John told stories clearly meant to showcase his competitive spirit, speaking gleefully about releasing flies at a competitor's restaurant and hosing down a McDonald's parking lot, knowing it would freeze overnight. These stories landed with a thud. Our team members who shared our values sat stone-faced. His unethical strategies weren't funny. Not to us.

As growth accelerated, Larry and I recognized that our old method of personally scouting every site was no longer feasible. We bolstered our real estate department, then led by my brother, Neal. A lawyer in Chicago, Neal and his partners, Carl Halperin and Richard Kaplan, had formed Rosenfield, Kaplan & Halperin, taking over the law practice that was started by my father and uncle, Rosenfield and Rosenfield.

With CPK's early success, Neal had convinced Larry and me to grant him and his law partners a franchise to develop CPK locations in Chicago. Entering a business transaction with a relative is always a sensitive matter, so I deferred to Larry to make the call.

With Larry's approval, they opened two restaurants in Chicago: River North and Water Tower Place (an iconic shopping center in Chicago's Magnificent Mile district). The first struggled, but the second thrived. Neal and his partners, hoping to expand, secured two prime sites at Oakbrook Mall and the Saint Louis Galleria, but they couldn't raise the capital to develop them, so CPK stepped in, salvaging the deals and taking over the locations as company stores.

It was a disappointment for all. But it underscored a brutal truth: In the restaurant business, one failed location can sink everything. Still, Neal's heart was set on restaurants, not law.

Larry, in a typically generous move, offered him the role of vice president of development. Neal jumped at it, moved to California, and joined us full-time. For us it felt like family coming fully into the fold.

As our development team ramped up, reality proved sobering. Lease negotiations dragged, construction and permitting crawled, and developers didn't always share our urgency. Our own hardball tactics sometimes slowed deals, though we felt justified in pressing our advantage. CPK was a prized tenant, and we told our team to act like it.

Still, the math was unforgiving. Over time we developed a rule of thumb: Only one in every two or three sites under negotiation actually came to fruition—at least in the timeframe we expected.

That meant keeping sixty to ninety deals alive at any given moment just to reliably deliver twenty-eight openings a year. And signing a lease was only the beginning—the easy part. After that came the real work: construction, hiring, training, and running each restaurant to our exacting standards. We were firing on all cylinders—and in danger of overheating.

As confident as we were in the concept and our expanding team, there were moments when it felt like we had bitten off more than we could chew.

On paper we pulled it off. We opened fifteen restaurants in 1993 and twenty-eight more in 1994. And while we celebrated these milestones, the challenges of scaling a full-service restaurant chain began to catch up with us.

In hindsight it's easy to understand what happened. We had unleashed a team of dealmakers whose primary objective was to make deals, and they did just that.

We had multiple deals in the works with all the major developers, but the reality was that there were only so many *A* locations available. Every major developer has top-tier, high-traffic, high-sales-volume locations, but they also have *B* and *C* locations. The developers always try to bundle locations into package deals, offering tenants a prime *A* location but requiring them to take on less desirable *B*- or *C*-rate sites as part of the overall agreement.

As hard as Larry and I tried to get our real estate team to resist, other forces were in play. The retail leasing world was a tight-knit community. Executives and leasing agents frequently moved between a small number of companies and restaurant/retail tenants, creating an unspoken culture of mutual backscratching. It was, in many ways, a good old boys network where everyone wanted to stay in each other's good graces because you never knew who you'd be working with next. It didn't pay to be a deal killer.

The cold, hard truth was this: We had sipped the PepsiCo Kool-Aid, thrown caution to the wind, and grown too fast, too soon.

When the smoke cleared, the results were predictable. In affluent neighborhoods and high-traffic retail centers anchored by heavyweights such as Neiman, Nordstrom, or Saks, we thrived. In centers anchored solely by Sears, Penney, or Macy's, we often struggled.

Yet another nuance became clear. Even within a strong mall, placement was everything. Near the high-end anchors, we soared. Near the others we stalled.

Demographics told the same story: When catering to families with household incomes above $100,000, we invariably succeeded; below $60,000, we often faltered unless the center itself was exceptionally strong.

While we had hit the growth targets to open the target number of restaurants as planned, the mixed performance had become a growing concern. But for CPK's future at PepsiCo, a seismic shift was underway—one that would ultimately shape CPK's destiny.

John Martin, the chairman of Taco Bell and the chief promoter of such rapid expansion, was replaced on our board by Indra Nooyi, PepsiCo's brilliant new head of corporate strategy. At the same time, our longtime ally, Ken Stevens, was promoted to president of Taco Bell. The writing was on the wall. The leadership change clearly signaled a shift in tone. We had a growing sense that the wind was not blowing in our favor.

We admired Indra right away. She was sharp, analytical, charming, witty, and refreshingly self-deprecating.

What we didn't know then was that she had been personally recruited by Wayne Calloway, PepsiCo's chairman, to lead corporate strategy. From her first day, she was the company's chief strategist, and a major shift inside PepsiCo was already underway. The ground was moving, and we didn't see the full picture yet.

However, despite our admiration, Indra was clear about her

disappointment in CPK's performance. Our push into middle-income demographic markets—an experiment encouraged by Taco Bell's John Martin—was dragging us down.

For the first time in our history, we were forced to confront a painful reality: We needed to close some underperforming restaurants.

PepsiCo made it clear: There would be no further expansion. They pulled the plug. Cold stop. Legally, under our agreement, it's doubtful that they even had the right to unilaterally halt funding our growth, but in the moment, it didn't matter. Larry and I were stunned. We didn't push back. We didn't argue. We were beaten down.

The fallout was swift and brutal. Layoffs rippled through every level of the company, from real estate and development to operations and even at the store level. Larry and I felt their pain, but it was beyond our control.

At the same time, our once-strong relationships with landlords took a hit as we abruptly pulled out of dozens of lease negotiations, fracturing trust that would be difficult to repair.

For us it felt like living a nightmare that was unfolding in real time. This was the lowest point in CPK's history.

How did we get to this point? In hindsight the cause was clear—a toxic brew.

With unlimited PepsiCo capital, combined with Larry's and my unbridled passion for the brand—plus our lack of experience in scaling at such a rapid pace—we drank the PepsiCo Kool-Aid, no question. The buck stops with us, but responsibility also rested with the PepsiCo executives who'd pushed us forward—Ken Stevens and, especially, John Martin. He wasn't just cheering us on; he was cracking the whip. With the full force of PepsiCo behind him, it was nearly impossible to say no. And we didn't.

Yet the very expansion they demanded was the one they abandoned. And now we were left holding the bag, wondering how no one saw it coming, least of all the ones who'd set it all in motion in the first place.

At the same time, even though they lacked the contractual right, PepsiCo pressed for more control of daily operations. They asked us to bring in Greg Trojan, a rising star from Pizza Hut, as executive vice president to take a leading role in operations.

From the start Greg impressed us. Bright, humble, and genuinely likable, he quickly earned our trust, and we had no hesitation approving him for the role. Once the decision was made, we introduced him to our senior team.

For Larry and me, stepping back from day-to-day operations was monumental. For the first time in our history, we were handing over the reins of the company we had built from scratch. There's no way to minimize the emotional impact this had on both of us. While it had felt right in the moment, we didn't yet realize this was the beginning of a shift that would echo in ways we couldn't have imagined.

Greg bonded quickly with our senior team, and it wasn't hard to see why. After the whiplash of rapid expansion followed by an abrupt stop, morale was badly shaken. Our team—young, tight-knit, and battle-tested alongside us—was bearing the brunt of the strain. Larry and I weren't exactly old-timers (I was fifty; he was fifty-two), but Greg, at thirty-six, was closer to their peer.

And this is where a not-so-subtle divergence began to show between Larry and me. I had other outlets—golf, especially. I'd just been honored to join the board at Callaway Golf, in its infancy. That only took a little time, but it added an exciting new dimension just when I was otherwise feeling down.

If I wasn't the one making the calls, I didn't feel the need to be in the office every day. It wasn't that I was entirely comfortable stepping back. These were troubling times, but under the circumstances, I was willing to give Greg the room he needed to lead.

Larry, on the other hand, had one hobby: menu creation. And if he wasn't in the test kitchen, he thrived on the day-to-day contact with the team at our Restaurant Support Center. His door was always open; if people weren't coming in, he'd roam the halls looking for someone to talk to. Stepping back was harder for him. He got along with Greg personally, but he remained ever-present—a watchful eye, eager to fill me in on anything that raised concern.

The deeper problem wasn't the shifting roles. Greg, under PepsiCo's marching orders, was charged with squeezing efficiencies and cutting costs. One of the most telling changes: Our fresh, high-quality mozzarella was replaced with frozen cheese pellets from a Pizza Hut supplier.

Sure, it may have looked like progress at PepsiCo's headquarters in Purchase, New York. But on the ground, it was corrosive—eroding the trust we'd built with our customers and, perhaps, even more critically, the pride our team members took in the product.

Bean counters always see the fat they can trim. They rarely notice when they've cut into muscle. With all due respect to Greg, and I truly have the greatest respect for him, he simply hadn't been around long enough to understand the depth of that trust. Like an unseen virus, the erosion spread. In the field our regional directors, all homegrown, were a tight-knit group. They communicated regularly with each other, far more with one another than with the home office.

Their phones were ringing off the hook. They could feel it. They saw the changes. And they were talking. We hadn't just bent our values; we had crossed a line. There was no pretending otherwise.

The truth hit me hardest one night in South Florida, where I'd gathered a group of store managers for dinner at the Forge, a legendary Miami restaurant. I expected it to be a treat. But as I spoke about our continued commitment to quality, I caught an assistant manager roll her eyes toward another manager, as if to say, "Does he really believe this?"

It was gut-wrenching. Back at the hotel, I called Larry and summed it up in two words: "We're screwed!" (Though candidly, I may have used something stronger.)

CHAPTER TWENTY-FOUR

BUT LONG BEFORE THE FULL DEPTH OF OUR PROBLEMS hit me during that dinner in Florida, I genuinely tried to be a good partner to PepsiCo. They had made what felt to us like a major investment, though to them it wasn't even a rounding error—and I felt a personal responsibility because of it. If they wanted me to step away from day-to-day operations, I was willing. My instinct was to be supportive, not a problem. I wanted to be available when needed, but otherwise, not to get in the way.

With less voice in the CPK's daily life, I found myself spending more time at my home in Indian Wells, near Palm Springs, in what Southern Californians simply call "the desert." Golf became a refuge, but even more it led to a friendship that changed my life. At my country club, the Vintage Club, I grew close with Ely Callaway, founder of Callaway Golf, who had just upended the industry with his revolutionary Big Bertha driver.

I'd first met Ely in the late '70s, when he had left as president of Burlington Industries to launch Callaway Winery in Temecula, California, making him a pioneer in the production of Southern California wine. Callaway Golf had recently gone public, and I had bought some shares. Whenever I bumped into Ely on the course or in the locker room, he'd give me the same advice, with a grin: "Don't sell your stock."

Ely was grateful for my support, and I was deeply honored when he invited me to join the Callaway Golf Board in 1994. That role became a constant in my life, and the greatest honor came when he asked me to succeed him as chairman upon his retirement (a story I'll return to in the prequel for those who choose to read on). Sadly, Ely passed away before that transition could take place, in 2001.

I remained on the board for twenty-three years, retiring in 2017 as the longest-serving director in the company's history. Today I proudly carry the honorary title of director emeritus. Under the leadership of Chip Brewer, Callaway's longtime CEO, the company has continued to thrive as the number one golf club brand in the world, a testament not only to Ely's vision and enduring legacy but also to the commitment of a strong management team.

Meanwhile, back at CPK, I was trying to be supportive of Greg's efforts and prepared to be called upon when needed. Larry spent much of his time in our test kitchen in Redondo Beach, developing new menu ideas. With PepsiCo's continued efforts to cut costs, directly affecting quality, CPK was still floundering. When we came to our offices, at the Restaurant Support Center, Larry and I often found ourselves aimlessly wandering the halls, doing what we could to keep morale afloat. The situation was bleak, and we couldn't see a light at the end of the tunnel.

Greg did his best with the hand he'd been dealt, but it was now obvious that PepsiCo had set him up for an impossible job. His mandate was narrow and unforgiving: manage the slowdown, impose discipline, and cut costs. He wasn't given the resources or authority to succeed. In hindsight PepsiCo hadn't brought in a builder; they had essentially sent Greg in as a caretaker.

Cutting off growth, cutting costs, and starving a business of capital isn't discipline. It's suffocation. Money, after all, is the mother's milk not only of politics but of business. In the end it turned out that Greg was only a placeholder. At least he wasn't the mortician.

Little did we know then that CPK's story was far from over and that one day, under very different circumstances, we'd see a familiar script unfold again.

As we wrestled with CPK's challenges—many of them tied directly to PepsiCo's tightening grip—something larger was brewing in Purchase. We were a small fish in a vast corporate ocean, unaware that Indra Nooyi, PepsiCo's brilliant new head of corporate strategy, had Chairman and CEO

Wayne Calloway's full attention. She was charting a tectonic realignment of PepsiCo's future, and we hadn't heard a word of it.

Our first clue came almost by chance.

Despite the tensions around CPK's struggles, we genuinely enjoyed our interactions with Indra. She was always straightforward, trustworthy, and frankly delightful. But beneath that warm, approachable exterior was a sharp intellect and a depth of strategic thinking well beyond her years. So when she invited us to join her and her husband, Raj, for dinner at their favorite Indian restaurant in New York, we gladly accepted.

Over a warm evening of great food and conversation, she casually dropped what felt like a quiet bombshell. Almost offhand, she said that PepsiCo shouldn't be in the restaurant business at all. Restaurants, she explained, were too capital-intensive and delivered the weakest returns. By contrast the real stars of the company were its high-margin syrup and soda business and, of course, Frito-Lay (which dominated the global snack market).

We weren't personally offended. She was clearly talking about the big three in PepsiCo's portfolio: Pizza Hut, Taco Bell, and KFC. Even though Indra sat on CPK's board, we knew that we were barely a blip on her radar screen. Still, her offhand comment was the first glimmer of light at the end of what had felt like a very long tunnel.

By coincidence, soon after that dinner, we spoke with Wayne Calloway. We hadn't interacted with him often, but every encounter left a mark. He was warm, approachable, and genuinely gracious—a true gentleman.

In that brief exchange, Wayne praised Indra and told us how lucky we were to have her on our board and added—almost matter-of-factly—that she was the smartest person at PepsiCo and that someday she should be CEO and chairman.

That was the final piece of the puzzle. You didn't need to be a rocket scientist to connect the dots. If the CEO believed she was the company's smartest mind, and she believed that PepsiCo should get out of the restaurant business, well, the writing was on the wall. It wasn't a question of if but when.

As a postscript, Wayne Calloway's prediction proved prescient. In

2006 she became PepsiCo's fifth CEO in its forty-four-year history, and the following year she was named chairman of the board. (She has since retired. Time flies!)

But let's go back. Now armed with that inside insight, we didn't know exactly how (or if) we could benefit. Soon enough, an opportunity presented itself.

One afternoon Greg Trojan walked into our offices looking uneasy. He'd just taken a call from someone in PepsiCo's Treasury Department, the division that managed capital risk and control rights. The question was blunt: How could PepsiCo justify having that much money—by then a $100 million equity investment plus a $150 million loan—tied up in a company they didn't control?

That question cut to the heart of our original deal. Thanks to our lawyer Bob Kahan's creativity and Larry and my stubborn refusal to surrender control, we had structured the agreement as a fifty-fifty balance. Neither party had control. Apparently, that was now becoming a problem for PepsiCo.

Greg laid out PepsiCo's proposal. On its face it looked like a generous offer. Because CPK was operating at a loss, PepsiCo could potentially use those losses to offset its own taxable income *but only* if it could consolidate CPK into its corporate tax return. To do that they needed control.

In exchange they offered to cut CPK a check for $2 million, equal to the value of the tax benefit, and to include our senior leadership in PepsiCo's rich employee stock program.

But the catch was glaring. To get the money and perks, we'd have to give up the one thing we had insisted on from the beginning: control. Or more accurately: the stalemate. Neither side truly controlled CPK. And now they wanted to tip the balance.

We voiced our concern to Greg. He was never our adversary. He was just the messenger in this process.

We told him that we trusted Indra and the PepsiCo executives and, in principle, were willing to grant them control. But we had one serious reservation: We believed that PepsiCo was going to exit the restaurant business in the near future. And if that happened, they could sell their interest to a buyer in CPK to someone we didn't trust or approve of.

So we made a counterproposal, crafted with our lawyer, Bob Kahan. We'd grant PepsiCo control but *only* if they agreed not to sell or assign their interest for five years without our written approval. And that approval didn't have to be reasonable; it was entirely at our discretion.

In other words, if we gave them control, we demanded complete veto power over whom they could sell us to for five years. Period.

As expected, PepsiCo wasn't exactly thrilled. They went ahead and drafted the documents on their terms anyway. Greg dutifully delivered them, but we refused to sign.

For months Greg stopped by, checking to see if we were ready to move forward. But it was a losing battle. We had no intention of budging. We weren't under any obligation to agree, and we were perfectly willing to let it play out.

If we're being honest with ourselves now, there was something else happening on a deeper, more personal level. Larry and I were hurting. As much as we appreciated PepsiCo's investment—and we truly did—it felt like they had pulled the rug out from under us. What once felt like a partnership, and indeed a friendship, had shifted. Now it was purely business.

It seemed that they viewed their investment in CPK as little more than a lab experiment gone wrong. A rounding error. But for us this wasn't going to be some journal entry or write-off. It was our lives. Our employees, our vendors, the extended families that relied on us—they were real people, not numbers on a spreadsheet. And now they were caught in the fallout. Collateral damage in a corporate strategy that we had no voice in.

We knew our rights. We had fought hard for them. When Larry and I are aligned and have our dander up, we're a tough act. We had absolutely no intent of compromising. Not an inch.

Finally, in June 1996, PepsiCo relented. We agreed to their terms on one condition: PepsiCo could not sell its interest in CPK without our approval for five years. Period.

With that settled PepsiCo named Greg Trojan as CPK's president, with our full support. Larry and I remained co-CEOs and cochairmen.

Then in another surprise twist, within a month or so, Greg informed us that he had been recruited and had accepted a position as CEO of House of Blues. We parted ways on the best of terms. Before he left, PepsiCo tried hard to keep him in their system, but he had other plans. Greg would later became CEO of Guitar Center and then BJ's Restaurants.

I've often wondered—had he known what was just around the corner, would he have stayed?

On September 27, 1996, just after Greg's departure, we were blindsided. Out of nowhere the editor of *Nation's Restaurant News* called to ask for a comment on a PepsiCo press release. We hadn't received so much as a whisper. Naturally, we told her we'd get back to her. Then we scrambled to track it down. When we read it, we were stunned.

The release covered several challenges PepsiCo was facing—including problems in its international bottling fiasco in Venezuela, where its longtime bottler had switched to Coke overnight and, adding insult to injury, had repainted all its trucks from Pepsi blue to Coke red.

But buried in the release was the real shock: PepsiCo was conducting a formal review to assess whether it would sell its casual-dining restaurants, *expressly naming California Pizza Kitchen*. Wall Street reacted instantly. PepsiCo's shares jumped. Apparently, no one cared about its casual-dining restaurants. That wasn't worth a yawn. Instead, it signaled a full-scale review of PepsiCo's entire business portfolio. Analysts began calling for a complete exit from the restaurant business. The casual-dining "review" looked to them like step one. Step two was obvious: Get out of the restaurant business entirely.

As for us? At first we were outraged. But as the dust settled, another thought cut through: opportunity.

For a while it felt like the CPK ship was taking on water, maybe even sinking. But now, unexpectedly, it seemed we were still afloat. Maybe, just maybe, the tide was turning in our favor.

Despite what the press release said or implied, one fact was crystal clear: PepsiCo could not sell its interest in CPK without our approval. Not that year, not that decade, not that century. Under our agreement, they couldn't sell a single share without our written consent for five more years.

We immediately reached out to Kathleen Luke, PepsiCo's lawyer, with whom we had a good relationship. "PepsiCo needs to issue a retraction,"

I insisted. "You may want to get rid of your dogs like Pizza Hut, Taco Bell, and KFC, but you just signed an agreement with us, and you'll be focusing on your one remaining core restaurant brand, California Pizza Kitchen, until the next century."

Kathleen told us to stay patient, and she'd get back to us.

It didn't take long for us to hear back. John Martin, from Taco Bell, called and asked us to meet for breakfast with a very senior PepsiCo executive near Taco Bell's offices in Orange County. We met, not sure what to expect, but what we got was our first and only truly ugly encounter in our history with PepsiCo.

There were no pleasantries. No diplomacy. They had sent an attack dog. This executive (whose name we'll refrain from mentioning) told us flatly that PepsiCo intended to sell its stake in CPK. When we reminded him that they needed our approval, he grew visibly agitated and, in a heated moment, declared, "If you don't cooperate, we will bury you!"

That line shook us. I don't recall anyone—before or since—saying something like that to me. It was unsettling. But Larry and I didn't flinch. After all, we'd built successful careers prosecuting major mobsters and hardened criminals. At this point in our lives, we weren't about to back down because of some boardroom tough guy.

If intimidation was the play, they'd picked the wrong guys.

Game on.

To PepsiCo's credit, after trying the hardball route, we soon received a far more welcome call—this one from Charles G. "Chas" Phillips, a partner in the Wall Street firm Gleacher & Company—a seasoned banker with the right bedside manner to navigate Larry and me.

Chas was refreshingly candid. He opened by acknowledging that we had the veto power over any deal. Then he laid it out plainly: PepsiCo planned to solicit buyers but would make it clear that any serious buyer needed to submit two offers—one for PepsiCo's stake and one for ours. Chas then summed it up in one line: "You guys just hit another lottery ticket!"

It marked the beginning of the end of our partnership with PepsiCo and the start of what would become a long and fruitful relationship with

Chas, a steady mediator who would later play a pivotal role in shaping CPK's future.

The transition wouldn't be without bumps. But once again the old adage proved true: When one door closes, another opens.

CHAPTER TWENTY-FIVE

BY THIS POINT PEPSICO WANTED OUT OF THEIR INVESTMENT in CPK. But they had a problem. Under the terms of our agreement, they couldn't sell their interest without our approval. After being threatened that they would "bury us," our dander was up. We had no interest in compromise. We held absolute veto power, and we had every intention of using it to our advantage.

Still, in the grander scheme, we were just a small irritant. Indra Nooyi's broader strategic vision was being carried out. PepsiCo was exiting the restaurant business entirely, spinning off the world's largest restaurant company with over thirty thousand units into a new company called Tricon Global Restaurants (later Yum! Brands), which would house Pizza Hut, Taco Bell, and KFC.

They had far bigger fish to fry than a standoff with CPK. At one point they approached us about folding into the spin-off, but we declined without hesitation. Our position was clear. It was time for CPK to stand on its own. Some would call it fate. We'd call it good lawyering. Sometimes they go hand in hand.

Chas cut to the chase. PepsiCo planned to conduct a formal auction, but every bidder would be told the same thing—no deal could close without our approval.

That was music to our ears. We had no intent of riding off into the sunset just because PepsiCo was ready to move on. We were staying put and living to fight another day. Chas made one firm point: Because PepsiCo was taking a loss, Larry and I would not receive a dime from the sale. We heard him out. But the moment we got off the call, Larry and I looked at each other and agreed. Oh yes, we were going to receive cash. That was the price they were going to pay for threatening us.

The process dragged on for a year, with presentations and suitors coming and going. One final bidder emerged that was acceptable to us: Bruckmann, Rosser, Sherrill & Co. (BRS), a New York City–based private equity firm with previous restaurant investments.

BRS's lead was Hal Rosser. In the courting phase, our interactions were smooth enough. And given PepsiCo's eagerness to exit, BRS was in the driver's seat. PepsiCo wanted a swift sale and cared little about price. Confident that he had our support, Rosser could set the terms, at least with PepsiCo. With us, not so much.

Larry and I together owned 30 percent of the company, our remaining investors another 3 percent. On paper that 33 percent was effectively worthless, buried under $150 million in PepsiCo loans used to fund expansion.

PepsiCo's debt was going to be wiped out in the transaction and replaced with a much smaller obligation. Tough, smart, and patient, Hal Rosser negotiated a purchase price of about $60 million for PepsiCo's interest, funded with about $25 million in cash and the rest borrowed through CPK's credit.

Separately, I was negotiating with Hal over our stake. He wanted our 33 percent interest subordinated, meaning lower on the totem pole to BRS's equity and the new debt. I pushed back, hard. After plenty of back-and-forth, BRS relented. Our group's 33 percent stake would be treated equally with theirs—pari passu. Just like them, we'd share the new debt burden no more, no less.

I also pressed Hal to push PepsiCo to absorb losses from some of our weakest restaurants. I gave him a list of ten restaurants, and he came back with a win. PepsiCo agreed to take back four low performers that soon closed. They would also assume liability for six that had already shut down.

It was a huge relief. Still, we felt our approval of the sale justified a "kicker" for our investor group.

From the outset we told Chas that we wouldn't sign off without cash as part of the deal. He insisted that wouldn't happen, but we all knew better. We held the ace (veto power), and we weren't afraid to play it.

Just as Chas predicted, we ultimately walked away with what felt like a lottery win for ourselves and for the loyal investors who'd stayed with us. At closing, not only was a massive debt wiped out, but our group received $10 million in "cash merger consideration."

Of course, it wasn't a lottery or luck. It was the product of years of discipline, strategy, and knowing exactly when to hold the line—with our lawyer, Bob Kahan, right there beside us.

Together, we had protected ourselves and our investors.

After the deal closed in late 1997, BRS assumed all control of CPK. For the first time in the company's history, Larry and I no longer had any decision-making authority. We hoped brighter days were ahead. Only time would tell.

CHAPTER TWENTY-SIX

AS THE PEPSICO ERA AT CPK DREW TO A CLOSE, WE couldn't help but reflect, not on the frustrations or missteps but on the highs. The PepsiCo years weren't just about expanding our footprint; they were a major leap in shaping the CPK brand.

Larry's and my vision (driven by the excitement around our innovative California-style pizzas, especially the blockbuster Barbecue Chicken Pizza) was generating buzz everywhere we went. Our growing in-house PR and marketing team, led by one of our earliest employees, Sarah Goldsmith Grover, seized the momentum and ran with it.

At every new opening, CPK attracted media attention. Local stations regularly featured our cooks and managers in on-air pizza demonstrations. The Barbecue Chicken Pizza was almost always the one they wanted to see, and it had become our calling card. This was before it showed up on menus everywhere, back when it was fresh, bold, and uniquely ours.

If Larry and I were in town, we'd often join in. Neither of us had the skills to actually work in the kitchen, but we could fake it just well enough to survive a live TV segment.

That buzz carried us to three appearances on *The Today Show*, where we had a great time with Katie Couric, Matt Lauer, Ann Curry, and Al Roker—all warm, gracious, and curious. We had the same fun on *Good Morning America* with Charles Gibson and Joan Lunden, another unforgettable chapter in CPK's rise.

We were also featured on *The Oprah Winfrey Show* and had a hilarious segment on *The Ellen DeGeneres Show*, where Ellen personally delivered CPK pizzas to the home of a very surprised customer. Print coverage followed: *Business Week*, *The Wall Street Journal*, *USA Today*, and *People* magazine.

One of most humbling and entertaining experiences was filming a segment for the reality series *Now Who's Boss*, where successful CEOs swapped roles with entry-level employees. Larry and I worked as dishwashers and servers in two CPK restaurants. (We split locations because, as we joked, we didn't want to overwhelm one location with our incompetence.)

Larry's biggest struggle came while waiting tables. He got slammed attempting to handle four tables at once and, in the chaos, forgot to card a young woman who ordered a beer—a definite no-no, as the trainer pointed out later (on video).

My own hard lesson came as a dishwasher. I learned that dishes needed to be sorted from forks and knives before being placed in the sink. "It's the forks that get you," I explained later.

What began as a rookie mistake turned into a system-wide change across all our restaurants.

More importantly, the experience gave us an even deeper appreciation of just how hard our teams worked—fiercely upholding CPK's service standards. We knew the segment would be a morale booster too. As Larry joked on camera, "I don't know what the national audience's reaction will be, but everyone at CPK who sees this will be rolling on the floor."

Looking back, that kind of enthusiasm has always been part of the CPK story. While we never specifically sought out celebrity visits or endorsements, they happened organically from the very beginning, and we were always happy to welcome the buzz they generated.

In our early days, George Hamilton would stop by our Beverly Hills restaurant for a glass of our bargain-priced Jordan Cabernet Sauvignon. After our friend and neighbor Paul Fleming told us that Clint Eastwood was the biggest celebrity who dined at his Ruth's Chris location across the street, we were thrilled to let him know when Clint came over to CPK for a meal.

Over the years the list kept growing. Michelle Obama regularly met friends and their kids at a CPK in Chicago. During the Obama White

House years, Sasha celebrated her ninth birthday at our Montgomery, Maryland, location—an event memorable not just for the cake but because the Secret Service briefly confiscated all customer cell phones.

Ronald Reagan became a regular after leaving the Oval Office, frequently ordering our Italian Chopped Salad for himself and his Century City office staff. On one occasion Larry, Joni, Esther, and I were honored to join him and Nancy for a CPK-catered luncheon.

Bill Clinton's visit to our Kahala Mall location in Honolulu caused such a stir that TV crews returned for days after his visit to film the exact spot where he'd dined.

Other political figures found their way to our tables as well. Dick Cheney, while secretary of defense, was a regular visitor at our Tysons Corner, Virginia, location, sometimes along with Ken Adelman, my lifelong friend and former director of the US Arms Control and Disarmament Agency.

Hollywood showed up in force. Because we didn't take reservations, Dustin Hoffman once held a large table at our Brentwood location while waiting for his family to celebrate his son Jake's ninth birthday. Years later Jake was our daughter Nicole's prom date—a fun footnote in the CPK story.

While in London, Katy Perry declared her devotion to CPK on Twitter: "I LOVE YOU CALIFORNIA PIZZA KITCHEN! Although I should be a shareholder since I have invested thousands of $ on BBQ Chicken Salads."

Viola Davis added her own, tweeting, "An end to a good day. Strawberry Basil Margaritas at California Pizza Kitchen."

Jane Seymour, one of our earliest investors, had a favorite seat by the window at our Beverly Hills location. (Okay, maybe we staged it.) She also drew a lot of attention at our Lenox Square location in Atlanta, where she signed copies of one of her books while the mall music system played "Somewhere in Time," the theme song from the famous film with Christopher Reeve.

Busy Philipps has recently become an official spokesperson for CPK, celebrating its fortieth anniversary—inspired by her having worked for CPK earlier and her true longtime love of the brand.

Even unexpected names pop up. I read that Mark Cuban came up with the $5.7 billion idea for Broadcast.com over a meal at CPK. Ryan Seacrest and Vanna White were recently spotted dining at CPK, which was no surprise since Ryan has long been a fan.

One of my favorite stories, though, happened at the Naples Winter Wine Festival in Florida, which raises millions for local children's charities. Esther and I were there as guests of Chairpersons Cynthia and Bruce Sherman.

At a charity dinner at their home, I was seated next to Christian Moueix, whose family owns Château Pétrus in Bordeaux, France, one of the world's most coveted wines. His wife, Cherise, spoke only French for most of the evening until she heard me mention California Pizza Kitchen. Suddenly, in perfect English she leaned across the table and said, "CPK! I was raised in DC, and whenever we get off the plane from Paris, Christian goes off with Daniel Boulud and his chef friends. I go directly to CPK at Sixtieth and Third [Upper East Side of Manhattan] and sit at the counter for my Barbecue Chicken Pizza fix!"

I told Cherise then, and I'll say it again now, that she had given me one of the best stories of my life.

But unquestionably, my favorite memory of boosting CPK's exposure came through the credit card giant American Express, and it showed the best of the synergy between Larry and me.

In 1994 Visa was running a big ad campaign featuring Wolfgang Puck, touting that his restaurants accepted Visa but not American Express. Spotting an opportunity, Larry asked our head of marketing, Sarah Goldsmith Grover, to pitch the idea that Larry and I appear in a competing ad—one declaring that CPK proudly accepted American Express. Sarah came back with the answer: Amex had politely declined.

In typical Larry fashion, he wasn't about to let it die. A little digging revealed the key decision-maker was Ken Chenault, head of Amex Travel Services. Larry called him directly and, after a brief conversation, came into my office grinning: "Ken's interested. He said we should come to see him next time we're in New York."

I didn't hesitate: "That's great! Call him back and tell him that we'll be there tomorrow!"

The next morning we were in Manhattan and were greeted at Amex headquarters by Tom Ryder, their national restaurants accounts manager. Tom wasted no time letting us know there was no way that Ken would approve our idea. He explained that lots of restaurants were clamoring for the same treatment and Amex couldn't single one out. He thanked us for flying in but made it clear—Ken had only agreed to meet with us as a courtesy.

That changed the moment Ken walked in.

We hit it off instantly with the charismatic Harvard-trained lawyer. Larry and I, maybe at our best Frick-and-Frack routine—playing off each other as we had for twenty years—pitched that the CPK brand was all about choices. And who better than CPK to carry that message?

Ken listened closely, and when we finished, he turned to Tom—who'd been sitting stiffly with folded arms and a face that radiated skepticism—and said, "How long will it take to produce this?"

Caught off guard, Tom stiffened, then fired back defiantly: "At least six months."

Ken didn't even blink. "Have it done in sixty days."

And just like that, we were on our way—headed straight into one of the most memorable moments in CPK history.

Within weeks production was underway. A film crew shot footage of Larry and me at CPK locations and on the beach in Santa Monica, capturing the California lifestyle that had become synonymous with our brand. One of the commercials—a sixty-second spot—went on to win an *Adweek* award for Best Spots in October 1994. The *Adweek* summary read,

> *In this commercial for American Express, Larry Flax and Rick Rosenfield, owners of California Pizza Kitchen, explain the concept behind their business as a fast-paced montage of images of life in Southern California is shown. 'California is what our restaurant is all about,' they say. 'It's about choices, innovation, freedom, and adventure. It's a place where adventurous diners can order pizza with almost any topping imaginable.'*
>
> *'American Express is welcomed at California Pizza Kitchen,' the announcer says. 'And wherever fresh ideas are cooking.'*

It was an exciting opportunity, though it didn't get quite the exposure we'd hoped for. American Express had planned to air the commercials heavily during the baseball season and the World Series. But in August the longest strike in baseball history began, wiping out the rest of the season, including the World Series.

Even so Larry and I enjoyed an unexpected perk. To appear in the commercials, we had to join the Screen Actors Guild. Once the spots aired, residual checks started arriving in our mailboxes—anywhere from $100 to $1,000. Opening the mail suddenly felt like Christmas morning. By the end each of us earned about $40,000 in residuals—a trifecta: great for the brand, a lot of fun, and surprisingly lucrative.

Looking back, it was more than just a commercial. It was proof of what could happen when we trusted our instincts, pushed past the initial no, and leaned into the unexpected. That lesson carried us far beyond marketing—it shaped how we built CPK itself.

Some would call it luck—and sure, a little luck never hurts. But I've always believed it came from taking leaps, refusing to take no for an answer, and sometimes stumbling into the right room at the right time with the right idea. That approach has served me well—from meeting my wife to launching a restaurant to becoming a card-carrying member of the Screen Actors Guild.

But it brings up something I've thought about often—and something I've shared with people I've mentored over the years. I don't pray for good luck. I figure I can take care of myself. What I pray for is the absence of bad luck—the things no amount of effort or planning can control.

CHAPTER TWENTY-SEVEN

JUST AS LIFE CAN BRING US UNEXPECTED WINS, IT can also deliver brutal blows. In 1995 the world was captivated by the O. J. Simpson trial, where he stood accused of murdering his former wife, Nicole Brown Simpson, and Ron Goldman, a young waiter and friend of hers from a nearby restaurant in Brentwood, California. Tragically, Ron was simply in the wrong place at the wrong time.

Like many in our social circle, Larry and I had connections to several people involved in the case. I knew Ron personally. He was a charming young man who had recently worked as a counter server at the CPK in Brentwood Gardens before taking a new job at nearby Mezzaluna.

Unfortunately, I also knew O. J. Simpson. We were both members of Sherwood Country Club and had played golf together. In fact six weeks before the murders, I'd invited him to join me for a round at Hillcrest Country Club. What I had expected to be a friendly afternoon had quickly turned sour. O. J. insisted on betting far more than the modest stakes that I had regularly enjoyed in games with friends. I went along, but as his game faltered, his mood darkened. He kept pressing—doubling his bets—and losing. By the end of our round, one thing was clear: This was a man who vehemently despised losing. Afterward, I quietly vowed never to play golf with him again, a remarkably easy promise to keep. Before leaving, he asked if CPK would donate pizzas for an event at his daughter's school. I agreed, gave him my number, and told him to have Nicole call me.

Weeks later, after the murders, detectives found the piece of paper with my number on Nicole's nightstand. I received a call from an investigator, but once I explained the context, the inquiry ended.

Larry and I were also friends with several members of O. J.'s defense team—Bob Shapiro, Rob Kardashian, and Shawn Holley (who was one of our original servers at Beverly Hills and had since become a rising legal star). Like much of the country, we were glued to the television throughout the trial.

A few months in, a dismissed juror (who happened to be an African American woman) claimed the jury was racially divided. Her comments made headlines and fueled speculation about deep divisions inside the sequestered jury.

Around that time Larry and I talked to Judge Ito's clerk about hosting the jury for a private meal at our downtown CPK in the Wells Fargo Center, just blocks from the courthouse. Judge Ito granted permission, and the jury dined with us twice. But it was their second visit that turned out to be particularly meaningful.

Out of curiosity Esther, Larry, Joni, and I dropped by to observe. Contrary to the media's portrayal of discord, the jury appeared completely at ease. The men sat at one table, the women at another—a familiar pattern from our own trial experience—but there was no sign of racial tension. They were laughing, relaxed, and genuinely seemed to enjoy the break from seclusion.

Coincidentally, Gregg Jarrett (then a young lawyer and reporter for Court TV, now a Fox News analyst and author) was also dining there that evening. Recognizing the jury, he observed the same thing and approached Larry and me. He mentioned he'd be appearing on *The Geraldo Rivera Show* and asked if we'd be willing to share our impressions. We politely declined. We had no interest in being drawn into the media circus.

Before leaving, the jury made a request: They wanted CPK T-shirts. Judge Ito approved the gesture, and we happily provided shirts for the entire group.

We knew the shirts included our signature yellow-diamond logo and, on the back, a message we'd always liked: "Fourteen ethnically different cultures peacefully coexisting on a thin, delicious crust."

What we didn't know—at least not yet—was the reason behind the request.

The next morning Judge Ito called the court to order and announced, "The jury is seated." Looking genuinely surprised, he added, "At least, I think it's our jury!"

Though viewers at home couldn't see them, everyone in the courtroom (including the press) recognized what was happening: Nearly every juror was wearing one of our shirts.

Only then did we realize: Their request had been less than subtle—it was a strong declaration of unity.

Since the jury had been sequestered for the entire trial, they technically shouldn't have known about the controversy surrounding the dismissed juror. Perhaps it was her attitude before she was excused that gave them a sense of the underlying tension. In any event their coordinated display was no accident. It was a quiet—but unmistakable—message.

On a related note, I happened to be at home watching *The Geraldo Rivera Show* when Gregg Jarrett appeared. Geraldo's guests included Oscar Goodman, the flamboyant Las Vegas defense attorney who later became the city's mayor. Oscar was infamous for representing mob figures such as Meyer Lansky and Tony "The Ant" Spilotro. Also on the panel was Stanley Goldman, a criminal law professor at Loyola Law School in Los Angeles and frequent analyst during the trial (no relation to Ron).

During the broadcast Jarrett described what he had observed at CPK and mentioned that the owners, Larry and I, had also been there and witnessed the same thing.

That was when Oscar Goodman interrupted: "I know those guys, and they're lying!"

Geraldo, clearly intrigued, leaned in: "Why would the owners of CPK lie? We'll find out after the break."

I was livid. I immediately called Larry. "We're going to sue that SOB Oscar!" I shouted into the phone.

When the show returned from commercial, Geraldo repeated the question: "Why would the owners of CPK lie?"

That was when Stanley Goldman stepped in. "I know one of the guys," he said. "He taught me criminal law. I don't believe he would lie."

I was stunned. I knew Stanley looked familiar but hadn't realized he'd been one of my students when I'd taught criminal law and procedure at Loyola Law School during my time as a federal prosecutor.

Oscar, laughing nervously, started to backpedal. "I was just kidding," he said. "Those guys were federal prosecutors, and they beat me all over town."

His retraction calmed me down. Sort of.

In the end the murders of Nicole Brown Simpson and Ron Goldman, and the trial that followed, had a profound impact on the nation. It captivated viewers and exposed deep divisions in how Americans viewed race, justice, and domestic abuse. We never imagined having any connection to that moment in history. That small, subtle display of unity wasn't something we'd sought or orchestrated. Still, I've come to realize that, in that brief moment, our shirts came to symbolize something larger: a sense of shared identity, however fleeting, during a time of deep division.

On a more personal note, I had sensed the depth of that division early on. A friend of ours from the US Attorney's Office, Paul Flynn, had become a superior court judge and was initially assigned the Simpson case. But after the public announcement, his appointment was quietly withdrawn because of concerns that his membership in the traditionally exclusive Los Angeles Country Club might not sit well with the broader community. In our view Paul would have been an excellent, impartial judge—one who likely would have run a tighter courtroom than the oft-criticized Judge Ito.

As the case unfolded, Paul shared a striking observation with us: Half of the African American judges he spoke with believed Simpson was innocent, not merely that he would be acquitted but that he was factually innocent. It was a sobering reminder of how the same set of facts can be viewed through entirely different lenses, shaped by lived experience, and a reflection of the deep, painful divides that continue to exist in our society.

Since the case marked such a pivotal moment in Los Angeles history, I want to offer a personal perspective—one shaped by my own experiences on both sides of the courtroom, first as a prosecutor and later as a defense attorney.

The city, still raw from the 1992 Rodney King Riots, was on edge.

Tensions simmered just beneath the surface. Against that backdrop, District Attorney Gil Garcetti's decision to move the trial from Santa Monica—a predominantly white, affluent enclave where it would normally have been held because the murders had occurred in neighboring Brentwood—to downtown Los Angeles was controversial. But in hindsight I believe it was the right call. The downtown jury pool was far more diverse, and the final panel was predominantly African American.

I shudder to think what might have happened if Simpson had been convicted by a mostly white West Los Angeles jury. The city was a powder keg. Garcetti may have wisely averted an explosion.

CHAPTER TWENTY-EIGHT

FROM THE MOMENT THE FIRST CUSTOMERS WALKED through the doors, alongside the immense relief Larry, Esther, and I felt, there was another emotion: pure gratitude. We knew how lucky we were, and we made a quiet commitment—once we had our feet under us, we'd find a way to give back.

Giving back soon became an integral part of CPK's culture. In every city where we opened, we partnered with local charities, volunteered, and donated food. We also used CPK for fundraising events benefiting schools, nonprofits, religious organizations, and civic causes. Grand openings were tied to local charities, and our employees were always willing to pitch in, strengthening both their comradery and our community ties.

Over the years Larry and I also coauthored three CPK cookbooks, with *all* proceeds going to charity. The first, *The California Pizza Kitchen Cookbook* (1996), featured twenty-five of our signature recipes (once kept secret). We wanted home cooks to be able to replicate our dishes as closely as possible. We weren't worried about competition. As Oscar Wilde once said, "Imitation is the sincerest form of flattery." Besides, all our ingredients were already listed on the menu.

Three years later our second book, *California Pizza Kitchen, Pasta, Salads, Soups, and Sides*, featured what we called our "Significant Others"—nonpizza dishes that had become customer favorites.

Our third cookbook, *California Pizza Kitchen Family Cookbook* (2008), was a tribute to the families who'd been at the heart of CPK since its inception.

In addition to donating cookbook proceeds, we partnered with dozens of nonprofit organizations. One of the most meaningful relationships was with the Starlight Foundation, which supports terminally ill children and their families. That effort was inspired by our friend and investor Jane Seymour, who was deeply committed to the cause. Over time our partnership with Starlight grew into something special, ultimately including over $1 million in donations and support.

By 2010 our CPKids Camps, developed in partnership with Starlight, had expanded to twenty-one cities across the United States, offering seriously ill children and their families a chance to enjoy recreational opportunities outside hospital settings. That same year CPK donated approximately $1.4 million to more than two thousand local community programs and children's charities nationwide.

We also supported organizations such as Elizabeth Glaser Pediatric AIDS Foundation, Make-A-Wish, the Juvenile Diabetes Foundation, the American Heart Association, and Childhelp. Esther played a leadership role in SHARE, a nonprofit founded by Hollywood wives to benefit children's charities. She's been a driving force in the group for more than three decades, serving as president, chairwoman, and director.

To further our philanthropic mission, we launched the CPK FOUNDATION—a nonprofit dedicated to supporting children's charities in the communities we served. A portion of its funding came directly from sales of our Original Barbecue Chicken Pizza. And given how popular that pizza was, it added up to a lot of support for a great cause.

While we were growing our charitable efforts, we were also building the CPK brand. From the start Larry and I had a strong aversion to traditional advertising. Right or wrong we believed our customers wouldn't respond to it—and, worse, it might send a subliminal message that we needed the business. CPK consistently spent less than 1 percent of its sales on marketing—an incredibly low number in the restaurant industry.

But that was entirely part of our philosophy: We didn't want *to* advertise; we wanted to *be* advertised. For us the best marketing was always word of mouth.

That said we did launch one marketing program that broke the mold and became one of our most successful and undeniably fun marketing campaigns in CPK history: the "Thank You Card" promotion.

Every dine-in or take-out customer received a sealed envelope, which could only be opened on a return visit in the presence of a manager. Inside was a prize: a 10 percent discount at minimum, but many held bigger discounts, vacations, cash prizes, and one grand prize of $100,000.

In one year alone, we distributed 2.7 million envelopes. The energy during the redemption period was electric. Customers at nearby tables watched intently as envelopes were opened, and when someone won a big prize, the entire restaurant erupted in cheers.

At its core it was a form of discounting, but it never *felt* like discounting. Instead, it carried the energy of a lottery while still being carefully structured to comply with legal requirements. Most of all, while the campaign generated excitement and drove repeat business, it did something even more valuable—it made our restaurants feel alive.

Beyond innovative promotions, we also secured some incredible brand exposure. CPK became the exclusive pizza provider at major California venues, including Dodger Stadium, Angel Stadium, and Staples Center.

Our relationship with the Dodgers was especially thrilling, thanks to our friend and former All-Star Steve Garvey. With his help we secured a spot on the centerfield scoreboard for a *CPK Strikeout Meter*. Each time a Dodger pitcher struck out a batter, a *K* was added to the meter, the lights dimmed, and a digital banner lit up the stadium: "California Pizza Kitchen Strikeout!"

Sitting next to Steve as fans lined up for autographs, watching the CPK banner light up the ballpark, it was the kind of surreal, pinch-me moment that reminded us just how far we'd come.

CHAPTER TWENTY-NINE

FROM THE MOMENT WE LAUNCHED THE CPK CONCEPT and successfully opened our first location in Beverly Hills, we knew our model would be copied. That's just the way the restaurant industry works. Indeed, we had borrowed inspiration ourselves—and our innovative pizzas, especially the blockbuster success of the Barbecue Chicken Pizza, attracted massive attention. When *Esquire* magazine named our small restaurant as one of the Outstanding Bars and Restaurants in America, a few months after we opened, we felt like the mouse that roared.

Knowing competition was inevitable, we made a strategic decision: Expand as widely and as quickly as we could. We were pioneering a new category with our unconventional toppings and wanted to lock down our position before the inevitable wave of imitators arrived.

We also knew our limitations. We didn't have the deep pockets or national ad budgets of the big chains. That part was unnerving. But we leaned into what we *did* have: a clear vision, a loyal following, and a name that said it all. Thanks to Larry's spot-on naming, we didn't just serve California-style pizza—we *owned* it.

That same mindset shaped our location strategy. We accepted that competitors would open nearby. But as long as we stayed true to our core constituencies—our employees, our customers, and the communities we served—we were confident we'd succeed.

When we opened our second restaurant in 1986 at the Beverly Center, mall dining was still dominated by fast food. By offering full-service casual dining in an upscale retail center, we helped pioneer a new category, paving the way for a new era of mall restaurants. It wasn't long before others followed.

The Cheesecake Factory, and later P. F. Chang's, catered to a similar crowd, but we never saw them as direct competitors. In fact we viewed them as synergistic. As CPK expanded nationally, they often followed our lead—opening in the same high-performing centers, sometimes just steps away. Over time we returned the favor—targeting their top-performing locations where CPK didn't yet have a presence.

After several years of success, Larry and I were invited to speak on a panel at a national restaurant convention. Sharing the stage with us was Robert Colombo, founder of Sfuzzi, a buzzy Dallas-based Italian chain, with a handful of units that had recently opened on New York's Upper West Side.

At one point the moderator asked Colombo about Italian competitors, specifically Olive Garden. Colombo, with a smug grin, dismissed it as little more than a gateway experience, saying that Olive Garden was fine for introducing people to Italian food, but once diners became more sophisticated, they'd naturally graduate to Sfuzzi.

From our seats we spotted Ron Magruder, the CEO of Olive Garden, sitting in the front row. He appeared visibly bemused by the comment. We stayed to watch his panel later that afternoon, curious to see how he might respond.

Sure enough, the moderator brought up Colombo's comment. Magruder's response was calm, thoughtful, and devastatingly funny.

"Perhaps it's different for dinner," he said, "but when it comes to lunch, we're all in competition, whether it's brown bagging, fast food, casual dining, or fine dining."

Then after a perfectly timed pause, he added, "But if the only purpose of Olive Garden is to educate Americans about Italian food, I can tell you—there's a lot of money in education!"

Naturally, the room erupted. It was one of the sharpest comebacks I've ever witnessed in the industry (or elsewhere).

One of our more interesting discussions about competition came shortly after PepsiCo purchased its stake in CPK. We were informed by

PepsiCo executives that some Pizza Hut franchisees were alarmed. They viewed CPK as a direct threat.

But from our perspective, CPK and Pizza Hut served entirely different audiences. Even if there was some overlap, the occasions weren't the same. A guest coming to CPK wasn't choosing between us and Pizza Hut any more than someone heading to Pizza Hut was weighing us as an option.

To ease concerns we suggested they check with the Pizza Hut franchisee at Kahala Mall, in Honolulu, where our CPK opened near a Pizza Hut that had been there for years. As we suspected, their review showed that CPK's presence hadn't affected Pizza Hut's sales at all.

The issue was never raised again.

But that conversation sparked a new idea. Pizza Hut International expressed interest in becoming a CPK franchisee in Europe. It sounded exciting—our first European restaurants.

Larry and I flew to the south of France, where the Pizza Hut team walked us through two proposed sites: one near the Flower Market in Nice and another next to the Casino in Cannes. On paper it was a dream.

Then came the due diligence. The European service model bore little resemblance to the hands-on, intensive training that defined our success. Strict labor laws added another concern. The deeper we dug, the less appealing the opportunity became.

Finally, weighing the risks and potential headaches, I turned to Larry and said, "This is one of our favorite places to visit. Why ruin a good vacation?"

By far the most memorable insight we ever received about competition came from Steve Wynn, the visionary behind Wynn Resorts. While socializing one day, we mentioned that given our success, we fully expected competitors to start copying our concept.

Steve looked amused. He said, "Guys, let me tell you a story. At the Golden Nugget, I had Waylon Jennings performing in my main showroom. At the same time, I had a performer named Wendel Adkins playing in the lounge. Wendel was a complete knockoff of Waylon. Whatever clothes Waylon wore on his last album cover, Wendel wore. Whatever songs Waylon sang on his last album, Wendel sang.

"One day I was walking through the casino and saw Wendel, I said, 'Wendel, I'm having lunch with Waylon. Want to come?' He was stunned and said, 'Really, Mr. Wynn? He's my hero. I've never met him, and I'd love to come!'

"So we sat down to lunch, and Waylon turned to him and said, 'You know, Wendel, I've seen your show, and you're really good.' Wendel, beaming, said, 'Really, Mr. Jennings? Thank you!' To which Waylon replied, 'There's only one problem, Wendel. You're always a song behind!'"

Steve's point was both reassuring and unforgettable. No matter how much someone tried to replicate us, as long as we kept moving forward, the imitators would always be one step behind.

We never forgot Steve's words of wisdom.

Perhaps the most bizarre knockoff experience we ever encountered came out of Vancouver, Canada. A real estate developer approached us with a prime property on Robson Street, Vancouver's most famous shopping district, and asked if we'd be interested in opening a CPK there. After we declined, he inquired about becoming a franchisee. But we only did limited franchising and only with groups that had real restaurant operating experience. He didn't qualify.

A few months later, we got a call from a Canadian friend who told us a new restaurant had opened on Robson Street under the name *California Pizza Kitchen*. I couldn't resist. I jumped on a plane. There it was. Same name, same decor, same branding, even the same menu. The developer had copied us down to the last detail. (We never tried the food, thankfully.)

We were stunned. Fortunately, we had legal protection in Canada for both our trademark and trade dress, and this was a blatant violation. Our attorney fired off a cease and desist letter, and the developer backed down quickly. Apparently, the entire stunt had been a costly attempt to entice us into opening there.

It didn't work.

We had zero interest in dealing with a knockoff artist. Desperate to keep the place open, he even launched a "Name This Restaurant" contest for the public, but it was no use. The knockoff was doomed from the start.

The restaurant shuttered not long after. Deservedly so. Turns out, you can fake the name, the menu, and the décor, but you can't fake karma.

Admittedly, Larry and I were naturally competitive. Let's face it—you don't choose a career as a federal prosecutor or a criminal defense attorney if you shy away from competition. That part of us hadn't entirely disappeared, even if those courtroom days were behind us. And truthfully, you don't set out to build a national restaurant chain without a healthy dose of competitive fire.

We thrived under pressure. Most of the time, we'd learned to let things roll off our backs, but every now and then, something would get under our skin. Not often but just enough to remind us that the spark was still there. And occasionally, our competitive dander would flare.

One such moment came at a national restaurant conference, during a panel discussion on restaurant design. Barbara Lazaroff, Wolfgang Puck's then-wife and business partner, was speaking about the new Wolfgang Puck Cafes they were developing. In front of the audience, she said they were "coming after California Pizza Kitchen," pointedly adding that they wouldn't have a "bumblebee design."

I'll admit, when we heard about it, that remark caught us off guard. Up to that point, our relationship with both Wolfgang and Barbara had been nothing but warm. In fact we'd always been grateful to Wolfgang for the early inspiration for our own leap into the restaurant world, though we've never been entirely sure he appreciated the gesture.

Still, I remember a flash of irritation. But discretion, as they say, is the better part of valor. I didn't respond. Instead, I made a quiet vow to myself: Let our success do the talking. No need for a comeback—let the scoreboard speak. And over time it did, louder than any words ever could.

In truth that moment was nothing more than an uncharacteristic blip. If anything, our experience in the restaurant world has been quite the opposite. We've found that most successful people in the industry—Wolfgang very much included—are incredibly generous with their time and open to sharing their knowledge. There's an unspoken understanding of just how tough the business is, and that tends to foster camaraderie more than competition.

We've had the honor of participating on many industry panels, and one of our favorite panels was at the Harvard Business School, where Larry managed to get a big laugh with his quip: "The only way I ever thought I'd make it to Harvard was in a bottle."

It was a good laugh—but also a proud moment. We were grateful to be there, not as students or professors but as entrepreneurs sharing the lessons of a journey we never could have scripted.

Another proud and humbling moment came when we were honored with the Golden Chain Award. Presented by *Nation's Restaurant News*, it's considered one of the industry's highest recognitions meant to celebrate leadership, innovation, and lasting impact in the world of food service. To be included among such respected peers was deeply meaningful and something we never took for granted.

For us these moments were never about personal glory. They were affirmations that Larry's and my vision that I'd first typed in my Beverly Hills office had grown into something bigger—something that touched millions of guests, created careers for thousands of employees, and left a mark on an industry we loved.

Rick Rosenfield, Esther Rosenfield, and Larry Flax in front of the original CPK in Beverly Hills.

Rick Rosenfield and Larry Flax in an early CPK restaurant.

Rick Rosenfield, Esther Rosenfield, and Larry Flax.
Esther's jacket is bright CPK yellow!

The original CPK in Beverly Hills, California.

CPK Lenox Square in Atlanta, Georgia (circa 1987).

CPK at The Mirage in Las Vegas, Nevada (circa 1989).

John Kaufman, an early standout who rose through the ranks to become CPK's first senior vice president of operations at age twenty-five; Gary Beauregard, who stabilized our kitchens after the original chef's early departure and became CPK's first culinary director. From that point forward, we never again used the title "chef."

CPKI going public! Larry Flax, CEO Fred Hipp, and Rick Rosenfield.

The Mirage in Las Vegas, Nevada.

Sarah Goldsmith Grover, CPK's first public relations hire, who later became chief communications officer and senior vice president of marketing and public relations; John Kaufman; Julie Carruthers, the original ROCKstar whose spirit helped define CPK's culture.

John Kaufman, CPK's first senior vice president of operations; Julie Carruthers, CPK's first employee and later vice president of human resources; Larry Flax.

CPK at 60th and 3rd in New York City.

An early CPK. Note the yellow ceiling and flowers, along with the white-pants uniforms.

President Bill Clinton at CPK Kahala Mall, Honolulu, Hawaii.

Rick Rosenfield, Merv Griffin, and Larry Flax at CPK's opening at Merv's Resorts Casino Hotel.

Freestanding CPK in Marina del Rey, California—the highest sales CPK in the mainland US.

Greg Trojan, who became CPK president during the PepsiCo period; Chris Ames, a vice president; and Larry Flax.

CPK in Beverly Hills. Third row, top left: Tim Gleeson, an early host who became vice president of business development. First row, third from the left: Rudy Sugueti, a then pizza cook who became senior vice president, global development and operations/executive director.

Rick Rosenfield and Larry Flax in rare business attire.

Larry Flax, Joni Flax, Rick Rosenfield, and Esther Rosenfield.

President Ronald Reagan and First Lady Nancy Reagan with the CPK team at President Reagan's office in Los Angeles's Century City.

CHAPTER THIRTY

WHILE NEITHER LARRY NOR I HAD EVER MET McDonald's founder, Ray Kroc, when we started our journey, we looked to his words for guidance. In his memoir Kroc admitted he couldn't control every detail of operations and instead chose to empower partners who could grow alongside him. McDonald's valued its vendors—most famously, Simplot, the Idaho potato company behind its french fries.

For us our first and longest vendor relationship was with Gayle Gannes, a young woman with a barbecue sauce based on her father's recipe. While we sampled sauces for our Original Barbecue Chicken Pizza, "Gayle's Sweet 'N' Sassy" was the clear winner. As they say, the rest is history! We could have replicated the recipe ourselves, but loyalty mattered. Gayle had helped us make history, and we stuck with her. We've remained friends with Gayle and her husband, Jeffrey Rosenthal, for decades.

Another enduring partnership began in 1987, in Atlanta, the site of Lenox Square, when we discovered Kenny's Great Pies. His key lime pie became a menu staple, and from what started in his one-room apartment, Kenny's business thrived and now operates out of a thirty-three-thousand-square-foot facility in Smyrna, Georgia.

Years later, in West Palm Beach, Esther and I sampled desserts from Judy Leibovit's Sweet Endings, one of CPK's most treasured vendors since 1998, and when we visited, she tearfully told us she started her business with $200 and "CPK made my life." Now she's building a sixty-thousand-square-foot facility.

Truthfully, it worked both ways. Our vendors shaped us as much as we shaped them. We also realized early on that design and construction coordination required real expertise. We turned to Aria Group, based in Oak Park, Illinois, whose work with Richard Melman's Lettuce Entertain You Group had impressed us. They took the design burden off our plate and gave CPK a professional polish.

After our early successes, we were approached by Bob Blessing, CEO of Vie de France, a national bakery-café based in the DC area. Bob proposed a partnership to expand CPK on the East Coast. He came with a prime location already secured at Tysons Corner Center in Virginia and introduced us to Jean-Louis Vilgrain, owner of Grands Moulins de Paris, Vie de France's parent company. Vilgrain invited us to Paris, where, over long dinners and great bread, he spoke enthusiastically about taking California-style pizza to France.

But the romance cooled quickly. The Tysons Corner restaurant didn't hit his first-year sales expectations. We weren't worried—it was simply ramping up—but Vilgrain wasn't convinced. Despite Bob's faith in CPK, the parent company decided to unwind the partnership. We agreed to reimburse their investment and parted amicably.

Sure enough, sales at Tysons Corner surged in year two, and within twelve months we had repaid their investment in full. Bob, ever gracious, later told us he regretted the decision—but the call hadn't been his to make.

As for Tysons Corner, it went on to become one of our consistent top performers and remains so today—an early flagship that planted the CPK flag on the East Coast and helped showcase the brand nationally.

From the start Larry and I were committed to developing exclusively company-owned restaurants. We were passionate about controlling quality and had no interest in letting others dilute it. People were often surprised to learn that CPK owned and operated more than two hundred restaurants across the United States, none of them franchised.

Our reasoning was simple: control. As lawyers, we wanted no part of the legal headaches that could come from franchisees who failed to uphold our standards.

We were, however, open to international franchising—but only under very specific conditions. The partner had to bring serious multiunit restaurant experience, and just as important, the chemistry had to feel right.

We never went out looking; we mostly just reacted to the steady stream of inbound calls. Entrepreneurs regularly asked, "How do I buy a franchise?" Sometimes it was for themselves; sometimes it was for their kids or as part of an investment group. Our answer was always the same: no.

Domestic franchising just wasn't part of the plan.

Naturally, we made an exception for Steve Wynn when he approached us about the Mirage—and later at the Golden Nugget. That deal paid off in spades (excuse the pun). The visibility and credibility it gave the brand was unmatched.

We also awarded a franchise to our friend Merv Griffin for his Resorts Casino Hotel in Atlantic City, adding another colorful and memorable chapter to our expansion and a reminder that while our principles guided us, we weren't afraid to bend the rules when the right opportunity came along.

The third exception—and ultimately the most consequential—was made for a young real estate developer who would go on to have a profound impact on CPK's future: Rick Caruso.

It was 1996. PepsiCo had slammed the brakes on our growth, refusing to allocate any new capital for expansion. At the same time, Rick—then just thirty-seven—was developing his first major project: the Promenade, one of the earliest examples of an outdoor "lifestyle center," in Westlake Village, a western suburb of Los Angeles.

Larry and I were eager to test a new fast-casual concept we called "CPK ASAP." Rick wanted it in his center. But PepsiCo wouldn't budge.

That was when Rick floated an idea: "What if I put up the money—and you guys run it?"

Just like that, Rick became our newest franchisee. None of us knew it then, but that single decision would later shape not just CPK's future but Larry's and my own roles within it.

Rick didn't yet have a restaurant team in place—though he'd go on to develop some highly successful dining concepts of his own. Instead, he reached out to my son, Ian, who had built solid hands-on experience with CPK, and brought him in as a consultant. For me it was a proud and personal moment—a meaningful connection between family and the business Larry and I had built from scratch.

Rick, of course, went on to become one of the most successful developers of lifestyle retail centers in the country. He also became a dear friend and eventually a member of the CPK board.

Years later, after his run for mayor of Los Angeles fell short, Rick continued to demonstrate his deep commitment to the city—using his resources, relationships, and relentless energy to help rebuild after the devastating wildfires.

Larry and I always tried to stay out of politics, but in Rick's case, I'll make a personal exception.

If he ever chooses to seek public office again, the city of Los Angeles—or the state of California—would be lucky to have him. Fingers crossed.

But another type of franchising soon crossed our radar. When Host Marriott Services (later renamed HMSHost) approached us about licensing CPK for their airport locations, our first reaction was hesitation. Airport dining is a different animal—bidding wars for locations, union labor requirements, and a customer experience far outside our full-service model. It wasn't a business we wanted to enter on our own, if at all.

We weighed the pros (early exposure for the CPK brand in some of the biggest travel hubs of the country) against the cons (giving up a measure of control and risking damage to the brand). In the end we trusted that many of our guests were frequent travelers, and they would welcome seeing CPK in airports, even if in a different format.

After extensive meetings with HMSHost executives—and reassured by their commitment to uphold our standards—we agreed. It turned out to be a terrific decision. They honored that commitment, and it's been an important partnership through the years.

By the time CPK went public, HMSHost operated twenty CPK ASAP restaurants in airports nationwide, providing exposure we never could have achieved alone. They proved that our brand could travel just as well as our guests.

But in an interesting twist, our relationship with HMSHost set the stage for a revelation that would prove monumental for CPK and, on a much broader scale, sparked a revolution that reshaped the pizza oven industry itself.

It began with something as mundane as building permits. Airport projects often raised concerns because building and fire departments were unfamiliar with wood-fired ovens. Bureaucrats often responded with a knee-jerk no when faced with something new.

By then CPK had installed nearly one hundred wood-burning pizza ovens around the world. After initially importing a few from Italy, we had turned to Wood Stone, a small, family-owned business in Bellingham, Washington, to build our ovens. Thanks to CPK's visibility and the prominent Wood Stone nameplate on our ovens, nearly everyone in America looking for a wood-fired oven bought from them. The exposure helped propel Wood Stone to become the largest manufacturer of wood-burning pizza ovens in the world. So when HMSHost encountered difficulties, we turned to Wood Stone for help. I remember the call when we asked if they could construct a gas oven that looked like a wood-burning oven. They were up for the challenge and amazingly pulled it off in short order.

HMSHost installed the prototype. From an operations standpoint, it was a revelation. The oven burned cleaner, was easier to maintain, and eliminated the logistical headache of storing wood. Even better, it simplified training for pizza cooks and the cooking process itself.

One of the biggest challenges of wood-burning ovens was the constant rotation required to avoid scorching pizzas near the fire.

The new gas oven, with its radiant floor with heating elements below the surface and controllable preset temperatures, solved all that with the push of a button.

The critical question, of course, was flavor. For years Larry and I had preached about the superior taste imparted by wood smoke. We believed it ourselves. We were sipping our own Kool-Aid!

To test it we flew with Brian Sullivan, CPK's head of culinary development, to Wood Stone's headquarters. We set up multiple blind taste tests, convinced the difference would be obvious. To our shock no one could tell. Each guess was a coin toss. The myth of wood smoke evaporated before our eyes.

But other hurdles remained: first, the "romance" of the wood hearth. More concerning, however, was that the California Pizza Kitchen logo had featured the term "wood-fired" since day one. It felt inseparable from the brand. Changing seemed risky.

As we pondered the decision, we were planning to remodel our restaurant in Boston's Prudential Center, a high-profile location that was one of our busiest restaurants. The two ovens there were worn out. With no small amount of trepidation, we installed the new gas model. We braced for complaints and committed privately: If customers noticed, we'd eat the cost and switch back.

No one noticed. Not a single comment.

That was all the proof we needed. Quietly, we removed "wood-fired" from our logo and never looked back. Over time every old oven was replaced with the new gas model. Not once did a guest raise the issue.

What started as a solution to a permitting problem became a watershed moment in American pizza-making history. CPK's shift catalyzed an industry-wide change. Wood Stone, once the king of wood ovens, became the leader in gas-fired ovens, too, driving a massive decline in the sale of wood-burning ovens across the country. Today, at every major pizza trade show, gas-fired ovens dominate the floor.

And Wood Stone never forgot. Keith Carpenter Sr., the company's founder, often credited CPK as the catalyst for their success. When he retired to Palm Desert, California, he became a regular at the local CPK. Upon his passing, one of his last wishes was to scatter some of his ashes in the plants outside the local CPK—a profound tribute to a partnership that helped change an industry.

CHAPTER THIRTY-ONE

IN THE MID-'90S, AFTER WOLFGANG PUCK'S LINE OF frozen pizzas debuted in supermarkets, Larry and I were asked by a trade journalist whether CPK planned to throw its hat in the frozen-pizza ring. While the idea had crossed our minds, we hadn't given it a lot of thought. Frankly, it was beyond our expertise, and we had more pressing projects on our plate.

Having sampled Puck's frozen pizzas, we felt the quality didn't meet his usual standards—probably the result of outsourcing production. To us it looked less like an extension of his brand than a dilution of it.

Nevertheless, we'd learned never to say never. So instead of dismissing the idea, we told the reporter it was something we were considering.

A couple of weeks later, we received a letter from Mary Kay Haben, the president of Kraft Foods' Pizza Division, inviting us to collaborate on a line of CPK frozen pizzas. At the time Kraft was the heavyweight of the category with its Jack's and Tombstone brands dominating freezer aisles.

Flattered by their interest, we agreed to visit their offices in Northbrook, Illinois.

From the start we were impressed by their professionalism and technical expertise. But we made one thing crystal clear: We wouldn't even entertain a deal until we had a product we could stand behind. This wasn't just about licensing a name—it was about protecting something we had built from scratch.

That kicked off months of research and development. Larry and I flew back and forth, rolling up our sleeves in their test kitchens, tasting iteration after iteration, and fine-tuning the recipes until we felt they captured the essence of CPK. We weren't trying to replicate our restaurant pizzas exactly—that was impossible. What mattered was that they lived up to standards that our customers would expect in the frozen case. Eventually, we got there.

By the time we were ready to discuss deal terms, Kraft had launched its DiGiorno line. They couldn't stop talking about its early success, proudly telling us that it had achieved $60 million in sales its first year and projected it to get to $100 million annually.

Being enthusiastic believers in the power of the CPK brand and, admittedly, with a healthy dose of ego, we shot back, "What's DiGiorno? It's a brand that you created from thin air. CPK is known nationally for its restaurants. If DiGiorno can do $100 million, so can we."

The Kraft executives humored us but remained skeptical. Nonetheless, we said that we were willing to bet on it and negotiated a tiered royalty schedule: lower percentages at the start, with rates increasing as sales climbed. If sales didn't materialize, we'd settle for a small royalty, but if CPK frozen pizzas soared, we wanted to share in the upside.

Just when everything seemed set, a curveball arrived. Kraft's lawyers warned that FDA regulations might prohibit us from labeling several of our signature pizzas—including our iconic Barbecue Chicken Pizza—as "pizza."

The issue? According to the FDA, a product couldn't be called pizza unless it contained tomatoes.

Larry and I were outraged. Of all the challenges we'd expected, the US government trying to tell us our bestselling pizza wasn't a pizza wasn't one of them. It felt like déjà vu—the same old "purist" critique we'd heard since the day we opened: If it doesn't have red sauce, it can't be pizza.

For those who cling to the misperception that pizza requires tomatoes, let me pause for a quick history lesson.

The origins of pizza trace back thousands of years. As far back as 700 BC, Etruscans and Greeks were baking flatbreads topped with oils, olives, garlic, and onions—none of which involved tomatoes. In ancient Rome, peasants milled farro into flour and used it to make discs of bread that served as edible plates for stews and sauces. By the Middle Ages, "pizza" was already a recognized term for certain baked breads in Naples, still without a tomato in sight.

Tomatoes didn't even reach Italy until the 1500s, after explorers returned from the New World. At first many Italians believed the tomato was poisonous. It wasn't until the late eighteenth century that it began appearing on pizzas, and even then it was just one of many possible toppings. In fact, when Queen Margherita of Savoy visited Naples in 1889, chef Raffaele Esposito created his now-famous tricolor pizza—tomatoes, mozzarella, basil—more as a patriotic gesture than a culinary rule.

By 1984, when Larry and I began researching California-style pizza, we concluded our version was more in line with authentic Italian traditions—individual-size, wood-fired, inventive toppings—than with its oversize American cousins. In fact some of the old Italian cookbooks we studied were far more adventurous than anything we dreamed up: clams and mussels (with shells!), octopus, snails, even tripe. Again, no tomatoes required.

The lesson was clear: Pizza had existed for centuries before tomatoes entered the picture. Which made the FDA's position—that our Barbecue Chicken Pizza wasn't "pizza" because it lacked tomatoes—not just wrong but laughably ahistorical.

For us the important point from the start was that pizza had originally been created without using tomatoes, thus paving the way for us to introduce a variety of new flavors centuries after its original inception. Pizza purists be damned.

Armed with that history, Larry and I were eager—almost giddy—at the idea of taking on the FDA. It had all the makings of a great fight—and even better PR. Kraft, however, didn't share our enthusiasm. They pointed out that Wolfgang Puck had sidestepped the issue by quietly adding a token amount of tomato to his frozen pizzas. That might have satisfied the bureaucrats, but it didn't satisfy us.

In the end Kraft devised a clever workaround. Instead of labeling the boxes "pizza," they let the brand name do the work. "California Pizza Kitchen," splashed across bright-yellow packaging, told customers everything they needed to know. Problem solved.

Frankly, Larry and I still would have preferred suing the FDA. But this time it wasn't our call.

The entry of CPK into the frozen pizza business was a genuine game changer for us and for the industry. Beyond generating a significant revenue stream, it created unprecedented brand exposure. Within a few short years, CPK frozen pizzas became available in twenty thousand retail locations nationwide. Our confidence in CPK and the tiered royalty structure had proven to be a smart bet. From 2004 to 2009, royalty payments grew significantly from $1.2 million to $7.7 million annually. Best of all, CPK didn't have to invest a dime of capital.

Just as in our restaurants, the frozen CPK pizzas struck a balance between innovation and tradition. The popularity of CPK's products reshaped the market landscape, shifting consumer preferences toward premium ingredients and innovative toppings. Industry insiders even coined a term for it: "the CPK effect." It was proof of the old adage "Imitation is the greatest form of flattery."

The success didn't go unnoticed. Following Nestlé's acquisition of Kraft's pizza business in 2010 for $3.7 billion, the chairman of Nestlé USA singled out CPK as the "super-premium" brand within the portfolio and as one of the key value drivers in Nestlé's $3.7 billion behind the deal.

By 2011 DiGiorno had become the dominant frozen pizza brand, capturing 20 percent of the market and topping $1 billion in annual sales. CPK held a 5 percent share nationally, but in California, where our brand awareness was strongest, CPK's share exceeded 15 percent. By comparison Amy's hovered around 1 percent, and Wolfgang Puck's frozen line barely registered at two tenths of 1 percent.

By this point CPK *owned yellow* in the frozen aisle, exactly as we had always envisioned. Our competitive instincts were satisfied. It was proof that the best response doesn't come in words; it comes in results.

Perhaps the most fun, though, was on the personal side. Our photos and the CPK story were splashed on the back of every box, which led to one of the most unexpectedly rewarding moments of the journey. While shopping at a local supermarket, a little girl recognized me and came running up to me with CPK box, asking for my autograph. Naturally, I happily signed it and bought the pizza for her. It was wildly flattering and utterly surreal.

Still, looking back, I don't think we ever fully imagined that frozen CPK pizzas would one day outsell the ones in our restaurants or that, for millions of people, their only taste of California Pizza Kitchen would come not from a table in one of our restaurants but from their freezer.

It was a strange, almost bittersweet realization. But even now, when I walk down a supermarket aisle and see those bright-yellow boxes, I smile. We poured our hearts into making sure that pizza reflected our brand. And happily, it still does.

CHAPTER THIRTY-TWO

WHEN LARRY AND I WROTE OUR INITIAL BUSINESS plan (the one we'd used to convince our bank to give us the loan to launch our first CPK), we boldly declared that California Pizza Kitchen would become an international brand. It was a gutsy prediction but, as it turned out, a prescient one.

Given our early success, it wasn't long before potential international franchisees came calling. While we were adamant that domestic CPKs remain company owned, with only rare exceptions, we were open to the idea of international franchising.

The exposure was enticing, but we weighed the risks, always aware of one of our guiding principles: "Do no harm." Ultimately, we decided that by selecting the right international partners, we could minimize the risk, maintain the integrity of CPK's reputation, and grow abroad without diluting the brand.

Our first international partnership was the Rodriguez family in the Philippines. We were particularly impressed by Archie Rodriguez, who was already operating upscale restaurants in Manila. The first CPK outside the United States, in Makati, launched a thriving franchise system that expanded to seven CPK locations across the Philippines.

Not long after, we partnered with Lucy Prananto, a savvy businesswoman from Malaysia. Her first CPK on Singapore's famed Orchard Road and the ribbon-cutting ceremony featured our first Lion Dance, a tradition meant to bring good luck. Standing there, swelling with pride, it certainly seemed like good fortune was on our side. Lucy went on to open CPK locations in Malaysia's iconic Petronas Towers and four more in Hong Kong.

My first trip to Hong Kong was unforgettable. From my Kowloon Hotel room, I gazed across Victoria Harbour at the forest of skyscrapers, their facades lit up in a dazzling laser show that made New York City feel modest. It was humbling to learn that Hong Kong had more skyscrapers than any city in the world.

Just as the ancients once believed the universe revolved around the earth, many egocentric Americans still believe the world revolves around the United States. It doesn't. Later trips to Dubai, Shanghai, and Tokyo only reinforced the point. I don't mean to sound unpatriotic because I'm not. But the energy was undeniable—each city felt like a glimpse of the future unfolding at a pace that left me awestruck.

Tokyo proved to be an early lesson on what not to do. We were first courted by the owners of one of Japan's largest supermarket chains. Flattered and curious to see Japan for the first time, we flew to Tokyo.

But the cultural divide was immediate and, in the suffocating summer heat, literal. After a long, unproductive day of meetings, Larry and I decided we couldn't stomach another in full suits—something we'd gladly abandoned after leaving our law practice. The next day we showed up in golf shirts. Not as a statement—just because we were too damn hot.

The deal was going nowhere, and after another round of fruitless meetings, we told them so. The next morning, as we were packing to leave, I got a call from the founder's son, pleading to see us at the airport. When he and his father arrived, they were both wearing golf shirts. It was a nice gesture, but our minds were made up. We passed.

Years later fortune brought us the right partners in Japan: Ken and Yoji Shimizu of WDI Group. Yoji had introduced Hard Rock Cafe to Tokyo in 1980 and built successful Tony Roma's franchises. Wolfgang Puck once said of them, "They gave me no choice but to open Spago in Tokyo. I said no, and they said, 'Then we'll open it without you.'"

But we were charmed. It didn't hurt that Yoji invited us to play golf at Kasumigaseki Country Club, one of the most beautiful courses in the world. During negotiations they hosted us for dinner at their fine-dining seafood restaurant in Ginza. The setting was stunning, fully staffed with tuxedoed waiters, but eerily empty—on a Saturday night.

It was a cultural chasm. In Japan they would rather lose money than lose face by closing the doors on loyal employees. In the United States, we would have made the painful call to shut it down. But their loyalty to their team told us everything we needed to know about how they'd treat us as partners.

And they proved us right. Our bet on WDI was one of the best we made. Similar to our experience in Japan, our entry into the Middle East became another lesson in the value of well-placed trust. The opportunity came through Sami Daud, a member of a prominent Omani family and the owner of Gourmet Gulf, a Dubai-based restaurant company.

The Middle East wasn't exactly on our radar at the time, but once again we trusted our instincts—and more importantly, we trusted Sami.

Larry and I, joined by his stepson, Peter Gillette, who oversaw our franchising, made several trips to the region to explore opportunities. We traveled through Dubai, the Emirates, Bahrain, Saudi Arabia, and Qatar, surveying potential locations.

At first I found the Middle East surprisingly comfortable compared with Japan and China. While I loved those Asian markets, venturing off the beaten path there was always a challenge—street signs written in characters I couldn't read, English rarely spoken, and our solution was to always hire a guide to keep us from getting lost. The Middle East, with its deep British influence, was different. Street signs were written in both Arabic and English, and spoken English was commonplace. For an American business traveler, that made the experience far less daunting.

Still, two experiences during those trips stand out as profoundly uncomfortable.

The first came during a short visit to Saudi Arabia. Esther and Joni had joined us on the trip, and while we were in Bahrain, we arranged to meet a potential franchisee: a young Saudi sheikh. The meeting was set at a mall just across the King Fahd Causeway, which connects Bahrain and Saudi Arabia.

Before crossing, we were bluntly advised: Our wives should not accompany us. At the time it was difficult—sometimes impossible—for American women to obtain visas to enter Saudi Arabia. Even for us there was a chance we might be turned away at the border.

Then came the second warning, one that cut even deeper. We were told that if our passports bore any evidence of travel to Israel, we would be denied entry outright.

For Larry and me, both Jewish, that hit hard. Larry had never visited Israel, but I had, back in 1983, when my son, Ian, celebrated his bar mitzvah at the Western Wall. Thankfully, that trip wasn't on my current passport. Even so, the idea that our heritage could bar us from entering a country left me cold.

Though we liked the sheikh when we met him, the experience unsettled us deeply. Between the treatment of women and the prohibition tied to Israel, we couldn't see a path forward. We chose not to pursue Saudi Arabia any further.

Many years later, long after we had sold CPK, Gourmet Gulf eventually opened a CPK in Riyadh. It's still there today. But at the time our values and instincts told us it wasn't the right place for us.

During one of our trips, we also met with a potential franchisee in Qatar and toured one of the restaurants they operated. At first glance the operation looked polished enough, but as the discussions unfolded, something felt off.

Most of the employees were from the Philippines, and as we asked questions, we learned troubling details. These workers were contractually bound to their employer, required to surrender their passports, and prohibited from seeking other jobs. That was alarming enough. But when we asked to see the dormitories where they were housed, the true picture came into focus.

The conditions were appalling—cramped, unsanitary, and dehumanizing. It wasn't just uncomfortable; it was unacceptable.

We knew cultural norms vary, and we always tried to approach new markets with respect. But this wasn't a matter of custom. This was about basic human dignity. There was no way we could attach the CPK name to a business that treated its people like this.

We cut the visit short and left Qatar with one clear conclusion: Sometimes the fastest decision you make in business is also the right one.

Our feeling about Gourmet Gulf and Dubai couldn't have been more different. From the start we liked and trusted Sami Daud, and we genuinely enjoyed visiting Dubai—a city that was as vibrant and cosmopolitan as anywhere we'd been.

Under Sami's leadership, Gourmet Gulf opened three CPK locations in Dubai, beginning with one in the Dubai Mall. As the largest mall in the world—with more than twelve hundred retail stores—it sat in the shadow of the Burj Khalifa, the tallest building in the world. What a sight: our yellow-and-black California Pizza Kitchen logo gleaming beside the most ambitious architecture on the planet.

The second location was just as surreal: the Mall of the Emirates, home to Ski Dubai, the indoor ski resort in the middle of the desert. Our CPK was positioned right next to the slope itself. Watching customers walk in from 110-degree heat, then out past an alpine ski hill, was an only-in-Dubai experience—and seeing our name there was almost too much to take in.

I felt something beyond pride. It was a surge of pure, palpable excitement. Back in the early days, we'd talked about building a global brand, but at the time it was hubris—just bravado on a business plan. Now, standing there with Larry, it was real.

I couldn't help but turn to Larry and express my appreciation for him coming up with the name. We always agreed that it would travel, but this was the moment that proved it. The name didn't just travel. It had wings.

Our entry into the Mexican market followed a familiar pattern: A group that shared our passion for the CPK brand approached us, and we granted them the franchise rights. To our absolute delight, when we visited their first restaurant in Mexico, we were greeted by a cheering staff chanting, "Roca! Roca!" (Spanish for ROCK). It was a fantastic start—lively, heartfelt, and filled with the kind of energy we always hoped CPK would inspire.

Later, with our approval, the group sold their interest to Alsea SAB de CV, a public company that had become the dominant restaurant operator in Latin America. Their portfolio read like a who's who of American dining: Domino's, Starbucks, and Chili's, among others. For the joint opening of CPK and P. F. Chang's in a small, upscale retail center in Mexico City,

Larry and I traveled down with our wives. Opening night was celebratory, with shared toasts and a sense of pride, along with Rick Federico, the CEO of P. F. Chang's, as we raised a glass to the launch of both brands in Mexico. The experience reinforced something we'd long believed: CPK and P. F. Chang's were not rivals but complementary-synergistic brands that could thrive side by side.

But Mexico also gave us a sobering reminder of the challenges of doing business abroad. The not-so-fun part was the security. Everywhere we traveled, we were shadowed by armed bodyguards. When our wives went shopping with the mother of one of Alsea's owners on Avenida Presidente Masaryk—Mexico City's equivalent of Rodeo Drive—they moved from stop to stop by car rather than walk the streets. It was unsettling, and it cast a shadow over what should have been an entirely joyful trip. Such a beautiful city, yet such a shame that such precautions were necessary.

Never ones to shrink from a challenge, we jumped headfirst when approached to open restaurants in mainland China. Up to that point, every international CPK had been franchised, but this proposal was different—and intriguing. The site was in the Mansions area of the French Concession in Shanghai, a historic district once called the Paris of the East.

We had our doubts about navigating Chinese bureaucracy but quickly learned that the government favored direct investment over franchising. Beyond some additional legal fees, the process was surprisingly straightforward. The sheer potential of Shanghai—its energy, its scale—was irresistible.

We went on to open a second location in a major mall near the convention center and airport. Both projects were exciting but ultimately sobering. As we had suspected from the start, international expansion worked best through local partners—people with the infrastructure, cultural fluency, and resources to thrive where we could not.

CHAPTER THIRTY-THREE

LOOKING BACK, THE PEPSICO YEARS WERE A ROLLER coaster—full of growth, exposure, and plenty of lessons. We'd expanded from twenty-five to sixty-seven company-owned restaurants and gained a national footprint. By the time we reached the end of that chapter, with new ownership under Bruckmann, Rosser, Sherrill & Co. (BRS), Larry and I felt a renewed sense of hope and a clean slate ahead.

We didn't work directly with Indra during the final sale, but our relationship with her had always been strong and cordial. We were genuinely honored when she came to the opening of our Park Avenue restaurant in Manhattan—a full-circle moment that meant a lot to us.

And for the record—sorry, Coke lovers—we stayed loyal to Pepsi in our restaurants. After everything, it felt like the least we could do.

But the next chapter was uncharted territory. For the first time in CPK's history, Larry and I no longer controlled our own destiny. We were now in the hands of private equity. BRS, our new owner, had the right to appoint a CEO while keeping us on as cochairmen.

At first things looked promising. They brought in Fred Hipp, the former CEO of Houlihan's, who quickly built rapport with our senior team. Larry and I wanted him to succeed and threw our full support behind him. To his credit Hipp saw value in keeping us as the public face of the brand, even ensuring our story and photos stayed on menus and pizza boxes.

Still, BRS made it clear: They were the professionals in charge, and they wanted us out of day-to-day operations. We'd seen this movie before under PepsiCo, and as Yogi Berra might've said, it was déjà vu all over again—only this time with one critical difference: We had no control at all.

But BRS wasn't there to see the dynamics day-to-day. Working with Hipp and the senior team, we set about restoring what had eroded under PepsiCo—quality food, generous portions, and a culture rooted in respect for our employees. Those changes paid off. Sales climbed steadily, margins strengthened, and customer loyalty returned.

Private equity's goal was always the same: Polish the company for a profitable exit. In this case that meant an IPO. By 2000, with stronger sales and a revitalized menu that introduced seventeen new items, we were ready.

The run-up to the public offering, however, underscored our uneasy relationship with BRS. We were excluded from the investor "roadshows," told by a board member not to speak to analysts, and essentially sidelined from the very process we had helped create. Still, Hipp and the new CFO, H. G. "Carey" Carrington, conducted an effective campaign, and the IPO was a success.

On August 4, 2000, California Pizza Kitchen went public. The stock debuted at $15 a share, jumped 35 percent on its first day, and within weeks had climbed above $24. Larry, Hipp, and I rang the opening bell at Nasdaq, our logo flashing across Times Square. For all the behind-the-scenes tension, it was still one of our proudest moments—proof that CPK had arrived on the biggest stage of all.

Yet our relationship with the BRS-controlled board was strained. They bristled at the continuation of our salaries we'd negotiated, as if we'd somehow taken advantage. Never mind that we'd given up bonuses and stock options to make it happen. Meanwhile, Hipp negotiated a far more lucrative package of salary, bonuses, and stock options. We didn't begrudge him—it came with the job. But the contrast underscored what the board thought of us: expendable.

From the outset, Hal Rosser, the BRS partner leading the deal, made it clear he didn't think much of Larry or me—other than as a face of the brand.

I was admittedly peeved that Rosser had such a short memory. He seemed to forget that the bargain deal he was so proud of wasn't his coup at all—it was ours to grant. Without us there was no deal, no bargain, and no CPK under his control.

What they never understood was that our true value wasn't measured in compensation packages. It lived in the loyalty of the people who worked for CPK: the VPs, regional directors, managers, servers, and cooks—the ROCKstars who believed in the culture we'd built and who had stayed because of it. That loyalty couldn't be bought, and it couldn't be replaced. The tight-knit, homegrown leadership team was the true core of the CPK family, and that's what mattered most. They would be there, loyal to CPK and to Larry and me, long after BRS executed its exit strategy.

Despite the smoldering tensions, Larry and I held a substantial ownership stake, and after fifteen years of stewardship, CPK was still our baby. We weren't going anywhere. We remained committed to CPK's success.

That didn't mean things were easy. In this strained environment with Hipp and the BRS-controlled board, we now had to negotiate our post-IPO employment contracts. They were content to keep us on as cochairmen but balked at paying us a salary—not exactly a promising sign for the future.

In the end we agreed that once the IPO was complete, we'd work without pay for the remaining two years on our contract. In place of salary and bonuses, we were offered stock options at the IPO price. At that point we had no real leverage, so we went along.

The irony, of course, was that while they didn't want to pay us, they still needed us. Not for strategy, not for management. Just for image. We were more valuable to them as a story than as executives. In fact the company's own SEC filings admitted as much, describing us as "the focal point of (CPK's) public relations and media efforts" and noting that our presence gave CPK a "competitive advantage."

The press followed suit: *Forbes*, *BusinessWeek*, *The Wall Street Journal*, *USA Today*, and even *People* magazine ran feature stories on us, boosting CPK's reputation nationwide.

By the time of our IPO, in August 2000, CPK had grown to 104 restaurants in twenty-one states, the District of Columbia, Guam, and three foreign countries (seventy-four company owned and thirty licensed or franchised). The numbers were impressive, but the message from BRS was clear: "Thanks for the story. Now stay out of the way."

CHAPTER THIRTY-FOUR

THE IPO WAS AN EXCITING MILESTONE FOR THE COMPANY. While we naturally harbored some bitterness toward the way we had been denigrated by Hipp and the BRS-controlled board, we remained excited about CPK's prospects. We were also thrilled that the IPO became an opportunity for our longest-standing employees to share in the success. Going forward, a favorable stock purchase plan for all employees allowed them to buy shares below market prices.

And many realized meaningful gains.

Larry and I continued to serve as brand ambassadors and stayed closely involved in menu development. But over time Hipp stopped inviting us to senior team meetings, a group largely composed of people we had hired, mentored, and promoted.

Frankly, it was humiliating. It felt like a rerun of a movie I'd seen play out during the final stretch of the PepsiCo era.

I had no desire to sit in a room where I wasn't wanted, and there was little satisfaction in simply showing up to occupy an office. So beyond my formal responsibilities, I quietly pulled back and retreated more often into my favorite outlet: golf.

It was during this period that something extraordinary happened outside of CPK. By then I had served on the board of Callaway Golf for six years and chaired its Management as Succession Committee. Ely Callaway, the legendary founder of Callaway Golf, honored me with a request I never expected: to succeed him as chairman when he retired. It was one of the most humbling and meaningful moments of my professional life.

But the opportunity slipped away after Ely's untimely passing, setting the stage for a bruising boardroom drama—including a clash with the powerful Vernon Jordan (a story I've saved for the prequel). Still, Ely's confidence in me remains one of the great honors of my career.

Meanwhile, back at CPK, the ground was shifting beneath us.

Larry, not being a golfer and ever the fighter, took a different approach. He stayed engaged, coming into the office, walking door-to-door, checking in with senior team members, and keeping me in the loop with what he saw and heard.

Larry also continued to throw himself in menu development, working closely with Brian Sullivan and the Culinary Development team. Brian wasn't a trained chef, nor was his predecessor. In fact the only time we used the term "chef" at CPK was during the brief period Ed LaDou worked for us. After that experience, Larry and I vowed that CPK would never again be held hostage by a chef's ego. Yet Fred Hipp wanted to channel everything through a newly formed menu committee, an idea that didn't sit well with Larry. He longed for the days when decisions rested with us alone. To him the only tastings that mattered came from Brian, from us, and from the CPK customers.

Before the IPO, Hipp had hired Tom Jenneman, a former Brinker International VP, to oversee new restaurant development. Our employment gave us the right to consult on site selection, but we were quietly shut out—a mistake that would come back to haunt them.

After fifteen years of opening restaurants, we knew how subtle differences in location could make or break success. It wasn't just data or models—it was instinct and gut, shaped by experience. For us, site selection was more art than science. But suddenly, no one was asking for our opinion.

Our employment contracts also gave us a role in shaping the aesthetic design of new restaurants. That, too, was ignored. One of the more baffling choices under Hipp's leadership was the large-scale purchase of colorful Mexican ceramic tiles to decorate exteriors. We were stunned. The tiles had no connection to CPK's brand or design DNA.

Yet the company was performing exceptionally well. By year end of 2000, just four months after going public, CPK had turned around dramatically. Net income climbed from a loss of $8.6 million in 1996 (the last full year of PepsiCo's ownership) to a profit of nearly $5 million. Comparable sales and traffic had increased noticeably, reflecting the efforts of the entire team in the post-PepsiCo era.

The momentum carried into 2001. Even though BRS maintained control, Larry and I remained the public faces and stayed deeply involved in menu development. A particular highlight was our frozen pizza partnership with Kraft, which was quickly gaining traction. We didn't realize it at the time, but it would prove to be one of the most powerful vehicles for putting the CPK name into kitchens across America.

CHAPTER THIRTY-FIVE

BY THE YEAR'S END, THE CPK FOOTPRINT HAD EXPANDED to 130 restaurants across twenty-five states, the District of Columbia, and four foreign countries, with 101 company-owned and 29 franchised locations. Revenues grew from $210 million in 2000 to $250 million the following year, and profits surged from $4.8 million to $13.2 million.

But beneath the good news, a troubling trend was emerging. Comparable store sales increased by 3.3 percent, but a closer look revealed that nearly all of it came from higher menu prices rather than an increase in customers. Customer counts were flat, a red flag for anyone paying attention. Relying on price hikes to mask stagnant traffic is a risky game that can't last forever. It should have set off alarms, but when we raised concerns with the BRS board, it was like talking to a wall.

The board at that time included Hipp, Bruce Bruckmann, Hal Rosser, Nick Valenti, and Brian Friedman, president of ING Furman Selz, a private equity firm BRS brought into the deal. Larry and I got along with Friedman like oil and water: He once instructed us that if a stock analyst managed to reach us, we should simply hang up.

Later, we added Chas Phillips, managing director of Gleacher & Company, the investment bank that had represented PepsiCo in the sale to BRS. Chas had real skin in the game. He not only invested Gleacher's fee into the deal but also put in his own money. Larry and I greatly respected him—smart, polished, likable, and smooth as silk.

In February 2002 we woke up to a gut punch: Our stock price plunged after BRS had quietly dumped most of its shares in a private transaction before the market opened.

Larry called me in a panic. But where Larry saw a crisis, I saw an opening. BRS no longer held a controlling stake. Finally, we had a chance to reshape the board with truly independent directors.

We moved fast. I called Hal Rosser and made it clear: At the next shareholder meeting, BRS would no longer control the board. Hal resisted until I told him we were prepared to launch a proxy battle to elect new directors. He backed down. By May 2002 three board members didn't stand for reelection. Rosser stayed, but BRS's grip was broken.

With the door open, we recruited new voices. Bill Baker was an Orange County businessman and a fellow Callaway Golf director. A Texan by birth, and a former lawyer, Bill had owned the Del Taco restaurant chain and had served as CEO of Red Robin. He was smart, ethical, and steeped in restaurant experience.

We also persuaded Rick Caruso—then a CPK franchisee and a rising star in Los Angeles real estate and politics—to come aboard. At the time he was president of the Los Angeles Police Commission, one of the city's most powerful posts.

Remarkably, Hipp didn't seem to notice the ground shifting beneath him. He kept operating as though the board were still a rubber stamp, just as it had been under BRS's control. But Larry and I knew better. The new directors were independent, thoughtful, and most importantly, respectful of what we had built. They would demand real oversight and fair judgment.

It was corporate governance working exactly as it should, and it was precisely what CPK needed.

Our employment contracts were set to expire on September 30, 2002. We wanted to stay. We still believed in the brand and its future. But we also knew we'd be wronged—refused salaries after the IPO and taken for granted by Hipp and the BRS-controlled board.

As the deadline approached, we were determined to right the wrong.

We met with Hipp in his office and laid out a modest proposal: Larry and I would share a combined salary equal to his own. Without hesitation he sneered, "The two of you aren't worth one of me."

We were stunned. Not just by the arrogance but by the sheer disregard for everything we had poured into this company. This was the business we had nurtured and created for seventeen years.

To be dismissed so casually was more than insulting. It cut deep.

Still, we weren't about to pick a public fight. We believed the board would have sided with us had we pressed the issue. But we didn't want to create turmoil. We had always tried to do the right thing for the people we worked with and for the brand we still loved.

As difficult as it was, and with heavy hearts, Larry and I made the decision to move on.

But Hipp's arrogance would later cost him. He hadn't just pushed us aside; he had underestimated us. As the saying goes, "When you strike at a king, strike him dead." He hadn't.

CHAPTER THIRTY-SIX

THERE WE WERE, AT AN EMOTIONAL CROSSROADS of our lives. By late 2002, after essentially being frozen out of the company we had built, Larry and I were restless. We needed a new challenge to keep our creative energies flowing. We began developing a full-service, upscale, casual-dining restaurant, which we called LA Food Show. The name captured our premise: to showcase the eclectic cuisine that made Los Angeles such a vibrant culinary city. It was designed to be different from CPK yet complementary—another riff on the "California-casual" spirit we had pioneered.

The menu was expansive and inventive. Appetizers labeled *Previews* ranged from an Ahi Poke Martini (yes, served in a martini glass) to a Chile Rennelo Egg Roll. Salads included a chopped BLT Bread Salad (another chance for Larry to sneak in mayonnaise), a Three Crunch Chinese Chicken Salad, and a Prime Steak Salad.

But the real stars were the *Featured Attractions*—entrées such as Thai Rotisserie Chicken, Garlic-Ginger Noodles, Fish and Chips, Grilled Sweet-Ginger Salmon, and Bangers and Mash. The most craveable of all: Fried Chicken and Waffles.

Desserts followed the same script: Banana Royale Bread Pudding (Larry's love letter to Bananas Foster), Chocolate Bread Pudding, Pecan Apple Cobbler, and Key Lime Cheesecake with a coconut-graham-cracker crust.

The CPK board fully embraced the LA Food Show concept and seized the chance to invest, taking a 25 percent stake. Larry and I funded the balance, with CPK retaining a right of first negotiation—positioning LA

Food Show as both our next act and a potential long-term benefit to the company. With the exception of Hipp, the directors weren't happy with his decision to force us out. Backing LA Food Show was their way of keeping us connected while giving us room to create a concept that could ultimately benefit the company too.

We secured a prime location at Manhattan Village Mall in Manhattan Beach, just steps from one of CPK's highest-grossing restaurants. Leaving our CPK offices behind and setting up shop in Manhattan Beach was nothing short of monumental—the end of one chapter, the uncertain beginning of another.

To help bring the new vision to life, we recruited Clint Coleman, a longtime CPK veteran who had risen from restaurant manager to operational VP. Clint had the operational chops, and with his eye for design, he helped us shape the restaurant's look and feel.

Larry and I threw ourselves into LA Food Show while continuing in our nonexecutive roles as cochairmen at CPK. On the surface the company seemed steady under Hipp and Greg Levin, our former controller turned CFO. Reports to the board—and the accompanying press releases—painted an upbeat picture.

Then came the first-quarter 2003 earnings report.

And there's no delicate way to put it: *The shit hit the fan.*

Public companies live and die by quarterly earnings reports. On April 22, 2003, CPK issued its first-quarter financial update, a press release so muddled that board members would later refer to it as the "gobbledygook press release."

Starting with the disappointing financial results, in a veritable word salad of excuses and finger-pointing, Hipp claimed that CPK's downturn was a result of "a convergence of unique circumstances." He blamed soft economic conditions, consumer spending, extreme weather on both coasts, and even the war in Iraq. It was a laundry list of excuses. But as I read it, something didn't add up.

One number jumped out: Comparable restaurant sales were *up* 2.7 percent year over year. That meant our mature restaurants (the bulk of the system) were outperforming the previous year, despite the supposed "convergence." So if the core restaurants were strong, what was dragging us down?

Thanks to my access to the company's internal data, I dug deeper. The truth stood out like a sore thumb: The problem wasn't the economy, the weather, or even the war in Iraq. The real drag was closer to home: The new restaurants—Hipp's and Tom Jenneman's sites—were dramatically underperforming. This wasn't just a case of soft sales or the slow ramp-up every operator expects. These were flat-out bad calls—poor locations that never should have been signed in the first place. The company had locked itself into long-term leases on losing sites that would weigh on our performance for years.

I immediately alerted the board. In response they formed a Special Real Estate Committee—consisting of Rick Caruso and me. Even though Larry and I had built the company on real estate choices that had helped reshape the industry, I was honored to serve alongside Rick. I had always been a bit in awe of him and felt fortunate to count him not only as a business associate but as a friend.

When Rick and I sat down with Hipp to present the facts, he brushed it aside, parroting the same excuses from his release.

As we walked out, Rick shook his head in disbelief. The moment reminded me of the classic punchline: *Are you going to believe me or your lying eyes?* Hipp's days were numbered.

Behind the scenes, Bill Baker floated the idea of Larry and me returning as co-CEOs. The votes were close. Larry's and my vote, along with Bill's, would give us three of the seven votes, but we needed a majority to resume our roles. One more would secure our return. There were two nonstarters, Hipp and Rosser. I wasn't sure where Chas Phillips would stand. We respected him, but he was part of the original BRS team. The swing vote was Rick Caruso.

I met Rick at his office at the Grove, his flagship development in Los Angeles. Sitting across from him, I cut straight to it: "Bill thinks that Larry and I should return as co-CEOs. Rick, do we have your support?"

Rick looked at me straight in the eye, quizzically, almost as if to say, "Why would you even need to ask?" Then he said it plainly: "You guys built this company. It's *your* company."

That was it. With Rick's support the outcome was inevitable.

With that Rick Caruso cemented himself in my mind forever as the quintessential stand-up guy—the kind of integrity and loyalty that was always in short supply, especially in business.

Unsurprisingly, Hal Rosser was opposed, but by that point, he and Hipp stood alone. Recognizing the inevitable, Rosser announced he would not stand for reelection. Hipp and his handpicked VP of real estate resigned. The BRS era was officially over.

In fairness BRS had advanced the company in meaningful ways, and Rosser, despite our occasional clashes, had always conducted himself as a gentleman—straightforward and honorable. But that chapter was closed.

Larry and I were back as co-CEOs, but the storm wasn't over. We were still being tossed about, but at least we were back at the helm, steering the ship ourselves.

CHAPTER THIRTY-SEVEN

WE HADN'T PLANNED FOR THIS. TRUTH BE TOLD, while we weren't happy with Fred Hipps's leadership, we certainly wished him to succeed. After all, we remained major shareholders and cochairmen. But when we stepped away to create LA Food Show, we did so with full commitment.

Now, unexpectedly, we found ourselves back at the helm—this time of a public company. And once we looked under the hood, it was clear: Things weren't in good shape. What we had stepped into wasn't familiar territory. This was a whole new ball game, with far higher stakes.

Our return as co-CEOs was not met with universal enthusiasm. While many longtime employees were thrilled, that support was not offered by everyone. At the grassroots level, we were well loved. We had always believed that the core of our business depended on the people on the front lines and their direct interaction with customers. We constantly reinforced the idea that CPK was a *work with,* not a *work for,* company. Despite the challenges, our continual focus on the ROCK mentality helped our employees understand that our hearts were in the right place.

However, at our headquarters (the Restaurant Support Center, as we had deliberately named it years earlier), the reception was cooler. We weren't exactly met with a victory parade. Some senior team members, particularly those who had aligned themselves with Hipp, didn't roll out the welcome mat.

In a span of eight years, they'd reported to PepsiCo's Greg Trojan, then briefly to BRS's Nick Valenti, and finally to Hipp. While Larry and I had remained the public face of the company, it had been a long time since we'd had true operational control.

During that stretch we'd been blamed for PepsiCo's overaggressive growth strategy and the cost cutting that had chipped away at CPK's quality. In truth those decisions were driven from Purchase, New York, not by us. But perception had hardened, and now we had to earn back trust.

Reestablishing ourselves wasn't easy. In hindsight it felt a bit like a parent-child dynamic: After years of answering to other "authority figures," some resisted the return of the originals. The good news was that most of the team had been hired and promoted by us. We knew, given time, we could win them back.

We liked and trusted the entire team—but one person never wavered: Rudy Sugueti. Rudy had started as a teenage pizza cook in our second restaurant and worked his way up to operational VP. He embodied the hands-on, hardworking "Don't do as I say—do as I do" ethic that defined our culture from day one. Rudy was a true ROCKstar. We could always count on him.

Still, there was no denying it. This was a fragile moment. Our return wasn't under the radar; it was unfolding under a microscope. CPK was a public company that had just reported disappointing results. We needed stability. So we turned to someone we trusted deeply: H. G. "Carey" Carrington, our former executive VP and CFO during the early BRS years. Widely respected by us, our senior team, and Wall Street, Carey agreed to return as interim president while Larry and I regained our footing.

We jumped in with both feet. Larry dove into operations, launching a weekly call with our regional directors, senior team members, and regional vice presidents, an invaluable real-time view of the restaurants. Meanwhile, I dug into the real estate and financial issues we were facing.

Larry and I had very different management styles. Larry was more emotional and reactive, while I was more measured and analytical. The team coined what they called the *twenty-four-hour rule*: If Larry dug in on an issue, wait a day and revisit it. More often than not, by then he had softened or at least opened up to other opinions.

Leading CPK as a public company was an entirely new experience for us. The good news: Eighteen years after we'd started, it had become a respected global brand. The bad news: The "professional management" had left us in a deep hole.

When we returned, we didn't know Greg Levin, CPK's CFO, all that well. While we respected him and worked together amicably during the transition, there was a quiet understanding on all sides: It was time for him to move on. When Greg left in January 2004, Sue Collyns, our controller, stepped in on an interim basis. An Australian native, she had joined CPK in 2001.

She and I vetted CFO candidates, but after several interviews, none felt like the right fit. Finally, in what we jokingly called a "Dick Cheney move," Sue convinced us that she was the best person for the job (much as Cheney once convinced President George W. Bush that *he* should be vice president).

By then I'd worked closely enough with Sue to see it was true. She was absolutely the right choice. We offered her the role, and she thrived. By 2009 she was promoted to chief operating officer and EVP.

At first Sue expressed reservations about stepping into such a high-profile role in a public company. I reassured her. "I've never run a public company either," I said. "But let's understand this: We're going to avoid any problems. There's a difference between telling the truth and being candid. You can tell the truth without being candid. We're going to be both truthful *and* candid."

The idea of running a public company, while certainly challenging, never intimidated me. One part of the job that many executives dread is the quarterly earnings call, where leadership reports financial results and then fields questions from analysts tracking the company's stock. But to me it was nothing compared with appearing before a federal district judge—or worse, a three-judge panel at the US Court of Appeals. In a courtroom there's no room to dodge a question. You answer, and you answer directly, or you risk the ultimate penalty: a loss.

On an earnings call, by contrast, I was in control. If a question strayed too close to sensitive territory, I could deflect by citing competitive reasons, confidentially, or any number of legitimate justifications.

But with Sue at my side, I actually enjoyed the process, and I think Sue did too. We made a good team. Her intense intellect, coupled with a polished Anglo-Australian accent, lent an instant credibility, and she earned a well-deserved trust in the investment community. Larry, on the other hand, was happy to stay out of it. He liked to say it was a left brain / right brain thing. His role was creative; mine was financial. But the truth was more nuanced. Larry was just as involved in shaping our financial strategy as I was in creative and operational decisions. Our division of labor wasn't rigid. It was instinctive, unspoken, and it worked.

Throughout our entire tenure as co-CEOs, Larry was physically present for nearly every quarterly earnings call. I always opened the same way: "Good afternoon, I'm Rick Rosenfield, the co-CEO of California Pizza Kitchen. With me today are our co-CEO, Larry Flax, and our chief financial officer, Sue Collyns."

Larry never spoke a word. Not once.

Often dubbed the Energizer Bunny and the Pied Piper of Pizza, Larry was the ultimate salesman for the CPK brand. He was an optimist by nature, always ready to paint the rosiest picture possible. But that wasn't what earnings calls demanded. My mantra was simple: Underpromise and overdeliver. To his credit Larry let me temper him in those moments. In that context silence really was golden.

Beyond that Larry was genuinely eager to throw himself back into the hands-on leadership of day-to-day operations. We hadn't played that role since PepsiCo had throttled CPK's expansion and effectively sidelined our influence on the business. Now we were back in control, free to apply the lessons we'd learned through every high and low of CPK's history.

It felt like coming home. In fact it was.

As we dug beneath the surface, the challenges were even more daunting than we anticipated. What we uncovered was deeply disconcerting. The restaurant locations chosen by Fred Hipp and Tom Jennemen—particularly the eighteen opened in 2002 and the twenty-two opened or planned for 2003—were significantly underperforming compared with our earlier restaurants.

We decided to address the issue head-on. In our reports we broke out the financial performance of these newer restaurants separately so investors and analysts could clearly see where the problems lay.

But it was painful. Larry and I had been completely left out of the loop when these sites were selected. Now that exclusion was coming back to haunt the company. It felt like history repeating itself, or as Yogi Berra quipped, "Déjà vu all over again." During the PepsiCo period, we had been seduced by the blank-check approach, chasing rapid expansion. Now years later we were dealing with the fallout from the same mistake—only this time, it wasn't ours.

It was obvious CPK could have benefited from our experience and counsel in site selection. Winston Churchill's warning rang in my ears: "Those that fail to learn from history are doomed to repeat it."

In restaurants the oldest rule still applies: location, location, location. Site selection is an art. Models and demographic studies can provide valuable insights, but they can't tell you if a place *feels* right.

After all our years in the business, we had developed the view that for a quality-oriented restaurant brand such as CPK, the most important drivers of sales were income levels and population densities. Our most successful restaurants had dense office populations or mall foot traffic during the day and an abundance of families at night.

The danger zone was always the "green-grass" suburban sites, built on promises of growth often near nothing more than grazing cows enjoying that grass.

That's why we believed so strongly in what we called "walking the earth." There was no substitute for visiting a site personally, standing there, and feeling it. We'd made that mistake before—delegating the responsibility to others.

When we returned as co-CEOs in July 2003, the restaurants already open, under construction, or about to break ground were beyond our control. Taking stock of the situation, we quicky began assessing the challenges ahead.

Since PepsiCo's departure in 1997, the company had opened seventy-two restaurants—forty of them in just 2002 and 2003. The underperformance of these newer locations leaped off the page.

By contrast our ninety-four established full-service restaurants were thriving, averaging weekly sales of $57,644 per unit with profit margins above 20 percent. That meant roughly $3 million in yearly sales and nearly $600,000 in annual profit per restaurant. In an industry known for razor-thin margins, CPK had always been an outlier. As we liked to say, our restaurants minted money.

The newer restaurants told a different story. The eighteen restaurants opened in 2002 averaged just $46,700 in weekly sales with margins of 11.6 percent, barely $281,000 in yearly profit. The twenty-two restaurants that opened the following year fared even worse, averaging just $43,275 per week at a dismal 4.7 percent profit margin. That translated to only $48,000 a year in profit on averages.

The truth is, many restaurants in this group didn't mint money; they burned it.

To tackle the problem, we created the Strengths, Weaknesses, Opportunities, and Threats (SWOTS) Team. Larry took the lead, working closely with regional and local managers. While we made immediate improvements, we understood the hard truth: Poor location is often insurmountable. Even the best concept, menu, or service can't rescue a bad site.

Our immediate priority was slowing growth. We scaled back to no more than twelve company-owned openings per year, focusing only on prime sites. To ensure the right choices, Larry and I reinstated a policy from CPK's earliest days, when every site was a winner. This meant that one of us had to personally evaluate each location, which was no small commitment. We also insisted on obtaining input from regional directors and local managers who brought invaluable on-the-ground perspective.

The most critical discipline we'd developed was the ability to say no. Rejecting questionable sites, even when growth targets loomed large, required clear-eyed objectivity. We'd learned our lesson. This time we weren't going to bend.

After reassessing the twenty sites inherited from prior management (but not yet signed), only two survived our more rigorous standards. It was sobering to see how close the company had come to disaster and a profound relief to know that we had returned just in time to avert what could have been catastrophic financial mistakes.

The sheer number of sites we needed to inspect raised a practical challenge: travel. To solve it we made an unconventional move for a public restaurant company of our size: We bought a corporate jet. At the time this wasn't typical for public companies operating under analyst scrutiny, but entrepreneurs with businesses our size often did the same. And with $360 million in revenue and strong cash flow, the decision was justified.

Admittedly, the decision raised a few eyebrows, but I don't recall analysts putting criticisms into their reports. In fact we remain convinced it was one of our smartest investments. Warren Buffett once quipped that the use of a private plane was *indefensible*, only to later call it *indispensable*. We felt the same. The jet allowed us to personally evaluate multiple sites in different cities in a single day. Considering each restaurant required about $3 million to open, this was a worthy expense.

Our new motto became President Reagan's famous line: "Trust but verify." A good location could generate millions; a bad one could destroy them.

Beyond efficiency, the jet also removed the grind from travel and gave us a unique benefit: uninterrupted hours for deep business discussions. We did, however, enforce one ironclad rule: no site visits to the Midwest or East during winter. After leaving Chicago for California sunshine, I had no desire to trudge through snow unless it was for skiing.

Eventually, we experimented with helicopters, too, scouting cities such as Atlanta, Cincinnati, and San Antonio from above. The aerial view proved invaluable. We could watch traffic patterns, study neighborhoods, and see retail centers side by side during peak hours. It offered insights no demographic model could match. Ray Kroc had discovered the same trick decades earlier when expanding McDonald's.

As we relished the chance to reevaluate every aspect of CPK's brand and business, it became quickly clear that the so-called professional managers had stripped away much of what once made CPK special. One glaring example was our wine list. Once a hallmark of the CPK experience, it had been watered down beyond recognition. For me it was personally disturbing—we had strayed from our original vision of offering exceptional wines at value prices. The selection process had clearly been handed off to people with little knowledge or passion for wine.

The decline hit home when Esther and I invited our friends Tony and JoJo Terlato to dinner at CPK. Tony was not only a terrific man but an icon in the American wine industry—instrumental in shaping the nation's evolving palate. In addition to introducing Americans to a broad variety of imported wines, including some of the world's finest, he was the one who discovered Santa Margherita and turned pinot grigio into a household name. Under his leadership, Terlato Wines became the country's largest importer of Italian wines.

Sitting across the table from Tony with our lackluster wine list in hand, I felt embarrassed. I confessed the problem and asked for his help. Gracious as ever, Tony agreed. Through his company—now run by his sons Bill and John and expanded to include ownership of wonderful wineries such as Rutherford Hill, Chimney Rock, and Sanford—the Terlatos helped us completely revamp CPK's wine program. Together, we curated a new list that featured high-quality pours across a range of price points.

The collaboration not only elevated our wine list but also made CPK the Terlato Wine Group's largest restaurant account. My embarrassment gave way to pride. CPK had renewed its commitment to offering guests excellent wines at reasonable prices—exactly as we had intended from the very beginning.

The necessity of reporting to shareholders on a quarterly basis is the bane of all executives. Our primary audience was institutional investors—the financial managers entrusted with massive sums on behalf of pension funds, endowments, and affluent clients. Within that world there are two kinds of analysts: buy side and sell side.

Buy-side analysts work inside firms that manage money, providing internal recommendations that drive investment decisions. Sell-side analysts, by contrast, issue research reports and recommendations to their firms' clients—reports that can move markets and sway a company's stock price.

Sue and I interacted with both groups, though far more often with the sell side. From the beginning we stuck to our foundational principle: Always be truthful and candid. That consistency built real credibility for CPK within the investment community. I was especially proud to work alongside Sue, an exceptional multitasker and an invaluable member of the team.

As we slowed down our expansion, we refined our site selection strategy to focus on markets where we already had restaurants. That way we could leverage familiarity with local demographics, attract talent in areas where we were known as a good employer, and strengthen our brand presence.

When I looked at our stock history, the story told itself. We'd gone public in August 2000 at $16 a share. It climbed as high as $35 before settling back into the mid-teens and twenties. By early 2002 BRS had mostly cashed out five to six times their money in just four years. Quite impressive.

When Larry and I returned as co-CEOs in July 2003, the stock was stuck around $17—barely above the IPO price three years earlier.

By the end of 2004, sales were climbing, profits were solid, and the stock closed near $32—a 40 percent jump in just twelve months and an 88 percent increase since our return seventeen months earlier. For us it wasn't just about the money. After years of being second-guessed by PepsiCo and sidelined by BRS, it was proof we could still steer the ship.

We used that stretch to rethink our restaurants. Guests didn't want ten-thousand-square-foot palaces, but they wanted more than cafés. They wanted spaces that felt warm, inviting, and grown-up—a place you could bring your kids, order wine or a cocktail, and feel at ease no matter the occasion.

So we began designing toward that vision and remodeling older stores to match.

By late 2005 the mood had shifted. Dining rooms were buzzing, guests were leaning in to try new dishes, and our team felt proud again. You could feel the energy in the restaurants. The stock followed, rising toward $34, but what mattered more was the spirit inside CPK: People believed again.

In 2006 we opened sixteen new full-service restaurants, and profits hit $20 million. Oddly, the stock dipped, but with confidence, the board responded by approving a $30 million buyback and investing $63 million in new locations and remodels, all funded by the cash our restaurants were generating.

But behind those numbers, something more important was happening: CPK was finding its soul again.

By the end of 2006, after the early dip, the stock was back up, outperforming the broader Nasdaq for the year. We entered 2007 with strong momentum and growing confidence in the road ahead.

CHAPTER THIRTY-EIGHT

IN FEBRUARY 2007 SUE AND I LED OUR QUARTERLY EARNINGS call to report on the final months of 2006. At the time everything looked golden. But I'm reminded of something my flight instructor always said: "Don't fly fat, dumb, and happy." His point was simple: Never get complacent—especially when you're flying through clouds with only your instruments to guide you. Take your eyes off the big picture for even a moment, and trouble can sneak up fast.

Looking back, maybe we should have taken that warning more to heart.

That morning everything sounded textbook. Sue and I read from carefully prepared remarks crafted with Tom Ryan and his team at ICR—one of the most respected investor relations firms in the country. Tom had an uncanny feel for messaging and how to communicate with Wall Street—clear, confident, but never overpromising—the very approach that mirrored my own credo. Of course, Tom would be the first to admit he didn't have a crystal ball. None of us did.

I led with the milestone I was proudest of. Since our return as co-CEOs, CPK had delivered thirteen straight quarters of same-store sales growth and increased guest counts, with more than three years of uninterrupted momentum.

While other casual-dining chains were wobbling, we still looked strong. Guests were showing up. Our model looked resilient. Confidence filled the air.

On paper we were firing on all cylinders. Takeout and delivery (which were already among the strongest in casual dining) were growing by double digits. Inside the restaurants, weekly sales averaged $66,000, a record for us. Adjusted for today's dollars, it was closer to $100,000. Looking ahead, we projected sixteen to eighteen new full-service restaurants in 2007, four smaller ASAP units, and a second LA Food Show.

I even slipped in a lighthearted line about the brutal East and Midwest snowstorms. "We love building restaurants in California," I told investors. "The costs are high, but the weather softens the blow."

The joke had truth to it. More than 40 percent of our restaurants were in California, and they consistently outperformed the rest of the country by 15 percent. Loyal guests, strong labor, and the ability to cluster locations made California our fortress. Or so we believed.

I spoke with certainty: "We remain extremely confident in our prospects and have never been better positioned to deliver on the 15 to 20 percent earnings growth range over the long run. We feel comfortable in saying that we can open sixty to one hundred company-owned, full-service restaurants in the next three to five years."

And I closed with genuine pride: "We're really starting to feel the momentum of the global brand Larry and I always envisioned for CPK. The leverage that this will create for shareholder value is the unfolding story."

It was the perfect ending to the perfect call. But in business, as in flying, clouds can hide mountains.

CHAPTER THIRTY-NINE

AS THE SAYING GOES, "THE BEST-LAID PLANS OF MICE and men often go awry." Just as CPK was firing on all cylinders, the Great Recession blindsided us (and the rest of the country). Officially, it began in December 2007 and lasted through June 2009, the longest and deepest downturn since World War II.

In June 2007 CPK was at its peak. Our stock hit an all-time high of $36.93—up 115 percent since Larry and I had returned as co-CEOs four years earlier. We were confident enough to approve a three-for-two stock split, aimed at making shares more accessible to new investors. On paper the math was simple: more shares, lower price. In spirit it was a victory lap.

But by our August earnings call, cracks were forming.

California's housing market was softening, but we still had forty-two straight months of same-store sales growth. California remained our fortress, outperforming the rest of the country by 10 percent, and our older restaurants were hitting weekly sales of $75,000.

Sue and I reassured investors: "We're not immune to economic pressure," I said, "but we're building for the long term, not chasing short-term numbers." Sue added, "We've never felt better about our business, despite the challenges. And those will pass." She was right, though none of us knew how long it would take.

By late 2007 the storm clouds darkened. Traffic slipped nearly 6 percent, and comps fell 2 percent. At first we thought we could ride it out. After all, CPK had weathered recessions in the '90s and post-9/11 period. But this time was different.

In early 2008 our stock slid to $16.00 ($24 presplit). By Q4 it bottomed at $5.24 ($7.86 presplit). From a $750 million valuation in June 2007, we'd lost 80 percent of value by November 2008. We were shell-shocked.

Still, instead of retreating, our board made a bold but calculated move: We secured a $150 million credit line and used $60 million of it to buy back stock at $9.00 ($13.50 presplit). For the first time, Larry and I were carrying real debt, and I'll admit, sleep didn't come easily. Confidence is one thing; gambling the company's future is another.

We decided to slow our pace and bet on the long game. Above all we believed in the CPK brand. Developers continued to pitch us prime sites, but the landscape was changing fast. With retailers closing, malls were reinventing themselves around restaurants and lifestyle concepts. It was what we'd long predicted—that restaurants would become the new anchors of retail centers. It didn't happen exactly the way we imagined, but it happened all the same.

On our Q3 earnings call, November 6, 2008, I didn't sugarcoat it. "We're restaurant operators, not economic forecasters. But it's clear we're in uncharted territory." Comps were down 7.3 percent, worst in California, Arizona, and Florida, where housing-boom markets were now leading the crash. Fear had replaced optimism almost overnight.

There was one moment of levity. Reports noted Michelle Obama would have to give up her regular lunches at a Chicago CPK once she moved into the White House. I joked that there was a CPK on Connecticut Avenue if she wanted to keep the tradition alive. It got a laugh, but no one missed the larger truth: The recession was reshaping everything.

As 2009 began, sales stayed soft—worst in the retail centers that had ridden the housing boom up and were now riding it down. There were bright spots. Our airport restaurants with HMSHost held steady; so did international franchise locations. But the biggest win was the frozen food aisle.

Our partnership with Kraft to sell CPK frozen pizzas had taken off. By year-end 2009 we were in twenty thousand stores across all fifty states and DC, with roughly $200 million in retail sales and $7.7 million in royalties. We'd negotiated a tiered royalty system—more volume, more rate—which was our way of betting on ourselves, and it was paying off in spades. We'd always cooked with fire in our restaurants, but now the frozen line had caught fire too.

A bonus: Kraft was contractually obligated to market CPK—and their national reach far exceeded anything within our budget. From the start we had operated lean, convinced that in restaurants such as ours, the best publicity came not from ad campaigns but from the credibility of word of mouth.

The recession changed other things in unexpected ways. Employee turnover dropped to an all-time low. In an industry where 100 percent churn is common, CPK consistently ran far below that, thanks to our strong ROCK culture.

There were moments that lifted us. In a *Honolulu Advertiser* readers' poll, CPK won Best Pizza, Best Salads, and Best American Food. For a pizza chain, that kind of trifecta was rare. For us it meant that our values traveled, that in a place as soulful as Hawaii, something about CPK resonated.

No one embodied that more than Eddie Spencer. He'd started as a teenage dishwasher at our Kahala Mall location and rose to area director, still bent on CPK quality every day in a wildly successful market. Eddie's arc was the point: Brands don't come alive because of locals or slogans. They come alive when local people make them their own.

It's said that all politics are local; I'd argue the same for national restaurant chains. There is a simple truth: No matter where a company is headquartered, it hires local people. Ultimately, the business succeeds or fails one neighborhood at a time.

Recognition kept coming even as the economy bit hard. Independent firms Zocalo and MARC Research ranked CPK the Most Recommended Casual Dining Chain in America. *Forbes* named us one of America's 200 Best Small Companies. Those nods didn't erase the pain, but they reassured us we were still earning trust.

Despite the hit, CPK remained fundamentally healthy. Before the downturn, we were proudly debt-free. In 2007 and 2008, we drew $74 million on our credit facility to buy back stock, ultimately repurchasing $110 million by the end of 2008 (funded with a mix of cash flow and modest borrowing). Then in 2009 we stopped repurchasing and paid down nearly $50 million of debt.

By 2010 comps were nearly flat. After years of decline, we thought we'd stopped the bleeding. But flat can be deceiving. We were now lapping a battered year. Stabilization wasn't recovery; it was simply not sinking further.

The math was unforgiving. At peak the average CPK did about $3.5 million a year. By 2010 it was closer to $3 million. That $500,000 gap wasn't just numbers on a page—it meant as much as a $200,000 hit to the bottom line per unit. Once fixed costs are covered, incremental sales translate directly to profit. This means that when sales fall, profit doesn't gently taper; it drops off a cliff.

We reminded our teams, "We put dollars in the bank, not percentages." Comps tell part of the story. Average unit volumes tell the truth.

Looking back, those were some of the hardest years. We had built CPK on optimism—on the idea that if you sweat the details and take care of people, good things happen. The Great Recession taught a more sobering lesson: It reminded us that even the strongest brands aren't immune to forces far bigger than themselves.

For Larry and me, it was humbling. We had known the thrill of expansion, of seeing our vision spread across the country and the world. Now we were learning the discipline of survival—of tightening our grip, conserving cash, protecting culture, and trusting that the storm would eventually pass.

It certainly wasn't easy to get through, but what lingers aren't just the sleepless nights; it's our people's resilience, our guests' loyalty, and the quiet satisfaction of steering the company through a once-in-a-lifetime crisis. We didn't just endure the recession; we came out with a deeper understanding of what really matters: not the ticker but the team, the guests, and the culture that got us through. That's what Larry and I held onto then. It's what we hold onto now.

CHAPTER FORTY

THE RECESSION TAUGHT US A PERSONAL LESSON THAT we hadn't expected. From the earliest days, we'd dreamed of building a public company. We nearly did before PepsiCo altered our path. But when the downturn hit, our stock cratered, control felt illusory, and the dream soured. Be careful what you wish for. The bloom was off the rose; running a public company was no longer fun.

The brand was still strong, the fundamentals were healthy, guests loved us, and we were respected in the industry. But the stock didn't reflect that strength. That disconnect breeds unrest, and it did. The phrase "strategic alternatives," including discussion of a possible sale, entered the boardroom.

For us it landed like a thunderclap. CPK had been our life's work for twenty-four years. We still believed in it. But a snowball began to roll.

In late 2009 the board authorized confidential outreach to investment banks. By spring 2010, with a better-than-expected first quarter, momentum built. We hired Moelis & Company—Ken Moelis's firm—with Carlos Jimenez and Jeff Raich guiding day-to-day. We built a strong bond with Carlos, prepared a confidential information memorandum, and Moelis contacted thirty-one potential buyers. Twenty-five expressed interest. When *The Wall Street Journal* leaked the process in April, we confirmed it. The stock jumped to its highest level since 2007.

Early nonbinding indications came in mostly from private equity firms—$20 to $24 per share. Golden Gate Capital (GGC) initially poked around at a lower range and stepped back. Then diligence turned grueling: meetings, plant-level questions, data rooms . . . rinse and repeat. By

July the "final" offers from two bidders were $15 and $16—disappointing. Moelis warned: Call it off and expect a stock drop and lawsuits; push forward at a weak price and expect a different set of lawsuits. Damned if you do, damned if you don't.

A handful of parties kept circling—some serious, some clearly in it for cocktail party bragging rights. One prominent local billionaire put us through exhaustive diligence, then lobbed in an insulting number. By late summer only one real bidder remained at $16. The board formed a special committee of independent directors to manage conflicts and decide when discussions should exclude us, since most buyers would want continuity in leadership, and we wanted to stay.

We played by the rules and stayed out of any talks about our own roles.

In the fall GGC reemerged with $17.00 to $17.50. A couple of "white knight" teases never materialized. In April 2011—nearly a year after we started the process—GGC came back at $18.00, contingent on final diligence. Their lead partner was Josh Olshansky, with associate Josh Cohen—the "two Joshes." Olshansky had recently inherited the firm's restaurant portfolio and was eager to land a trophy brand. That deal heat helped us nudge the number. After a timely call from Director Chas Phillips, GGC lifted to $18.50.

When the deal closed on July 7, 2011, Larry and I could finally sit down with Olshansky for a conversation free of any potential conflict. He told us that GGC wanted us to remain as cochairmen, with compensation to be worked out later. We felt optimistic—after all, they'd just paid $470 million for CPK. He also promised we'd be consulted before any new CEO was hired.

At Olshansky's request, and to reinforce that stability, we held an all-hands meeting at a nearby hotel, where he introduced himself to the two hundred employees at the Restaurant Support Center. Spirits lifted when he announced that Larry and I would remain as cochairmen. That was the high point.

From there things unraveled quickly.

In early August, over lunch at the Casa del Mar hotel in Santa Monica, Olshansky introduced us to G. J. Hart, informing us that GGC had already hired him as CPK's new CEO. So much for consultation.

He praised Hart's tenure at Texas Roadhouse. We later learned that Hart and founder Kent Taylor had built a strong public company, but with a model that couldn't have been further from ours: a dinner-only steakhouse with line dancing servers and peanut shells on the floor, aimed squarely at secondary markets and working-class families. CPK, by contrast, thrived in major urban centers and an upscale, educated demographic. Research during the sale process confirmed it: Our guests ranked highest in income and education among all national chains.

A few days later came the real blow. Olshansky called, sheepishly saying that during final negotiations, Hart insisted on being named executive chairman and CEO. Larry and I would no longer serve as cochairmen, as previously agreed.

We were stunned. For twenty-four years, CPK had been our life. To be pushed aside so casually and so quickly felt like a gut punch. Still, after talking it through, Larry and I came to the same conclusion: We couldn't walk away. Not yet. We owed it to the brand, to the people, and to ourselves to try to see it through.

So we showed up—again—at the same hotel ballroom where Olshansky had only recently assured the entire Restaurant Support Center staff that Larry and I would remain as cochairmen.

This time the tone was very different. Olshansky introduced G. J. Hart as the new CEO and executive chairman. Larry and I stood silently off to the side.

Hart took the mic and launched into his life story: how he'd immigrated from the Netherlands at age five, not speaking a word of English, and had gone on to succeed at every turn. Then came the line that stopped us both cold. He emphasized proudly that he had *never failed at anything.*

As we left the room, Larry and I exchanged a glance. Later, we said the same thing. That was odd. There was no question Hart had been successful indeed, highly successful. But really, *who in life can claim they've never failed? Why did he feel the need to say that?*

Meanwhile, nothing had been clarified about our roles or our compensation. And with Hart now firmly in charge, everything felt up in the air.

Then Olshansky called, asking us to meet him and Hart at the

Ritz-Carlton in Marina del Rey. That alone told us everything. Larry and I had seen this movie before. We weren't being invited to a coronation. We were being summoned to a hanging.

In the private conference room, Hart began with a lengthy monologue about his understanding of California and the CPK brand. It felt rehearsed—more presentation than conversation. I remember wondering why he felt the need to persuade us at all. I was simply waiting for the blade to fall.

And then came the moment we had anticipated.

"I don't have any money or stock for you," he said flatly. "I don't see a role for you going forward."

Across the table, Olshansky sat silent. Not a word. Not even a half-hearted attempt to acknowledge the promises he'd made to us—or to the hundreds of CPK employees he'd reassured just days earlier. His silence told us everything.

Only later did the full picture come into focus. Kent Taylor, founder of Texas Roadhouse, was blunt: It had been Taylor, not Hart, running the show. Hart's contract made the point in black and white: If he were fired or resigned, his severance was "a crisp $100 bill." Translation: Don't let the door hit you on the way out.

So when Hart stood in front of our team declaring that he'd "never failed at anything," the moment came into focus. He wasn't trying to persuade them. He was speaking to himself.

Years later, in a 2016 *Los Angeles Times* interview, Hart reflected on why he had taken the CPK role. "I wanted to see if I was any good," he said.

By then there was no real surprise in how things unfolded. What lingered wasn't anger so much as disappointment. After nearly forty years together, I didn't need to check with Larry. I knew how he felt.

I stayed composed: "That's fine. The check cleared."

Then we stood, walked out, and closed the door behind us.

It's hard to describe what that moment felt like—walking away from twenty-five years of passion and partnership, knowing it was over. That was the last time we saw either Hart or Olshansky.

As for Olshansky, the consequences flowed from his own choices.

After standing before our team and offering his reassurances that Larry and I would remain as cochairmen, only to later reverse course, his credibility eroded in ways that no explanation could repair. Words matter—especially when they're spoken to people who have built their lives around a company.

From there the authority to shape what followed rested with Hart and GGC.

To be clear Olshansky didn't violate any legal obligation. He was entitled to change direction. What was lost was something less tangible but no less real: trust. In our world a person's word still counts.

Hart, for his part, owed us nothing—legally or otherwise. He'd been handed the keys to the kingdom and moved quickly to chart his own course.

CHAPTER FORTY-ONE

FROM THE MOMENT HART ASSUMED THE DUAL ROLE of CEO and chairman, it became clear that he intended to remake CPK—something he was, of course, entitled to do.

His decision to cast us aside was personally devastating. We had never imagined a future for CPK without us in it. It wasn't about compensation. To us it was about identity, legacy, and the abrupt severing of what we had poured our lives into. We weren't emotionally prepared for it. Honestly, we never saw it coming.

But as painful as it was to be pushed out, what followed was harder still: standing on the sidelines as the company moved in directions we no longer recognized. Decisions that emphasized financial engineering over relationships and culture began to reshape the organization, touching every corner of the business.

The reality was stark: From the moment GGC's deal closed in July 2011, control of the company rested with G. J. Hart and GGC, led by Josh Olshansky. What follows is a matter of public record. Less than a decade later, CPK entered Chapter 11 bankruptcy in 2020. GGC lost control, debt holders absorbed losses reported to exceed $220 million, and the company emerged carrying approximately $177 million in debt—its future uncertain.

Admittedly, we are not neutral observers. But our concerns were not shaped by hindsight. We experienced the early signs firsthand. From our vantage point, decisions were being made that felt increasingly disconnected from the culture and long-term health of the company. We were frustrated, powerless, and heartbroken, watching the business we had built struggle under pressures that seemed avoidable.

CPK was never just a business to us. It was something closer to a child—created, nurtured, and grown into the global brand we had envisioned.

One of the earliest signals came with the transaction itself. To finance the $470 million acquisition, CPK assumed approximately $335 million in debt, while GGC contributed approximately $135 million in equity. Two years later the company refinanced—taking on a new capital structure that included a $370 million first-lien loan and a $30 million revolving credit facility. That refinancing enabled a reported $50 million dividend to GGC—funded from the company's balance sheet.

At the same time, a familiar private equity financial playbook took hold: tight cost control, freeze growth, and an overriding focus on servicing debt. To some observers those shifts may have appeared prudent. From our perspective they reduced flexibility and narrowed the range of options for a business that had historically thrived on momentum, creativity, and long-term relationships.

Those relationships had always been central to our growth and success. CPK was built alongside the nation's leading mall and retail developers—Simon, Westfield, Taubman, Macerich, General Growth, and others. These were not just transactional arrangements; they were strategic partnerships cultivated over decades, grounded in trust, shared growth, and mutual long-term commitment.

By the time of the sale, we had just emerged from the recession and were poised for a wave of expansion. We'd fine-tuned our site selection process and had ten to twelve new leases, plus key renewals sitting on my desk, ready to be signed. Some even included creative structural protections to limit downside risk.

That momentum ended abruptly when Hart and GGC elected not to proceed with any of the pending deals. From a financial perspective, the decision was consistent with a conservative capital preservation approach. From the standpoint of how the business actually functioned, however, the consequences were immediate and lasting. Within days Larry and I began receiving calls from developers who were openly frustrated, indeed angry, by the sudden change of direction. At a major developer's conference not long afterward, a senior executive captured the prevailing mood with blunt clarity: "Screw them. They won't be getting new locations. And when the renewals come up, they'll be lucky if we let them stay—and it won't be cheap."

Hart and GGC had underestimated a basic reality of the business: Developer relationships are built on consistency and trust, and once disrupted they are not easily repaired. The reality was simple—CPK was one option among many. There is always another "hot" concept waiting in the wings. The consequences were swift, lasting, and entirely avoidable—an inauspicious beginning.

CHAPTER FORTY-TWO

IN THE AFTERMATH CPK'S FOOTPRINT BEGAN TO SHRINK, predictably losing prime locations as leases expired. At its peak—on the day GGC assumed control—the company operated 205 restaurants, with additional revenue from franchising and frozen pizza bringing total sales to approximately $642 million. *Nation's Restaurant News* ranked us 63rd among the Top 100 Restaurant Chains in America.

Today that footprint has fallen to roughly 140 restaurants. System-wide sales are estimated at $406 million, and the brand now ranks 123rd on the Top 500 list. On paper the trend was unmistakable: fewer restaurants, declining sales, and diminished scale.

But the real cost was not captured on a balance sheet. It was human.

The decision to load the company with substantial debt may have made sense from a transactional or financial perspective, but to us it placed sustained pressure on a brand whose strength had always depended on investment, continuity, and trust.

Our concern was never for GGC's investors or lenders. They understood the risks. It was for the people—the roughly fourteen thousand team members who poured their hearts into CPK every day—and the long-standing partners who had put in their passion and money—and built their own businesses alongside ours. And deeper still, it was for the brand itself. When a brand weakens, everything connected to it follows.

Sustaining a world-class brand is a delicate balance. You can reduce costs, or you can build momentum—but rarely at the same time. We'd seen this dynamic before under PepsiCo. When development slows, morale dips, innovation stalls, and forward momentum fades. In our view the strategy that followed the sale repeated that patten—with results that, unfortunately, seemed predictable.

For Larry and me, the hardest part was watching from the sidelines as the culture we'd built—our ROCKstar culture—began to disappear. From the beginning we believed deeply in growing leaders from within. At the time of the acquisition, CPK had thirty-two regional directors with an average tenure of nearly fourteen years. Nearly all had started as cooks, servers, hosts, or managers and worked their way up. They weren't just employees—they were stewards of the brand. Loyal to the brand and each other.

That culture of trust and teamwork eroded quickly. Many long-tenured leaders were let go, and their roles were filled by executives brought in from other organizations, including Texas Roadhouse. The new structure stretched regional oversight well beyond what we had ever considered effective and did so without the institutional knowledge that had long underpinned CPK's operations. That is not to question the abilities of those people who were brought in, many of whom were undoubtedly capable, but rather to note they were placed in an extraordinarily difficult situation.

At the same time, financial incentives at the senior level were reoriented toward aggressive profit targets. The result was a steady exit of experienced managers—people who had helped build the company and carried its values forward day-to-day.

I'll never forget visiting one restaurant not long after the sale and hearing a server, through tears, describe the abrupt firing of a general manager she deeply admired—replaced by someone new to the team with no shared history. That moment has stayed with me.

What was missed was something fundamental: The restaurant business is a team sport. When you remove trusted leadership, you don't just lose experience—you lose morale, cohesion, and forward momentum. Once that foundation weakens, the rest of the structure inevitably feels less stable.

There were the symbols too.

After taking over, Hart relocated to Newport Beach, an hour away from the Los Angeles headquarters, and purchased a yacht. At a time when the company was carrying significant new debt, it struck many inside the organization as a curious contrast—and not one that inspired confidence.

We had always been very deliberate about symbols—the small, visible details that quietly defined the CPK experience. From the beginning we set a clear tone: Pressed white shirts, black aprons, ties—even the short-lived white pants—were statements of professionalism, pride, and polish. These weren't gimmicks. They conveyed to our guests that we took the experience seriously—and that we respected the people we were serving.

Those standards were later set aside. Crisp whites gave way to black shirts. Ties disappeared. Servers were allowed to wear blue jeans—any wash, any style. What may have felt more "casual" on the surface carried a subtler message: The old standards no longer applied.

To us that shift reflected a misunderstanding of what made CPK distinct and special. Texas Roadhouse's boots-and-peanuts aesthetic worked for their brand. But CPK had always occupied a different space—urban, polished, and professional. Guests weren't looking for rustic. They came for a dining experience that felt elevated yet approachable. For twenty-five years that balance had defined us.

Esther and I felt the change firsthand during a visit to the CPK in Palm Desert. Some members of the staff looked less put together. The energy felt flatter, less purposeful. We began hearing similar comments from longtime guests—not complaints exactly but a recurring refrain: It just didn't feel like CPK anymore.

Symbols matter. They reinforce what a company stands for. Change them without understanding their meaning, and you risk sending a message that's hard to undo.

Then came the menu.

Under our leadership, CPK's offerings always evolved but deliberately. We expanded carefully from the original lineup of pizzas, pastas, and salads into a broader mix that still felt unmistakably "California"—or, at least, unmistakably CPK. We had come a long way since introducing the Barbecue Chicken Pizza to the world—adding signature favorites such as Spinach Artichoke Dip, Szechwan Chicken Dumplings, and Avocado Club Egg Rolls. But every new dish had to clear a simple test: Did it feel like it belonged on a CPK menu?

The approach that followed took a different direction. Under what was called the "Next Chapter" strategy, the menu was streamlined and the pizza lineup reduced by nearly half. For Larry, our self-appointed "Pied Piper of Pizza," that was particularly painful. His long-held vision was for CPK to be the Baskin-Robbins of pizza—thirty-one flavors. We never quite reached thirty-one flavors; we topped out at twenty-nine. But cutting the list down felt like a retreat for a brand built on expanding what pizza could be.

Then came the additions. First, a hamburger—unexpected but manageable. Later, a fire-grilled rib eye. At that point the menu began to feel less like an evolution and more like an identity crisis.

The moment that crystallized it for me came when I walked past a CPK and saw a sandwich board out front. That alone felt foreign. What really took me aback was a hand-drawn chalk cow promoting the steak. Whatever the intent, the image was jarring. CPK no longer felt rooted in Los Angeles or California cuisine—it seemed to be borrowing cues from somewhere else entirely.

The menu had changed. And with it, the signals of what the brand stood for were changing as well.

Hart also oversaw a redesign of CPK's interiors, replacing the contemporary aesthetic with rustic oak floors and reclaimed wood tables. For longtime guests the shift was disorienting. What had once felt distinctly California, or at least unmistakably CPK—urban, polished, and modern—was slowly being recast in a very different image.

And yet the clearest measure of what was happening wasn't in the comments we heard; it was in the numbers. Reports from Moody's and Dun & Bradstreet told the story plainly: CPK was carrying an unsustainable debt load. Ratings were downgraded, bond values eroded, and the implications were unmistakable. Res ipsa loquitur—the thing speaks for itself.

In January 2019, after eight years at the helm, Hart resigned. His chapter ended there, though GGC remained in control of its investment.

Jim Hyatt, formerly CEO of Ruby Tuesday and global chief operating officer at Burger King, was brought in to replace Hart. Hyatt was a seasoned operator and widely respected by those who worked with him. But by the time he arrived, the reality was unavoidable: Much of the damage had already been done.

That spring Hyatt invited Esther and me, along with Larry and Joni, to CPK's new Playa Vista headquarters to mark the company's thirty-fourth anniversary. It was a gracious gesture. We were shown the Honor Wall, where longtime contributors were recognized. Our names were at the top. I'll admit—it meant something. For a brief moment, I felt a flicker of pride and connection to what we had built. But sentiment wasn't going to change the company's trajectory.

By late 2019—months before COVID-19—CPK was already edging toward default. Debt covenants were tightening, lenders were circling, and the company retained Guggenheim Partners and Kirkland & Ellis to explore a sale or restructuring. Nothing materialized in time.

Then came the pandemic.

In July 2020, CPK filed for Chapter 11 bankruptcy. As industry journal *FSR Magazine* reported,*

> *COVID only exacerbated issues that were already occurring. In court documents, California Pizza Kitchen blamed its bankruptcy on the rise of fast-casual [dining], decreasing mall traffic, and the growth of third-party delivery services. Pre-pandemic, the company faced liquidity problems for multiple years and hired a management team to trigger a turnaround effort. In the fall of 2019, the brand began exploring M&A and even initiated a marketing process to sell itself, but COVID halted those efforts.*
>
> *As part of its bankruptcy restructuring, California Pizza Kitchen completed a debt-for-equity swap and eliminated more than $220 million in existing funded debt. Substantially, all of California Pizza Kitchen's equity is now held by CPK's prepetition lenders.*

By then the leadership responsible for many of the earlier decisions had already moved on. Yet the consequences remained. Debt holders absorbed losses exceeding $220 million. Employees, franchise partners, vendors, and loyal customers bore the uncertainty and disruption that followed. Whatever the intentions behind the strategy, the human toll was unmistakable.

Private equity often operates on portfolio math: Gains in one deal are expected to offset losses in another. But when an investment falters, the impact is not confined to balance sheets. It is felt most acutely—the people who gave the brand its soul. Those losses are harder to quantify and harder still to repair.

In CPK's case the combination of heavy leverage and constrained operating flexibility proved difficult to overcome. Viewed in hindsight, the risks embedded in that structure were substantial. Once momentum slowed and external pressures mounted, the outcome followed a course that, regrettably, was not surprising.

So it leaves the obvious question: Should we have sold the company? The answer is not simple. The reality is that once a public company contemplates a sale, the process takes on a momentum of its own. You don't guide it; you hang on. I've described it before as a snowball—rolling downhill, gathering size and speed until no one can stop it. That's what the CPK sale became.

And selling to private equity is a different kind of gamble. It's like handing over your child to a stranger and hoping they'll raise it with love. Sometimes they do. Sometimes they don't.

In Delaware, where we were incorporated, the law is unambiguous. Once a public board contemplates a sale, its fiduciary duty narrows to one thing: Maximize shareholder value in the short term.

Everything else—the culture, the people, even the founders' vision—gets pushed aside. Not because the board didn't care but because the legal mandate leaves little room for anything else.

We believed we'd have a continuing role. That reassurance mattered at the time. But those assurances never materialized. By the time it became clear, the deal had closed, and our influence was gone.

Looking back, we thought we were doing the right thing. But helping set the process in motion came at a cost we deeply regret—for the people, the culture, and the brand itself.

We, too, paid more than just an emotional price. During the bankruptcy, Jim Hyatt, then CEO, chose to reject CPK's contractual obligation to pay our promised retirement benefits (about $200,000 each per year for life). He could have honored it. He didn't. That left a bitter taste.

But our loss wasn't the real loss. Far more painful was seeing the impact on the people who poured their hearts into CPK. Many lost their jobs. Vendors and partners who had believed in us suffered financially. And yet many on the team stuck it out anyway, working tirelessly to keep the brand alive. They deserve enormous credit.

In December 2022 CPK's lenders appointed Jeff Warne as CEO, with a résumé that included Perkins, Marie Callender's, and TGI Fridays.

By then we were long gone. And in all the years since, Hart, Olshansky, and Hyatt never once picked up the phone. Not a call. Not a question. Nothing. I used to say at CPK, "If you include me in the decision, I'm your partner. If you don't, I'm just the judge."

So (for what it's worth) here's my judgment:

If GGC had kept its promises—to us and to the employees—and left Larry and me as cochairmen, CPK's story could have been very different.

We weren't just former executives. We were part of CPK's DNA. We'd spent decades cultivating relationships with developers, landlords, suppliers, and guests. We understood our customers. And we cared—deeply—about their experience. Hart never gave us a seat at the table. There was no negotiation, no discussion how our institutional knowledge might fit into the next chapter. One day we were stewards of the company we had built. The next the chair had been kicked out from under us.

And yet, despite it all, we remain hopeful. CPK's story isn't finished. In recent times the company has expanded its franchise program, partnered with Litehouse Foods, on a new line of salad dressings now appearing in grocery stores and even begun testing vending machines in airports. The frozen pizza line thrives, too, selling more pizzas today than in the restaurants themselves.

In March 2025 CPK marked its fortieth anniversary by recommitting to its core values: culture and innovation. We were invited to the celebration by CEO Jeff Warne, and we were grateful for the reconnection. It was long overdue—and it felt like more than a reunion. For us it was a moment of genuine pride, seeing how many people remained deeply committed to the brand—still carrying forward the spirit we started with all those years ago. It truly felt like a bridge to the future, as much as a look back.

Then in December 2025, the moment we had long hoped for finally arrived: CPK was acquired by a new investor group deeply committed to its future. The group was led by Consortium Brand Partners and backed by financial heavyweights, including Todd Boehly's investment firm, Eldridge Industries, and Bain Capital.

Jon Weber—chief executive officer of Convive Brands, part of the investor group—was named CEO of CPK's restaurant division, while Michael Beacham, who had served as president of CPK, would lead the company's consumer-packaged-goods business.

In announcing the deal, Weber emphasized what he saw as the brand's next chapter. "California Pizza Kitchen is a brand with a remarkable history and an even brighter future," he said in a press release. "As we look to realize its exceptional potential, our focus remains on honoring CPK's legacy, empowering the teams who drive its success every day, and welcoming the next generation of guests to experience the flavors and hospitality that will continue to set it apart."[*]

In that same press release, Jonathan Greller, president and co-founder of Consortium Brand Partners, echoed that enthusiasm as he outlined the group's ambitions. "California Pizza Kitchen is an iconic American brand that has inspired generations of fans through creativity, flavor, and innovations. We are thrilled to partner with Eldridge Industries, Aurify Brands, and Convive Brands to build on CPK's rich heritage by expanding its global restaurant footprint, growing its grocery presence, and exploring new product categories that celebrate California creativity and flavor."

Cory Baker, founder of Consortium Brand Partners, echoed that optimism in an interview: "CPK has extreme brand loyalty for something that's been around for so long . . . and there's an incredible amount of opportunity left."[†]

The new ownership group made clear that franchising would remain

---

* California Pizza Kitchen. "Consortium Brands to Acquire California Pizza Kitchen® in Partnership with Aurify Brands, and Convive Brands." Press release, reported by *Businesswire*, December 16, 2025.

† Abigal Summerville, "Exclusive: California Pizza Kitchen Reaches Buyout Deal, Names New Leadership," *Reuters*, December 16, 2025.

the cornerstone of domestic expansion, focusing on partnerships with a small number of seasoned operators in strategic markets. The company expects to select three or four new multiunit franchisees each year and has already begun engaging with potential partners in Florida, in the mid-Atlantic, and along the East Coast.

To Larry and me, the news was music to our ears. For years it had been painful to sit on the sidelines, watching CPK struggle while controlled by a group of creditors whose primary focus was managing debt rather than growing the brand. It was hard to imagine attracting new franchisees under those circumstances, although one deal was sealed for CPK's successful Nevada region along with Utah. Now with fresh capital and an energized ownership group attacking the business from every direction, the future suddenly looked bright again.

Not long after the announcement, Jon Weber reached out to both of us, eager to meet and hear our perspectives on the brand's history and possibilities ahead. After all these years, that invitation was thrilling—and deeply reassuring. It gave us real confidence that this new team understood what CPK had always been about and where it still might go.

For the first time in a long while, we felt something we hadn't allowed ourselves to feel.

Relief.

CPK had always been bigger than any one group of owners, bigger even than the two of us. It was built on people—line cooks, servers, managers, Restaurant Support Center teams, franchise partners, field leaders, dishwashers, and designers—on thousands of small decisions made every day in kitchens and dining rooms around the world by people who deeply cared. Seeing a new generation step forward with energy and conviction didn't feel like losing something. It felt like the natural next chapter of a story that was still being written. And for the first time in years, we could finally read the opening lines of that chapter with optimism.

To this day nothing means more to us than walking into a CPK and being greeted by longtime employees. The words are always the same: *We miss you.* The feeling is mutual. We miss our CPK family. But in a real sense, we're still connected—bound by the love of a brand that changed our lives, and many others, in ways we once only imagined.

Looking back, it's incredible—but not unbelievable. In 1985 two friends opened a small restaurant in Beverly Hills, inspired by a radical idea I first typed on a word processor in my law office: California Pizza Kitchen would redefine pizza. And it did. We introduced Barbecue Chicken Pizza to the world—and in doing so, we expanded what pizza could be. What began as a bold vision became a reality beyond our wildest dreams.

From the start Larry and I never chased personal fame—we wanted the story to be about the brand, not about us. Still, the unlikely tale of two former federal prosecutors creating a global pizza phenomenon caught people's attention. We leaned into that when it helped the company (and yes, sometimes ourselves too). Our names were never in lights, but every so often, when someone finds out we're the co-founders of CPK, the reaction is always the same: "Wait—you're one of the lawyers?"

Along the way we met extraordinary people—cooks, servers, managers, investors, developers, and vendors—who took a chance on our dream and brought it to life. To all of them, and to everyone who celebrated milestones, shared meals, or made memories inside a CPK, thank you.

You brought the magic.

No matter what happens, CPK will always be our baby. And here's our final consolation: The world is full of former CEOs. But there's no such thing as a former founder.

PREQUEL
(and Then Some)

CHAPTER FORTY-THREE

ENDING THE STORY WITH CPK WOULD'VE BEEN EASY. Clean. Simple. But it wouldn't have been the whole story. CPK didn't happen in a vacuum—everything that came before put Larry and me in a position to make it happen.

And for those friends who've encouraged me to write this, it's often the law stories they've loved most. But my life has been about more than the law. And truthfully, it's been about more than CPK too. It's about the people—the family and friends who've shaped me—and the passions that have brought meaning and joy to my life.

When I set out to write this memoir, I even offered to include Larry's personal story alongside my own. He graciously declined, saying he wanted it to be my memoir. That gave me the freedom to lean into my own perspective while knowing he fully supported the project.

So this "prequel" begins before CPK: through my years as a federal prosecutor, Larry's and my days in private practice (where our partnership deepened and where we discovered we were as strong outside the courtroom as we had been inside it), and my childhood roots in Chicago. From there the timeline loosens, wandering across lifelong friendships, mentors, and hobbies that carried me forward and back, always, to where it all began.

Growing up, I assumed my future was already mapped out. One day I'd join the Chicago firm of Rosenfield and Rosenfield, founded by my father and his brother, a well-known criminal lawyer.

My older brother, Neal, stepped in after my uncle passed away, and it seemed only natural that I'd follow.

But just as that path was coming into view, another door opened—one that felt almost too good to be true. I had just graduated as valedictorian from DePaul University's College of Law, eager to begin my legal career, when an earlier decision came to fruition. Before my final year, I'd been accepted into the Attorney General's Honors Program—the highly selective gateway into the Department of Justice.

Looking back, I hadn't set out to be valedictorian. At the University of Illinois, I'd been a solid B student, more focused on getting into law school than excelling in college. But something shifted at DePaul. From day one I was fully engaged, and when I ranked first after the first semester, I was determined to stay there all the way through graduation. That drive stuck with me.

As an Honors Program appointee, I had my pick of assignments at "Main Justice," the storied building at Tenth and Constitution in Washington, DC. Without hesitation I chose the Appellate Section of the Criminal Division. I wanted to follow in my uncle's footsteps as a criminal lawyer, and at just twenty-four years old, I found myself writing briefs in the United States Supreme Court and arguing cases in federal appellate courts across the country. (A bit of DOJ trivia: Because I was hired through the Honors Program, my starting salary was $11,000 a year instead of the standard $8,000—a monumental difference at the time.)

The Appellate Section was the government's first filter for criminal cases seeking review by the Supreme Court. We reviewed petitions, worked closely with the Solicitor General's Office, and supervised criminal appeals across the circuits. For a young attorney, it was a dream assignment. Not only did I supervise cases, but I was also entrusted to select and argue some myself. At twenty-four it felt almost surreal.

The section was small (barely a dozen attorneys), but it was led by Beatrice "Bea" Rosenberg, one of the most revered lawyers in DOJ history. Bea wasn't just respected; she was legendary. She joined the Antitrust Division in 1943, when few women (let alone Jewish women) held such roles. She rose through brilliance and sheer tenacity. Over her career she argued more than thirty cases before the US Supreme Court—more than any woman in history at the time.

In 1970 I stood in DOJ's Great Hall as Bea became the first woman ever to receive the Tom C. Clark Award for Government Service, bestowed on Washington's most outstanding career lawyer. Supreme Court Justices William Brennan and Thurgood Marshall, both of whom knew her well, considered her the finest lawyer ever to appear before the court. Praise doesn't come higher.

Even after her passing, her legacy lives on. The DC Bar created the Beatrice Rosenberg Award for Excellence in Government Service, still given annually. I've been invited to speak at the ceremony, a privilege I embrace with pride and gratitude for an unforgettable mentor.

Bea was a mentor who gave freely of her time. She reviewed my briefs with a red pencil—line by line—walking me through every edit. It was an incredible education. I often sat in the court to watch oral arguments, but nothing compared to seeing Bea. The atmosphere shifted the moment she stepped to the lectern. Finger raised for emphasis, she spoke with unshakable confidence, and the justices rarely interrupted. It was as if they knew they were in the presence of someone extraordinary. They were.

She mentored many lawyers over the years, young and old. I'm sure some thought they were her favorite. But between us, I've always believed I actually was. What I know for certain is that I was profoundly fortunate and forever grateful for her trust, her guidance, and the foundation she gave me as a young, unseasoned lawyer.

I also learned from others. Theodore "Ted" Gilinsky was a gifted lawyer with a quiet demeanor. I leaned on him often, and he was always there. Only later did I learn that his pronounced limp came from a wound at the Battle of the Bulge, for which he received a Purple Heart. He never mentioned it. That humility stayed with me. Ted embodied the Greatest Generation—men and women who carried their burdens quietly and simply got on with the work in front of them.

Another was Jerome "Jerry" Feil, whose brilliance and depth of experience earned him deep respect across the Solicitor General's Office and US Attorney's Offices nationwide. Jerry was generous with his time, quick to lend perspective, and a helpful force for a young lawyer like me.

Bea, Ted, and Jerry set the standard. And together with the lawyers in the Solicitor General's Office, with whom we regularly interacted, it made every day feel like a graduate seminar in constitutional law.

Not long after I started, I was chosen to represent the Criminal Division for a *Washington Post* profile on the Honors Program—no doubt thanks to Bea's quiet pull. The reporter was Ken Clausen, who later become Richard Nixon's press secretary during Watergate. He asked what I thought of Attorney General John Mitchell, whose law-and-order rhetoric was already divisive.

I answered carefully: "My work is in the Supreme Court, and it remains the same from administration to administration. It doesn't really matter who the attorney general is." The next day's paper opened with "Richard Rosenfield, 25, says he doesn't care who the Attorney General is."

I could only imagine how that landed in the Mitchell household, but it taught me an enduring lesson: Be careful with the press because once you've spoken, you don't control the story.

I met John Mitchell only once, in October 1970, alongside William Rehnquist—then an assistant attorney general, years before he became chief justice. I'd been tapped to represent the Criminal Division in a DOJ initiative tasked with visiting campuses after the Kent State shootings to reassure students and faculty that the Justice Department wasn't spying on them. I repeated those words at the University of Cincinnati and the Claremont Colleges in California. Naively, I believed them to be true.

Then in March 1971 activists broke into an FBI office and exposed COINTELPRO—the bureau's covert program targeting antiwar groups. *The Washington Post* published the files. It was one of my earliest lessons: Even inside the DOJ, you don't always get the truth. A lesson, sadly, that's been proven true too often in the years since.

Those were turbulent years. Vietnam War protests raged, once erupting right outside my office window, where I watched police swing batons into a crowd of demonstrators. When volunteers were sought to report back from the streets, I'll admit, I kept my hand down.

Amid that chaos, I still felt that working in the Appellate Section was an extraordinary privilege. We were a small, tightly knit team, with a hand in every single federal criminal case reaching the Supreme Court. For a young lawyer, it was surreal: Walking into Main Justice each morning knowing I had even a modest role in shaping legal precedent was nothing short of awe-inspiring.

Though I left the practice of law decades ago, the imprint of those early days has never faded. I still follow the court, often listening to arguments and reading opinions. The law, especially at that level, never really leaves you. It shapes how you see the world, long after you've stepped out of the courtroom.

CHAPTER FORTY-FOUR

IN THE MIDST OF THE VIETNAM WAR, MY ASSIGNED SPECIALTY (thanks to Bea) became cases involving conscientious objectors. Congress had exempted those who opposed *all* wars on religious grounds, but in *Welsh v. United States* (1970)—a case I helped brief—the Supreme Court expanded the exemption to include those guided by moral, not just religious, beliefs.

That gave rise to a new type of resister: men who admitted they would have fought in a "just" war such as World War II but who believed Vietnam was morally indefensible. The government classified them as "selective conscientious objectors" and denied them exemption. In *Gillette v. United States*—another case I worked on—the court agreed.

Given my experience in these cases, Bea assigned me one of the most consequential cases of the era: *Cassius Clay a.k.a. Muhammad Ali v. United States.*

Ali was not only the heavyweight champion of the world—he was also a lightning rod for controversy. After his draft board denied him CO status, citing his affiliation with the Nation of Islam, he refused induction and was convicted of draft evasion, sentenced to prison, and stripped of his titles.

Much has been written about the court's deliberations. Bob Woodward's *The Brethren* and HBO's documentary *Muhammad Ali's Greatest Fight* suggest the justices were initially poised to uphold his conviction until Justice John Marshall Harlan II changed his mind after reading more about the Nation of Islam. According to those accounts, the court then "compromised" by reversing the conviction on a technicality rooted in *Sicurella v. United States*, a prior CO case.

I've always found those portrayals surprising. As the most junior lawyer on the case, my job was to review the full record and draft the government's brief.

What I saw was clear: The government's case was fatally weak. The local board's technical errors made the conviction unsupportable. I recommended the government "confess error" and ask the court to overturn the conviction.

I wasn't in the room when Solicitor General Erwin Griswold made the final call, but I know Bea agreed with my conclusion. The government stopped short of confessing error, but our brief openly acknowledged the flaws and cited *Sicurella* four times. That gave the court the legal path to reverse.

Which is why I've never believed the tale of a law clerk's "last-minute discovery" of *Sicurella*. It was right there in the brief. The case wasn't a mystery. It was law applied to fact, and the right result followed.

The larger lesson, though, is sobering. If five justices really did vote to uphold Ali's conviction, only to shift later, it shows how outcomes even at the highest court can turn not just on precedent but on human judgment and the mood of the times. It is the inescapable reality, one that resonates even today. Justice may be blind, but it is ultimately rendered by human hands.

For me the case was unforgettable. At twenty-five to have a role in *Muhammad Ali v. United States* was surreal. I wasn't thinking in terms of history. I was just doing my job. But years later, when books and documentaries revisited the case, I couldn't help but look back in awe. I had been there, in the thick of it, seeing firsthand how fragile justice can be and how, at its best, it still finds its way.

CHAPTER FORTY-FIVE

ANOTHER EARLY CASE THAT HELPED SHAPE MY PERSONAL views was *United States v. Thirty-Seven (37) Photographs*, after US Customs agents seized thirty-seven black-and-white photographs from a traveler and the Justice Department moved to have them declared obscene.

You may remember Justice Potter Stewart's famous line that he didn't know how to define hardcore pornography, "but I know it when I see it." I went to the Supreme Court to examine the evidence myself. What I saw left me shaking my head, not because the images were shocking but because they *weren't*. They were simple black-and-white nude studies, almost artistic, the kind of thing you could imagine hanging in a gallery.

By then I had already had strong opinions about privacy and government overreach. I believed the government had no business interfering in private matters between consenting adults. Yet I carpooled with two young lawyers from the Criminal Division who spent their days screening "stag films" and "dirty" photographs, then laughed about it in the car while prosecuting the very people who made them. The hypocrisy was almost comical, if it wasn't such a waste of taxpayer dollars.

The irony didn't stop there. Bob Woodward's *The Brethren* later revealed that the Supreme Court justices themselves held regular "movie days," screening potentially obscene films with their law clerks. I've often joked that my rewrite of Justice Stewart's line would be "I don't know how to define pornography, but I know what I like!" I have no doubt that at least the clerks enjoyed their government-sponsored showings.

After reviewing the thirty-seven photographs, I walked straight into Bea's office and said, "I want off the case, and I don't want anything to do with obscenity cases." Without hesitation Bea nodded. She understood completely.

CHAPTER FORTY-SIX

DEFINITELY AMONG MY MOST INTERESTING CASES WAS *United States v. The Founding Church of Scientology,* a civil forfeiture brought by the FDA in the church's early days. Agents had seized the now infamous "E-Meters," along with stacks of literature, claiming they contained "false and misleading labeling" under the Food, Drug, and Cosmetic Act.

At the center was the so-called Hubbard Electrometer. According to Scientology, it could diagnose and cure disease. When I went to inspect one at the Supreme Court, I found myself staring at two Campbell's Soup cans wired to a meter. Not "soup-can-like." Actual Campbell's Soup cans. As a scientific instrument, it looked more like something from the telephone game we played as kids than a medical device.

The legal problem snag was obvious. Scientology had clearly exaggerated the E-Meter's powers, but the FDA had gone overboard—confiscating not only the devices but also truckloads of church literature. In their zeal they'd managed to turn a straightforward false-labeling case into a fight over the First and Fourth Amendments: religious freedom and unreasonable search and seizure. From the start it was a losing battle in the Supreme Court.

Still, I did my part—drafted the government's brief, had it approved by Bea and the Solicitor General's Office, and watched the case predictably die when the court declined review.

Hard to imagine then, but that soup-can contraption (something that looked like a playground toy) would go on to power one of the most controversial institutions in Hollywood and one of the most polarizing movements in the world. What seemed laughable in the courtroom turned out to be a force with real and lasting consequences.

CHAPTER FORTY-SEVEN

IN THE WINTER OF 1969, AN OPPORTUNITY AROSE THAT nudged me toward California. In addition to handling Supreme Court cases, the Appellate Section also supervised appeals in the federal circuits—including those from the Virgin Islands, which went to the Third Circuit in Philadelphia. Naturally, the judges preferred to hear those cases in January in Saint Thomas rather than in icy Philadelphia. That seemed like a splendid idea to me, so I chose a case to argue there.

Departing Washington's snow, I landed in sun-drenched Saint Thomas, where an FBI agent in a floral shirt scooped me up at the airport. A couple of cold Heinekens—"greenies," as the locals called them—at a waterside bar and I was already feeling the tug of island life.

After spending time with the US attorney, Robert Carney, a transplanted New Yorker, he even offered me the lofty-sounding role of "first assistant United States attorney." In reality it was a two-man office. The lifestyle was tempting, but with my then-wife expecting our son, Ian, and my love for the work in Washington, I passed.

Still, when I got back to DC, shivering in the cold, I couldn't shake thoughts of warmer weather. With cousins in California, I'd always imagined retiring there someday. Then it hit me: Why wait? Why not take the California Bar now and keep my options open?

So, heart pounding, I walked into Bea Rosenberg's office with a proposal: a temporary assignment at the US Attorney's Office in Los Angeles during the Supreme Court's summer recess. Trial experience, I argued, would perfectly complement my appellate work. To my relief Bea agreed.

With her legendary reputation, one call to US Attorney Robert "Bob" Meyer in Los Angeles was enough to make it happen.

When I saw the draft of Bea's glowing introductory letter, though, I asked her to add one condition: I wouldn't touch pornography cases. Los Angeles was ground zero for those prosecutions, and I wanted no part of them.

Sometime after I arrived, Meyer brought it up with a raised eyebrow. "Would we have a problem if I asked you to handle a pornography case?"

Without missing a beat, I answered, "We won't have a problem—as long as you don't ask." To his credit he never did.

That summer in Los Angeles turned out to be life-changing. It was when I met Larry Flax. We clicked right away. Larry looked like he'd stepped straight off a movie set—tall, handsome, prematurely gray, charismatic, and tan. California personified. Years later I'd give him the nickname that stuck: Hollywood Flax.

The US Attorney's Criminal Division in Los Angeles was small then—barely twenty lawyers compared with more than a hundred today. The camaraderie was instant, and I was welcomed with open arms. After trying my first jury trials, I carved out two weeks to study for the California Bar. Having just taken the Illinois Bar a year earlier, I felt confident.

Before I returned to Washington, Meyer sweetened the deal by offering me a permanent position as an assistant US attorney, with the added promise of creating a new Appellate Section and naming me its first chief. The lure of California, the friendships I'd made, and the professional opportunity were irresistible.

But above all, I didn't want to disappoint Bea. When I called her, she was characteristically blunt, playing on my Jewish guilt with a single line: "I sent you out there on this boondoggle, and you owe me."

That settled it. Out of respect for Bea, I committed to another year in DC.

Still, Meyer kept checking in. On one especially brutal winter day in Washington, he called, his voice tinged with mischief. "So how's the weather there?"

"It's minus forty with the windchill," I admitted.

"It's ninety here in LA," he replied.

The 130-degree difference was the tipping point. I laughed and told him, "Bob, I'm coming."

True to my word, I honored my commitment to Bea and stayed another year in DC before heading west. The move was deeply upsetting to my father and brother, who had always hoped that after my time in Washington, I'd return to Chicago and join the family firm. But I couldn't see myself practicing law there. After my time in Washington—working with the DOJ's brightest minds and seeing the law at its highest standards—I couldn't imagine returning to a system where corruption was still whispered about as routine. I dutifully kept up my Illinois Bar membership, but I never practiced a single case there.

To be clear not everyone in Chicago's system was compromised. My lifelong friend Judge James "Jimmy" Linn built an extraordinary career there, first as a prosecutor and defense attorney and later as a widely respected judge. His last case, the trial of actor Jussie Smollett, drew national attention, and his scathing but fair sentencing remarks went viral—a testament to his integrity. Jimmy assures me corruption in Chicago's courts has largely been rooted out. I believe it's true as to Jimmy. I've watched him in court. He's one of those rare judges that either side would be happy to have presiding over their case. Still, I'm just not sure about the system as a whole.

Back in DC, working under Bea, my moral compass was reinforced daily. More than once, when I concluded a conviction was legally defective, I'd walk into Bea's office and explain my reasoning, and she never hesitated. I would draft the government's brief confessing error, and the Supreme Court would reverse. To have the power to do the right thing at that level was indescribable.

Yet California was calling. When I went into Bea's office that final time, she looked at me with the warmth and clarity I had come to rely on. "Don't let them corrupt you," she said. It wasn't just a farewell; it was heavy with emotion. Bea had taken me under her wing from the start and took pride in my growth. She wasn't just a mentor; she was something close to family. She knew me then as I was: a young lawyer who loved the law and believed deeply in doing the right thing. Her words weren't only about the challenges of trial work; they were a reminder to hold tight to integrity and purpose.

I didn't realize it at the time, but that moment would become my North Star in a very different world to come.

Leaving Washington meant leaving behind a city where I had found my footing and purpose, lifted by colleagues who inspired me daily. As the plane lifted toward Los Angeles, I stared out the window. Just a few years earlier, I had been a kid from the South Side of Chicago. Now I was stepping into the unknown.

It was no small leap. For as long as I could remember, the plan had been to return home and join my father and brother in the family practice. I loved my father deeply, and breaking from that path came with real emotion. Looking back, I see how much of the man I became traces directly to him—the way he lived and the passions that drove him. He set the tone, not only for my career but for how I aspired to move through the world.

CHAPTER FORTY-EIGHT

WHEN I ARRIVED IN LOS ANGELES—THIS TIME FOR good—I was once again welcomed as if I'd never left. It felt like home almost immediately. From my summer stint the year before, I already knew that Bob Meyer, the US attorney who'd recruited me, believed in me. Standing firmly beside him was Robert "Bob" Brosio, chief of the Criminal Division—the steady hand and institutional backbone of the office. His brother, Fred Brosio, led the Civil Division. Together, the Brosios were fixtures of the Los Angeles legal community; the *Los Angeles Times* once described them as "virtually an institution within an institution."

Bob Brosio was a true Renaissance man: equally at ease discussing history, film, or Stanford football, always with authority and wit. His influence in the office was such that after his twenty-eight-year career, the main conference room was named in his honor, anchored by a full-length portrait of him in a dark suit, flanked by smaller portraits of the former US attorneys he had outlasted and, more than once, outshone.

I had no doubt their confidence in me stemmed from Bea Rosenberg's early imprimatur. Her reputation carried weight in every US Attorney's Office in the country, and Bob Brosio spoke with her often. Bea, ever loyal, made a point of checking in on me regularly.

I landed on what became known as the *Frontier Hotel Case*, thanks to perfect timing. It spun out of the infamous Friars Club "card-peeking" scandal—where celebrities such as Zeppo Marx and Phil Silvers were fleeced in rigged poker games. Spotters hid above the room, peering through drilled holes in the ceiling and signaling hands electronically. Losses totaled $400,000 (roughly $4 million today).

That prosecution convicted mob figure Johnny Roselli and, with him, Maurice "Maury" Friedman, president of Las Vegas's Frontier Hotel. Friedman flipped, confessing to FBI Special Agent Wayne Hill that he'd helped Detroit mobster boss Anthony "Tony Z" Zerilli and "Capo" Mike Polizzi conceal unlicensed interests in the hotel, with Anthony "Tony" Giordano, the St. Louis boss, also involved. Eight men were charged under the "Travel Act"—a prequel to RICO.

The case was led by Tom Kotoske, a former marine and ex—Purdue defensive back. I was brought in for my appellate experience and given an early pivotal task: Get charges against Emprise Corporation reinstated. Emprise (founded by sports concession magnate Louis "Louie" Jacobs) was alleged to have helped finance the hidden stake.

The hearing landed before Judge Gus Solomon, a visiting judge from Portland. I flew to Oregon to argue the issue—a technical but critical question of corporate criminal liability. I hadn't been speaking long when Judge Solomon cut me off: "Mr. Rosenfield, I've heard enough. I'm going to rule in your favor."

I kept pressing until he gave me a lesson I never forgot: "When I say I'm going to rule in your favor, you sit down."

After the Portland win, I was named coprosecutor on the marquee trial in downtown Los Angeles. It was 1972, and to me, at twenty-six years of age, it was the trial of a lifetime.

The defense table was a who's who. Emprise had Joseph "Joe" Ball, revered nationally and senior counsel to the Warren Commission; his partner, former Governor Pat Brown, gave the firm political heft, while his son Jerry was on the rise. John P. Frank—who argued and won *Miranda v. Arizona*—rounded out the Emprise bench. Zerilli had William Weinstein, a marine major general turned lawyer. Giordano had Irl Baris, with two Supreme Court wins. The rest were backed by some of Los Angeles top attorneys, including several former federal prosecutors. It was the most formidable defense phalanx I'd ever seen.

On our side: Tom Kotoske, me, and Wayne Hill—one of the most ethical and experienced agents I ever had the honor of working with. On paper we were outgunned. (Pun intended.)

Tom prosecuted like a battering ram—loud, relentless, and forever testing the edges of propriety (the Ninth Circuit later said as much). He'd inflame the defense; I'd mop up the legal mess—drafting responses to a blizzard of motions backed by teams of associates who were billing by the hour. I worked around the clock—on a government salary.

The trial ran forty-eight days (spread over four months): 11,022 pages of transcript and 321 exhibits. The Ninth Circuit later opened its opinion with a shrug: The appellants had lobbed 534 pages of arguments, so a long opinion was "unavoidable."

With allegations of hidden Mafia ownership in a Vegas casino, the press feasted. Zerilli and Polizzi had recently appeared by name in the Congressional Record as mob figures. The public was riveted.

Early on the defense moved to dismiss, claiming the case was tainted by illegal electronic surveillance—warrantless bugs ordered years earlier by Attorney General Robert Kennedy in his war on organized crime. The DOJ had already disclosed a Detroit bug at the Giacalone Brothers' "Home Juice Company" office (yes, orange juice). One brother, Tony "Tony Jack" Giacalone, would later be infamous in the Hoffa saga—as the person Hoffa was going to meet for lunch before he disappeared.

Our case had nothing to do with any of that. The spark was Friedman's cooperation. Still, when the judge ordered a check, I asked the DOJ to search FBI files. Back came the surprise: Both Zerilli and Polizzi had been overheard on those Detroit bugs. Boxes of transcripts arrived—thousands of pages from 1962 to 1965. It fell to me—the twenty-six-year-old kid from Chicago—to read every word from those transcripts and later prove our case was built wholly independent of those tapes. Alone at night with those transcripts stacked high, I felt as if I were staring into a world I wasn't meant to see.

Meanwhile, *The Godfather* hit theaters mid-trial and turned our courtroom into pop culture catnip. Defense counsel cried that the jury pool was poisoned. (They weren't sequestered; avoiding headlines in Los Angeles over four months was fiction.)

It was the kind of tension no law school classroom could ever prepare you for. And for me it was baptism by fire.

The most explosive moment came when Mike Polizzi took the stand. Let me pause here with a brief observation: When an organized crime defendant decides to testify, he's not just throwing caution to the wind—he's inviting a hurricane.

Polizzi threw out the gauntlet, insisting that he had been falsely labeled as a Mafia member by the government. We would never have introduced that label, but he opened that door and ripped it off its hinges. Given the media atmosphere, he drew a bright-red circle around the elephant in the room. The courtroom, already crackling with tension, now felt like the set of a Coppola film.

Polizzi was lying. We knew it then, but years later his own son testified in another case that his father admitted to being a "made" man and holding an illegal ownership interest in the Frontier Hotel—exactly as we had alleged.

Evidence 101: The government can't use illegally obtained information in its case in chief, but if a defendant lies on the stand, he "opens the door" to impeachment—even with evidence otherwise off-limits.

Tom didn't miss a beat. At sidebar he argued that Polizzi's perjury opened the door to the Detroit tapes. He vividly described the hierarchy and operations laid bare in those transcripts, the very pages I had painstakingly flagged.

But the drama didn't stop there.

The next morning the *Los Angeles Times* splashed a front-page story: "Transcript Shows U.S. Bugged Mafia Talks." Somehow their reporter had obtained a sidebar transcript. Needless to say it caused a firestorm. Tom and I were called to court and asked to state, on the record, that we hadn't leaked it. I did not. To this day I don't know how the reporter got it.

Publicity aside, the evidence had its own drama. A bank vice president testified about a meeting in a Las Vegas suite where Friedman pushed for a bigger construction loan, while Zerilli sat there silently.

When asked what security they could offer, Zerilli finally spoke. "Cash in a suitcase." The Jewish banker turned to Friedman and, referring to the bank's owner, muttered in Yiddish, "What's the old man going to say when I show up with a suitcase full of $1.5 million?" You could hear a pin drop.

Then came Hattiesburg. Both the banker and Friedman said one other man was in that suite: T. W. Richardson, a Mississippi "point holder" in the hotel. We subpoenaed him, but he claimed he was too ill to travel.

We invoked a rarely used tool: a criminal deposition. Off we went to Hattiesburg, with the defense attorneys and many of the defendants, including Zerilli.

Richardson testified and claimed, under oath, that he remembered nothing. His feeble excuse? "I was so tired from my trip, I fell asleep on the couch in the hotel suite."

Of course, he was lying. And while I couldn't see it clearly in the heat of battle, I've since come to a reluctant truth: Who could blame him? Zerilli had flown to Mississippi for one reason—to sit there, stone-faced, and stare him down.

Still, Richardson gave me what I needed. After four months of trial, the defense delivered fourteen hours of closing arguments across several days—hours of pounding the same themes: vendetta, holes, missing witnesses. Table-pounding theater.

But we had the last word.

I stayed measured and calm, sticking to the evidence, and then closed: "Ladies and gentlemen, after fourteen hours of defense counsel pounding the podium and attacking the prosecutors, I'm reminded of the old saying: When the law is in your favor, pound on the law. When the facts are in your favor, pound on the facts. But when neither is in your favor . . . pound on the prosecutors—and pound on the table."

And then I finished: "You've heard a lot about the awesome power of the federal government. With all that power they ask, why didn't we bring this witness or that one? Well, let me tell you something about power. With all the awesome power of the federal government at our disposal . . . *we couldn't wake up T. W. Richardson on that hotel suite couch*."

Silence. Punch landed. Zerilli's trip to Hattiesburg backfired.

I was quite flattered when several defense attorneys later told me my closing argument had been devastating. They'd convinced themselves that their clients wouldn't be convicted. They were wrong.

Zerilli, Polizzi, and Giordano each received four-year prison sentences.

Emprise Corporation was also convicted and fined. (Corporations can't be jailed.) Though Louie Jacobs had died before trial, he was named as an unindicted coconspirator. The evidence showed intimate involvement.

The fallout was swift. Liquor licenses at ballparks, racetracks, and arenas were yanked. *Sports Illustrated* put Louie on the cover as "The Godfather of Sports," with "What Louie Has Wrought."

Years later his uninvolved son Jeremy rebranded Emprise as Delaware North and built a multibillion-dollar hospitality empire, bought the Boston Bruins, and became a respected philanthropist. He will be remembered for his own achievements, not his father's sins.

People sometimes ask if I was afraid to prosecute the mob. Honestly, no. I was twenty-six and felt indestructible. I knew the Italian mob historically avoided targeting prosecutors or FBI agents. They didn't want to bring that kind of heat.

We even bantered in the hallways. Just before my closing argument, Giordano, boss of the St. Louis mob, approached me: "Ricky, are you going to mention me today?"

Of all the defendants, our case against him—the single conspiracy count—was the thinnest. I smiled. "Tony, you've sat through months of trial and barely heard your name mentioned. But today is your day."

He didn't laugh.

CHAPTER FORTY-NINE

ON APRIL 13, 1972, RICARDO CHAVEZ ORTIZ STORMED the cabin of Frontier Airlines Flight 91, a pistol in his hand and desperation in his eyes. He forced his way into the cockpit and ordered the pilots to Los Angeles, then Mexico. At LAX he released the passengers, summoned Spanish-speaking reporters, and delivered a rambling speech about the plight of Mexican Americans before finally surrendering.

The headlines came instantly. To activists he was a folk hero. To the rest of the country, a hijacker. The protests were so loud, the courthouse installed magnetometers for the first time—an innovation that spread across America.

Fresh off the four-month Frontier Hotel mob trial, I was handed the case. Just past my twenty-seventh birthday. My first solo major prosecution. And it had all the ingredients of a spectacle.

The law was clear: Air piracy carried twenty years to life. But his lawyers—a blend of public defenders and MALDEF (Mexican American Legal Defense and Educational Fund) attorneys—tried to have it both ways. He was both a principled activist and insane. They leaned on his own words: The gun was unloaded, and he had hijacked the plane "to save America and the world."

The trial landed before Judge Charles H. Carr, a man whose reputation preceded him. A Southern transplant with a taste for intimidation, named the meanest federal judge in the nation in a book, *The Benchwarmers*, Carr wielded sarcasm like a whip. He once sentenced a seventy-five-year-old bank robber to twenty-five years. When the man protested that he was too old to serve, Carr replied, "Just do the best you can."

I braced myself. On day one I rose at the lectern: "Richard Rosenfield, for the United States."

Carr cut me off mid-sentence. "Counselor, don't waste the court's time. Make your appearance from the table."

The next morning, obediently, I did just that.

He pounced again. "Counsel, have you no courtesy? Make your appearance from the lectern!" With Charlie Carr you were damned either way.

The defense pushed insanity. At that time juries weren't told that an insanity verdict meant freedom, not treatment. They tried to have it both ways: martyr and madman.

Our expert, Dr. Seymour Pollack, testified that Ortiz knew exactly what he was doing. At the crucial moment, I asked him the defining question. Carr, with theatrical flourish, cut me off.

"Counsel, are you familiar with a Ninth Circuit case directly on point? How come the government didn't know about it?"

"Your Honor," I shot back, "I have more than a passing familiarity with that case. I represented the government of the United States in the court of appeals."

The jury leaned forward. Carr barked at his clerk to fetch the law book. Moments later, with the jury still in the box, he read aloud, "Richard L. Rosenfield, on behalf of the United States."

Then he looked at me. "Why didn't you tell me earlier?"

"When the issue came up, Your Honor, you ruled in my favor so fast. You didn't give me time."

The room broke apart in laughter. Even Carr allowed himself a grin. The defense table looked stricken.

But the real drama came the night before closing arguments. My voice was gone. I could barely whisper. A Beverly Hills doctor shoved a vile solution up my nose and told me not to speak. That night, in the dark, I whispered over and over: "Ladies and gentlemen of the jury . . . ladies and gentlemen of the jury . . ."

The next morning I tested the microphone with a whisper. "Ladies and gentlemen of the jury—"

Carr exploded: "Mr. Rosenfield, what are you doing? Speak up!"

And just like that, my voice came roaring back. His bark had jolted me into full strength. Without realizing it Judge Carr had saved my closing argument.

Six hours later the jury returned a verdict: guilty.

The protests outside didn't matter. The speeches didn't matter. The unloaded gun didn't matter. What mattered was that Ricardo Chavez Ortiz had hijacked a plane, terrified its passengers, and crossed a line no cause could excuse.

He wasn't a martyr. He wasn't a hero. He was guilty. And justice had been done.

CHAPTER FIFTY

I HAVE ONLY FOND MEMORIES OF MY TIME AT THE DEPARTMENT of Justice. In Washington it meant walking each morning into the stately entrance on Pennsylvania Avenue, surrounded mostly by career lawyers quietly devoted to the craft of doing justice. In Los Angeles it meant working alongside assistant US attorneys who, like Larry and me, were young, ambitious, and eager to prove themselves. In both places there was a shared sense of passion and purpose.

Every time I stood up in court—whether in district court or in a court of appeals—I felt a surge of pride announcing, "Richard Rosenfield, on behalf of the United States." I briefed and argued cases in four circuits—California, Pennsylvania, Illinois, and Florida. And during my stint in Washington, I not only worked on cases in the Supreme Court but also had the extraordinary opportunity to sit in on virtually every criminal argument heard there. For a young lawyer, it was intoxicating.

I never lost a case I prosecuted. But then again, why should I have? I only prosecuted guilty people, and at the time the US Attorney's Office had a 95 percent conviction rate, thanks in no small part to guilty pleas.

I wasn't a hard-liner across the board, though. I reserved my sharpest edge for defendants who were truly bad actors. At my core I believed in fairness and in the Justice Department motto that the government wins whenever justice is done.

While I loved being in California and the heat of battle in trials, I stayed in touch with Bea and other colleagues in Washington. One day Bea called to say the Criminal Division wanted me back to lead a program rewriting sections of the Federal Criminal Code. After some persuasion, I agreed to return for six months.

It was great to see old friends, but drafting legislation bored me to death. I missed the fight of trial work. Before I left, Herb Hoffman, counsel for the House Judiciary Committee, called. His first question was unforgettable: "Can you say with a straight face that you're a Republican?"

Growing up in Chicago, I'd probably never met a Republican. My DOJ appointment had been apolitical through the Honors Program. I told him half-jokingly, "I'm like a willow tree—just tell me which way the wind is blowing."

Herb offered me a job as counsel to the House Subcommittee on Criminal Law.

It was flattering, but I wasn't interested. I wanted to get back to Los Angeles. Much later, as I was preparing to leave government for private practice with Larry, Herb tried one last time: "Rick, you could be majority or minority counsel. Your choice. Two years on the Hill, back to Justice as assistant attorney general, then counsel to the president. You can be another John Dean!"

In 1973 that still sounded like a golden path. Of course, when Dean's role in Watergate was exposed, I couldn't resist calling Herb: "Herb, thanks so much for the opportunity!"

And with that the die was cast. I turned down Washington power, threw caution to the wind, and leaped into private practice with Larry—a decision that would change everything.

CHAPTER FIFTY-ONE

OUR FIRST BOLD LEAP WASN'T INTO THE RESTAURANT business—it was leaving the security of our jobs as federal prosecutors for the uncertain world of private practice. Larry went first in 1972, joining the Los Angeles firm of Stern, Lewann & Hanessian. It was more step than leap; he had the safety net of an established firm.

From the moment he left, Larry urged me to follow. I wasn't ready. I loved my work at the US Attorney's Office and had exciting cases ahead. Still, I never saw myself as a career prosecutor, and teaming up with Larry was tempting. I wasn't in a rush—but I knew it would happen. Larry knew it too.

A year later I gave in. From the outset we built a unique arrangement that foreshadowed our bond: a true partnership, splitting clients and fees right down the middle.

Our time at that firm didn't last long. I had just finished my first civil jury trial when Larry and I went with a client to Las Vegas. Lounging by the pool, I got a call from one of the partners ordering me back to Los Angeles to help him prepare for a case. That was my breaking point. I hadn't left the government to take orders from another lawyer.

Larry and I had already floated the idea of starting our own practice. That phone call pushed us off the diving board. This wasn't a step; it was a leap. We didn't have a client base yet, but we were determined. Ready or not, the law firm of Flax & Rosenfield was officially open for business.

Looking back, it was the earliest sign of our entrepreneurial spirit. In March 1973 we opened in Century City, sharing space with lawyers who became lifelong friends. Among them was Bob Kahan, who from the start of

CPK became our personal lawyer, staying by our side through the PepsiCo years and every deal that followed. Another was Bob Mandler, founder of Chin Chin on the Sunset Strip. His wildly successful restaurant—launched just a year before CPK—was both inspiration and education, and he generously shared his playbook.

Running our own firm gave us more than independence; it gave us the confidence to bet on ourselves. That instinct—back then just a survival skill—would later become the foundation for CPK.

We also had the good fortune of working with an extraordinary legal secretary, Mary Craig Calkins. She ran our office while attending Loyola Law School at night. When she graduated and left to build her own career, she became one of the city's most respected litigators. It was a loss for us but a source of pride.

A couple of years later, we commissioned a Tiffany glass artist in Aspen to design our partnership logo: the three monkeys—"hear no evil, speak no evil, see no evil"—with a banner reading "Flax & Rosenfield, Established 1973." It hung proudly in our office.

My walls were a collage of reminders and inside jokes. Next to a DOJ plaque signed by John Mitchell were two cartoons. One showed a fisherman holding up his catch: "If he hadn't opened his mouth, he wouldn't have gotten caught!" The other had a judge slipping into his robe while telling a colleague, "At home, I'm a plain, ordinary schlub. But here, I put on my robe, and by God, I'm it!"

And behind my desk, in bold letters, hung my favorite maxim: "When you've got them by the balls, their hearts and minds will follow."

That mix of irreverence and grit defined our practice. We took the law seriously but not ourselves—and that balance kept us sharp. The same instincts that shaped our office culture—confidence, humor, and a willingness to bet on ourselves—would later drive us to take an even greater leap. From the courtroom to Century City to Beverly Hills, the spirit was the same.

CHAPTER FIFTY-TWO

OUR FIRST CLIENT WAS A TRUE HOLLYWOOD CHARACTER: Allen Wells, owner of the once-famous Classic Cat, a topless-and-bottomless bar on the Sunset Strip. The "performances" were little more than simple nudity, but that was enough to put the so-called obscenity police on high alert. With the California Supreme Court having just upheld Los Angeles's antinudity laws, local authorities staged a sweeping crackdown, raiding twenty-eight establishments—including the Classic Cat. I always suspected some of the officers were far more eager than reluctant to conduct these raids, just as certain former colleagues of mine at the DOJ had seemed a little too enthusiastic when reviewing obscene materials in their cases.

To fight back, Larry and I filed for a temporary restraining order and injunction. Our argument turned on a narrow exemption in the ordinance: Venues classified as a "theater lounge" were permitted to feature nudity. At the hearing Larry passionately made our case—but in his zeal, he went a step too far, telling the judge, "Your Honor, think of the Classic Cat as a small Dorothy Chandler Pavilion."

The comparison between a Sunset Strip nude bar and Los Angeles's most prestigious performing arts venue nearly sent me out of my chair. Worse, a *Wall Street Journal* reporter sitting in court picked up the quote and printed it.

We lost, of course. And I never let Larry live that analogy down.

Undeterred, Wells tried to rebrand. He dropped "Cat" from the name, called it simply the Classic, and for a brief time, staged a surprisingly good production of *Jacques Brel Is Alive and Well and Living in Paris.*

Unfortunately, it bombed. The customers on the Sunset Strip were looking for something quite different—and Wells had also lost his most reliable audience: the undercover cops who'd been so determined to "protect" the citizens of Los Angeles from themselves.

CHAPTER FIFTY-THREE

ANOTHER EARLY CLIENT WAS JACK GINSBURG, A WILDLY successful pornographer. The business was unseemly, no doubt, but I've never apologized for representing him. My view was simple: Unless it was child pornography or shoved on people without consent, the government had no business interfering. But honestly, it wasn't about principle—we were hired guns. Everyone deserves a defense, especially when they're paying the bills. And Jack? He was rolling in money.

He liked to spread it around too. He took Larry and me to some of the best restaurants in Los Angeles, and he was the first to introduce us to Dom Pérignon. Not bad fringe benefits for two young lawyers.

Jack also loved cars. In 1974 Jaguar had just given its four-door sedan a facelift, and he wanted a look. I'd driven my friend Burton Goldberg's '67 XK-E convertible in Miami—gorgeous to the eye, junk under the hood—and Jack agreed. But the new sedan had potential.

We walked into the local Jaguar dealership: me in a sharp Italian suit, looking every bit the young successful lawyer, and Jack in a scruffy beard and clothes that made him look like he'd wandered in off the street. The salesman ignored us. Finally, I told him my friend wanted to test-drive the sedan. He barely looked up, muttering that the cars were back-ordered for months.

I pointed to a British-racing-green sedan sitting right on the showroom floor.

"How about that one?" I asked.

Reluctantly, the salesman admitted it was available. Jack asked, "How much?"

"Seventeen thousand," came the smug reply.

"I'll take it," Jack said, pulling a thick stack of hundred-dollar bills from his pocket.

The look on the salesman's face was priceless. And for me it was a reminder of something I'd learned years earlier selling sporting goods during law school: Treat everyone with respect. You can't judge a book by its cover.

It was a lesson I carried with me into everything that followed—especially CPK, where respecting people, no matter who they were or how they looked, became part of the culture that defined us.

CHAPTER FIFTY-FOUR

BECAUSE LARRY AND I HAD JUST LEFT THE US ATTORNEY'S Office, most of our defense work was white collar. We knew the rules of federal court, the culture of prosecutors, and the temperaments of judges. That gave us an edge. But every now and then, we found ourselves face-to-face with cases that blurred the line between high finance, labor unions, and organized crime.

Our first major client was Joe Hauser, a Beverly Hills high roller who lived in a tennis-courted estate but was being pursued by Dick Crane, head of the Justice Department's Organized Crime Strike Force in Los Angeles. Hauser was under investigation for bribing union officials to steer business to his Miami insurance company.

No client ever protested his innocence louder than Joe. He insisted it was a witch hunt. Charismatic and a high-stakes gambler, he could drop $50,000 in a single night in Las Vegas (the equivalent of $300,000 today). As the saying goes, that's why they build the casinos.

Joe's world was a swirl of union bosses, politicians, and shadowy organized crime figures. He was persuasive, apparently sincere, and devoted to his family—everything a con man needs to be until the truth catches up. We did our job, gave him the best defense we could, and—admittedly—enjoyed the ride.

Early in our representation, Joe introduced us to his close friend Bernard "Bernie" Rubin, a powerful South Florida labor leader. Rubin was no stereotypical thug. A decorated veteran of World War II and Korea, he carried himself more like a diplomat than a union boss: handsome, gray-haired, impeccably dressed, with a beautiful home, a lovely family, and a cellar of fine Bordeaux. With Bernie, I tasted wines I couldn't yet afford.

The Strike Force, however, wasn't interested in his charm. Rubin headed four Laborers' Union entities, and when investigators audited them simultaneously, they found a brazen scheme. Bernie routinely double-, triple-, and quadruple-billed expenses. A $2,000 conference suddenly became $8,000 in reimbursements. The total ran into hundreds of thousands—all cashed, never deposited.

Indicted on 103 counts, including racketeering under the brand-new RICO statute, Bernie claimed he used the money as a cash pool to help union members in distress. We brought witnesses to support that story, but accounting for all the money proved impossible.

Larry and I defended him in Miami federal court. It was grim. Our only real hope was jury nullification in the form of a hung jury. For a moment we thought we had it. One elderly Jewish woman on the panel grew furious at the prosecutor during cross-examination, shouting, "You sit down and leave him alone!" A gift from heaven. But she soon developed a painful case of diverticulitis and had to be dismissed. So much for divine intervention.

Then came my closing argument. Midway through, a juror broke down crying and fainted. Bernie thought it was a good sign. We had to tell him the truth: "If she were ready to acquit you, she wouldn't be so troubled."

He was convicted, as we expected. He hadn't expected it at all.

Only later did we learn the full picture. Hauser and Rubin were deeply entangled in a nationwide scheme: Hauser bribed Rubin and other union officials to secure contracts for his insurance companies. Both men eventually pleaded guilty in Arizona, their downfall detailed in a 215-page Senate report.

To their credit—or perhaps their cunning—they never tried to involve us. They wanted us to believe in their innocence. Discovering the full extent of their crimes later was deeply disheartening.

Not everyone in their orbit escaped unscathed. Richard Kleindienst, the former US attorney general, was suspended from practice for his involvement. Hauser, seeking leniency, turned government witness in the FBI's "Brilab" sting, helping convict New Orleans boss Carlos Marcello—the man long rumored, though never proven, to have ties to the Kennedy assassination.

By then Joe and Bernie were long gone from our lives. But their shadows lingered—a reminder that sometimes the most polished, charming men are the ones running the dirtiest games.

Both the Hauser and Rubin cases went to trial because negotiating them out wasn't an option. Both men claimed innocence and demanded their day in court. Yet in 90 to 95 percent of our cases, we never saw a jury. Our strength was in pretrial negotiation: knowing when to push, when to settle, and when to tell a client the hard truth—that their best option was to flip.

But every so often, bold action was the only defense. And sometimes the irony cut both ways: Hauser and Rubin had tried to fool us into believing in their innocence. In this next case, the client himself had been the one fooled.

CHAPTER FIFTY-FIVE

IT BEGAN WITH A PERSONAL FRIEND OF MINE, A WEALTHY man with homes in Houston, New Orleans, and the Cayman Islands. Pale and shaken, he confessed that he was about to be indicted in Washington, DC, under the federal Corrupt Practices Act. His story spilled out in one breath: He had flown his private jet to Mexico and hand-delivered $250,000 in cash—stuffed into a rolled-up architect's blueprint tube—to the president of his company, who was supposed to pass the money along as a bribe to a Mexican official to approve a power plant.

It sounded like the plot of a bad movie, and it was about to become a federal indictment.

Larry and I contacted the prosecutor, confirmed the charges were imminent, and secured time to investigate. What followed was a whirlwind—trips to Mexico, then to Manchester, England, chasing paper trails and interviewing anyone who could shed light. The prosecutor warned us his star witness was ready: the company president himself, prepared to testify that the bribe had been made.

Then came the break. We uncovered that shortly after the supposed payoff, the president and two Mexican associates each deposited about $75,000 into their personal bank accounts. The math was undeniable: The $250,000 cash delivery hadn't gone to a government official—it had been pocketed. Our client had been scammed by his own partner.

When we presented the evidence, the prosecutor saw the problem immediately. His only witness was the very man who had stolen the money. The case for bribery collapsed. At best, he could argue "intent to bribe," but even that looked flimsy with a tainted witness.

The result: The corporation was indicted and fined. Our client, who had braced himself for handcuffs, walked away clean.

Justice served—and another reminder that in federal court, the truth is often stranger than fiction.

CHAPTER FIFTY-SIX

I'VE OFTEN REFLECTED ON HOW DIFFERENTLY LARRY AND I had experienced the criminal justice system. My Chicago upbringing, in a family full of lawyers—including my uncle Harold, a renowned criminal defense attorney—meant I grew up on stories of corruption and shady deals. Later, in Washington, I encountered lawyers whose ethical "flexibility" was just as troubling.

Larry, by contrast, had been largely shielded from that world. One reason I chose to practice in Los Angeles was the prevailing culture of trust among federal court lawyers, where deals were often sealed with nothing more than a handshake. In all my years there, I never once encountered outright corruption. That's not to say there weren't bad actors. In addition to the occasional prosecutor who crossed the line, one successful civil litigator made a sport of sending letters that blatantly misrepresented our phone conversations. Every call was followed by one of his phony "summaries," forcing me to fire back with letters flat-out accusing him of lying. It was maddening.

Larry's education in hardball lawyering came in a drug case. We represented a mule—a low-level trafficker—who was ready to plead guilty in exchange for probation and testimony against the kingpin. Larry assured me the prosecutor in the Southern District of New York had agreed to the deal. Drawing on my own experience, I warned him: *Get it in writing.*

But Larry, confident in his charm, didn't. Sure enough, the prosecutor reneged, denying any agreement. Larry stormed into my office, enraged and on the verge of tears. Then his creativity kicked in. Right in front of me, he picked up the phone and told the prosecutor, "We just left being federal prosecutors, and I'm going to call in my cards. I'm going to call the attorney general, tell him I want to take a lie detector test, and demand that you do the same."

That ended it. Larry got the deal. Justice was served.

CHAPTER FIFTY-SEVEN

ANOTHER EXAMPLE OF OUR SYNERGY CAME IN A CASE that could have been pulled straight from a law school ethics exam. A Beverly Hills dentist walked into our office with a twenty-five-year problem: two sets of books. One showed his real income, the other the sanitized version sent to the IRS. For decades his trusted office manager had kept the system humming—until he fired her.

In retaliation she revealed she had copied both sets and now demanded $40,000, threatening to turn him in if he didn't pay.

It was a true conundrum. Ethically, we couldn't advise him to cover up a crime by giving in to extortion. Practically, paying rarely ends it—it usually emboldens the blackmailer. I thought of Sir Walter Scott's old line: "Oh, what a tangled web we weave when first we practice to deceive."

Larry and I debated the options for days. Finally, we turned to Henry Rossbacher, a federal prosecutor with a bulldog reputation. We'd faced him before and knew, beneath the toughness, he was fair. We laid out the situation carefully—without exposing more than necessary.

Henry listened, leaned back, and asked, "What do you want me to do?"

We had a proposal:

"Henry, we can all agree tax fraud is bad. But extortion is worse. How about this? Our client pays his taxes, cooperates, and wears a wire to pay her off. You prosecute her."

He agreed. The sting worked. The office manager was caught, convicted, and jailed for extortion.

Our client paid his back taxes and a fine.

Justice, in the end, was served.

CHAPTER FIFTY-EIGHT

OUR REPUTATION AS FORMER FEDERAL PROSECUTORS became the lifeblood of our defense practice. In 1975 George "Blackie" Dardeen, a legendary Las Vegas casino executive I'd met during the Frontier Hotel case, sent two new clients our way. Blackie always treated us generously (room, food, beverage . . . all comped) even though we weren't gamblers. This time, though, the gift wasn't a suite at the Desert Inn. It was a case that looked like a dead end.

Robert "Bobby" Huntley and Gibson "Stud" Hemphill had already been convicted in federal court in Wichita Falls, Texas, for a $96 million cotton-securities and check-kiting scheme that allegedly sank the First Bank of Vernon. They'd been sentenced to ten years in prison before I ever met them.

I took on their appeal, but the odds were grim: They'd waived a jury trial, the record was thin, and now the local prosecutor wanted to pile on state charges. To any layman this looked like "double jeopardy." But the Supreme Court says otherwise—under the doctrine of dual sovereignty, federal and state governments can each prosecute for the same conduct.

When I arrived in Wichita Falls to argue venue, the courthouse felt like something out of the Old West. At the clerk's desk, a man in a plaid shirt introduced himself as the judge. Every witness I'd subpoenaed—shopkeepers, barbers, local business owners—knew Bobby and Stud personally and blamed them for the bank's collapse. After a few rounds of this, the judge turned to the prosecutor and said, "Looks like we have no choice. I'm transferring this case to Fort Worth." A courthouse lynching was avoided, but the outlook was still bleak.

The new judge, Byron Matthews, was a former criminal defense lawyer with a sharp wit and an even sharper reputation for his personal life. (Legend had it that when his wife once caught him in bed with another woman, he said, "I'm warning you—next time you catch me like this, I'll divorce you!")

The trial itself went about as badly as expected. The prosecutor was determined to tack on another ten years. At one sidebar Judge Matthews warned me, "Mr. Rosenfield, you need to slow down. We don't speak that fast in Texas, and the court reporter can't keep up." I replied, "Your Honor, if I slow down, you'll know which pod the pea is under." The prosecutor scowled, but I caught the twinkle in the judge's eye.

Our one sliver of hope came from an unlikely source. Esther, whom I was dating at the time, sometimes attended the trial in her Delta stewardess uniform. She brought a flash of color into that dreary courtroom, and one juror clearly noticed. He stared a little too long, smiled a little too broadly, and even tried to strike up a conversation in the elevator. Esther, to her credit (as coached by me!), never said a word. Still, the way he looked at her told me everything: There was at least one sympathetic face on that jury.

When the verdict came down, there was one holdout for acquittal. It was him.

Rather than face a retrial, the prosecutor relented. With the judge's help, we negotiated guilty pleas with concurrent state sentences—no extra time beyond their federal term.

Justice was served. And maybe, just maybe, a little courtroom charm had made all the difference.

CHAPTER FIFTY-NINE

THERE WAS ONE OTHER MEMORABLE COURTROOM moment with Esther I'll never forget, and it came in the only traffic case I ever defended. I took it on out of pure principle.

One afternoon Esther swung by to pick me up in front of my office in Century City. She pulled across the street and stopped in a "No Stopping" zone. By the time I walked out, a police officer was already mid-ticket, writing her up for "Failure to Obey Signs"—a moving violation.

I pointed out, respectfully but firmly, that the car hadn't moved an inch. At most it was a parking infraction, not a moving violation. He didn't see the distinction and handed her the ticket anyway.

I told Esther we'd fight it. On the court date, Esther came straight from LAX in her Delta stewardess uniform and met me in West Los Angeles traffic court.

As I sat in the courtroom, I noticed it was packed with uniformed officers, all waiting for their cases to be called. When our turn came, as I laid out the facts to the judge, midway through my explanation, a murmur rose from the back row. The chant began: "Bad ticket . . . bad ticket . . ." Within seconds the entire gallery of officers had joined in. The judge, suppressing a grin, let the chant build before finally raising his hand.

"Well," he said, looking around the room, "it seems the jury has already reached a verdict. Case dismissed."

And that's how I preserved my perfect record in traffic court: one case, one win.

CHAPTER SIXTY

THAT TRAFFIC CASE WITH ESTHER WAS A FUN DISTRACTION. But my legal career was serious, and the case that changed my perspective—and set the course for my future—came in 1980, in federal court in San Francisco. I was defending Rudy Tham, a prominent Teamster leader accused of misusing union funds to entertain none other than "Jimmy the Weasel" Fratianno, a confessed mobster and star government witness.

I detailed earlier in this memoir how the prosecutor's misconduct, and the judge's refusal to curb it, planted the seed of my eventual decision to leave the practice of law. I won't repeat that moment here.

In the aftermath my cross-examination of Fratianno circulated nationally among defense lawyers bracing for the wave of cases in which he was expected to testify. That notoriety led directly to one of the most surreal chapters of my career.

Later that year the Justice Department unsealed an indictment against Aniello "Neil" Dellacroce—John Gotti's mentor and reputed underboss of the Gambino crime family. The charges were staggering: racketeering and ordering the murder of an FBI informant. But the government's real ambition was bigger.

For the first time, prosecutors set out to establish in court what law enforcement had long asserted but never tried to establish before a jury: that La Cosa Nostra was not a myth or a movie script but a national criminal empire, that the Gambino family was one of its most powerful clans, and that Dellacroce was the boss.

The case became front-page theater in Fort Lauderdale, where the case was tried. The newspapers splashed Dellacroce's name and face across their pages daily. The press painted him as a living archetype of the Mafia—ice cold, silent, a man whose presence alone carried menace.

One reporter even claimed that, sitting at the defense table, Dellacroce formed a pistol with his hand, pointed his finger at a witness, and pulled the imaginary trigger.

TIME magazine had recently anointed him as *capo di tutti capi*—the don of all dons. The FBI cast him as John Gotti's godfather, the true power behind the Gambino family.

This was no ordinary trial. It was theater, myth, and menace colliding—and the stakes were nothing less than proving the Mafia's very existence.

I was brought in to handle Fratianno, if he testified. He didn't, but I stayed on, quietly helping Dellacroce's Florida lawyer, who wasn't a seasoned criminal litigator. My role became that of strategist: drafting cross-examination questions, steering the defense behind the scenes.

Dellacroce himself was everything the rumors suggested—ice cold, polite but intimidating, carrying the gravity of a man who understood exactly how much power he wielded. But the case against him was astonishingly weak, perhaps the weakest federal case I had ever encountered.

The government's star witness was a convicted burglar, later memorably described by the judge as the leader of the "dinner-set burglars"—men who slipped into the second stories of South Florida mansions while the owners were being served on the main floors. He claimed that on a Monday in 1974, he overheard Dellacroce order the killing of an informant at Lanza's, an old-school Italian restaurant in Little Italy. His story was supposedly corroborated by his brother-in-law, also a convicted burglar—both of them hoping to shave time off their sentences.

The defense unraveled it quickly. The owner of Lanza's testified that the restaurant had been open since 1904 but never once opened on a Monday. Then came the knockout: Government records proved Dellacroce was in Atlanta federal prison at the time of the supposed meeting.

The jury hung, but Judge Norman Roettger—conservative and usually prosecution-friendly—granted a rare judgment of acquittal, ruling that the government's evidence was so weak, it left reasonable doubt as a matter of law. Later, he rebuked the prosecutors for wasting the court's time.

I hadn't played the lead, but Dellacroce—who was present at every strategy session—came to respect me. He listened carefully when I spoke, and I could sense he valued the perspective I brought. After the acquittal, he asked that I sit beside him at a celebratory dinner in a North Miami restaurant with reputed mob ties. Later, he even invited me to dine with him at Grotta Azzurra in Little Italy—his favorite haunt.

I never took him up on it.

Not long after, I declined an invitation to join the defense team of Frank "Funzi" Tieri, reputed boss of the Colombo family. Fratianno testified in that case, and Tieri was convicted.

I would defend anyone's rights in court—that was sacred—but after the Dellacroce case, I knew this was a world I would not enter again. Whatever power or legend swirled around those men, I closed that door forever and left those cases to others.

The postscript: In 1985 Dellacroce was indicted once more, this time in New York, in the famous Mafia Commission Trial. The government set its sights higher than ever, claiming "the Commission" was no myth but the secret ruling council of all five New York crime families. At the helm of the prosecution stood a young, ferocious crime buster named Rudy Giuliani.

The trial was a thunderclap. One by one the bosses of New York's families were convicted, each handed a one-hundred-year sentence—a collective death knell for an era. But Dellacroce never lived to hear his fate. Cancer took him before the gavel fell.

What followed belonged to legend. Just weeks later Paul Castellano—the Gambino boss in name—was cut down in a storm of bullets outside Sparks Steak House. He had been on his way to meet Dellacroce's son, reportedly to apologize for missing Neil's wake. According to testimony from Sammy "the Bull" Gravano, the ambush had been orchestrated—and silently witnessed from a nearby car—by John Gotti.

The whispers that followed gave it the air of destiny: Dellacroce had forbidden Gotti from striking Castellano while he lived. With Dellacroce gone, so, too, was the last barrier. The legend of the "Teflon Don" began.

By then I was thousands of miles away, already absorbed in the early days of CPK and happy to have left that world far behind.

CHAPTER SIXTY-ONE

OUR FINAL TRIAL—THE SWAN SONG—SET THE STAGE for our exit from the practice of law. It was the spring of 1984, and I once again found myself in San Francisco, entrenched for months in what would be our last courtroom battle.

Our client was James C. "Jay" Krosp, a successful Los Angeles businessman who owned a commodities trading firm. He was also a partner in a sprawling fifty-thousand-acre ranch in Elko, Nevada, with an associate named Richard "Rick" Waggoner. They shared offices in Los Angeles.

That was where the trouble began.

Waggoner was the architect of a sweeping commodities scam that siphoned millions from California investors. His playbook was classic boiler room fraud, wrapped in international jargon. He set up shell companies in Panama with names such as Currency Specialists Inc. and Systems Monetaire International, then placed newspaper ads: "$2,500 can return $6,500 in 90 days. Call Currency Specialists Inc."

When people called, they reached a boiler room full of slick-talking salesmen, fluent in fast promises and foreign currency—in deutsche marks, Swiss francs, dollars. It sounded sophisticated. It was all fiction. No trades. No profits. Just money disappearing offshore.

Eventually, prosecutors caught on. Waggoner and eleven others were indicted. By then Waggoner had fled to Panama. Extradited back to the United States, he pled guilty—and promptly blamed Krosp. According to Waggoner, Krosp had been the mastermind.

From the start, Krosp never wavered. Polished, steady, and almost unnervingly calm, he insisted on his innocence.

And that was when we stepped in.

My first move was procedural. I challenged a search that had violated attorney-client privilege, took it all the way to the state court of appeals, and won. That bought us time, but the government wasn't backing down.

They leaned on three witnesses. First was Waggoner, a desperate man with every incentive to shift blame. Second was Dr. Jones, a computer scientist who claimed she had worked with Krosp to design programming that enabled the fraud. The prosecutor never missed a chance to polish her credibility, repeating "Doctor" at every turn. Third was Murphy, a Los Angeles printer who said Krosp had ordered letterhead for Systems Monetaire International . . . and he produced a receipt.

We were confident we could convince a jury that Waggoner would say anything—lie, shift blame, even invent stories—if it meant saving his own skin. But Jones and Murphy were another matter.

Then we caught a break.

A potential defense witness, Dunlap (vice president at the firm), told us that Waggoner and Dr. Jones were romantically involved.

That opened the door.

If true, it meant that Dr. Jones had a personal motivation to protect Waggoner—perhaps even lie for him. That was something the jury had to hear.

We called Dunlap to the stand. At the end of my examination, I asked one final question: "Do you know whether Dr. Jones was sleeping with Rick Waggoner?"

A pause. "Yes."

"No further questions," I responded as I sat down.

The ripple through the jury box was palpable. But the real fireworks came when the prosecutor tried to rehabilitate her credibility—and ended up stumbling into the single most unintentionally comic courtroom exchange I ever witnessed.

The prosecutor, clearly rattled, rose like a wounded animal.

Prosecutor: "How do you know that Rick Waggoner was sleeping with Dr. Jones?"

Witness: "She led me to believe it."

Prosecutor: "Did you see them sleeping together?"

Witness: "No."

Prosecutor: "Did Rick Waggoner tell you that he was sleeping with Dr. Jones?"

Witness: "No."

Prosecutor: "Did Dr. Jones tell you that she was sleeping with Waggoner?"

Witness: "Not exactly, but she led me to believe it."

Prosecutor: "And how did she do that?"

Witness: "She came into the office one morning with burns on her elbows and knees. I asked what happened. She said she'd spent the night with Rick."

The courtroom went still. You could hear a pin drop.

But the prosecutor, oblivious, pressed on. You could see it in his face. He thought he'd found a gap.

Prosecutor: "Did you see any burns on her back?" he asked triumphantly.

Witness: "On her back? No. I couldn't see her back."

And then, convinced he'd trapped the witness, the prosecutor made the fatal mistake.

Prosecutor: "If you couldn't see her back, can you explain to the jury why, if Dr. Jones had burns on her elbows and knees, you believed she was sleeping with Rick Waggoner?"

Without missing a beat, the witness leaned into the mic and said, "Sure. They were doing it doggy style."

The courtroom exploded. Jurors were doubled over in laughter. The judge nearly toppled out of her chair. It took several long minutes to restore order. The only person *not* laughing was the prosecutor, who stood frozen at the lectern, shell-shocked, still not understanding what happened.

After the lunch recess, the court reporter—entirely on her own—handed us a printed transcript of the exchange. I was told it quickly made the rounds in legal offices across San Francisco. It became an instant classic.

With that Dr. Jones's credibility went up in smoke, right alongside Waggoner's. But we weren't out of the woods yet. Murphy, the printer, still loomed large.

He took the stand and seemed highly credible—clean cut, pleasant, the kind of witness jurors instinctively trust. He testified that Krosp personally came into his shop and ordered the stationery for the phony company. Then he produced the copy of the receipt he had handed over to the district attorney's investigator. To cap it off, he unhesitatingly pointed Krosp out in the courtroom. After that bit of theatrics, court adjourned for the day with our cross set for the next morning.

Krosp was unwavering. He insisted he'd never met Murphy and never touched System Monetaire International stationery. I believed him. But the obvious question nagged: Why would Murphy lie?

Back at Burton Goldberg's San Francisco home, where we were staying, the place looked like a war zone with papers and exhibits spread across every surface. I kept circling back to Murphy's receipt, the supposed smoking gun.

Then it hit me.

If you're running a scam through a fake Panamanian company, the last thing you want is a receipt. You'd pay cash and leave no trail.

And then I saw it: a subtle but telling detail. On all of Murphy's receipts, the top line was left blank. His handwriting always began on the second line. All of them, except one.

The Systems Monetaire International receipt.

There, the company name was handwritten neatly across the top line. It didn't fit the pattern. The more I studied it, the clearer it became. The receipt had been doctored *after the fact*, manufactured to satisfy the district attorney's investigator when he came knocking. A forgery meant to protect Murphy himself.

I told Larry, and we plotted our approach. In a perfect world, we'd confront Murphy in court and catch him off guard, and he'd crack, admitting to doctoring the document to save his own skin.

That was our hope. Still, it was a long shot.

We'd split trial duties, and Murphy was Larry's witness. Never in my career had I wanted to cross-examine a witness more than Murphy. But it was Larry's turn, and I trusted him completely.

What followed was as close to a *Perry Mason* moment as I've ever seen.

Larry, who is a large, imposing figure, walked toward the stand with quiet intensity, a stack of receipts in his hand.

"Mr. Murphy, do you see here that on all the receipts, the top line is blank . . . except one? The one from Systems Monetaire International?"

"Yes," Murphy muttered.

Larry pressed. "When the district attorney's investigator came to interview you, you were nervous—because you had been paid in cash?"

"Yes."

"You were worried they'd think you were part of the scheme, weren't you?"

"Yes."

"So you took a blank receipt from another job—one that had nothing to do with Systems Monetaire International—and you wrote the name in, to cover yourself."

Murphy looked down, almost with relief. "Yes."

Larry turned to the judge. "Your Honor, I believe this witness should be advised of his Fifth Amendment rights and given an opportunity to consult with counsel."

The judge nodded. "I agree. We'll recess."

That was the last anyone saw of Murphy. After consulting an attorney, he invoked the Fifth. His testimony was stricken. The prosecutor's star witness was gone.

Piece by piece, we had dismantled the case. And the finale was pure Rick-and-Larry synergy at work.

Still, you never know what a jury will do.

The jury stayed out for days of deliberation. We paced. And finally, the word came: hopelessly deadlocked. Most jurors favored acquittal.

The judge declared a mistrial. Soon after, the district attorney announced they would not retry.

That was it. Our swan song. When we returned to Los Angeles, we knew it was time. Time to stop grinding out cases and finally pursue our dreams. The rest is history.

CHAPTER SIXTY-TWO

EVERY STORY HAS A BEGINNING. LONG BEFORE California Pizza Kitchen, before Washington, DC, before the courtroom battles that shaped my adult life, there was Chicago. The place where it all began. The city that molded my instincts, my tastes, and many of the values I carried forward. But more than the city itself, it was my family—especially my father—who planted the seed for the person I would become. And then there were the friends—some lifelong—whose influence still echoes today.

While I've always thought of myself as a baby boomer—one of the post–World War II babies—I technically arrived just a bit early. I was born on May 21, 1945, exactly two weeks after Victory in Europe (VE) Day (when Germany surrendered to the Allies) and just months before Victory over Japan (VJ) Day (which brought the war to its final end).

It was a time of relief and celebration, especially for families like mine. All the men had served.

My father, Theodore ("Ted" or "Teddy" to friends) was a lawyer who'd enlisted in the navy after Pearl Harbor. He was pushed through the "ninety-day wonders" program, a crash course that produced officers at record speed. Commissioned as an ensign, he rose to lieutenant commander. In that position he commanded a merchant ship on Atlantic crossings and later a submarine chaser out of New Orleans. There weren't many subs in the Gulf, which left him time to explore the city and to fall in love with its cuisine. That passion for food, in turn, was passed down to my elder brother, Neal, and me.

His brother and law partner—one of three "Harolds" in the

family—also served as a lieutenant commander in the Pacific. The other Harolds were my mother's younger brother, Harold Iglow, and my aunt's husband, Harold Odell. Family gatherings later on could be confusing, but it gave "Harold" a certain mythic weight in our household.

My uncle Harold Iglow enlisted in the marines at nineteen and fought at Iwo Jima. He witnessed the iconic flag raising on Mount Suribachi—an image etched into American memory. Years later, after becoming a lawyer, he even represented Ira Hamilton Hayes, the Native American marine immortalized in that very photograph.

After the war my father and his brother returned to Chicago and their law practice, Rosenfield and Rosenfield. My dad specialized in personal injury (PI) law, a field often mocked as ambulance chasing. But he carried himself with pride. He genuinely loved connecting with people from every walk of life, treating each client with respect, regardless of background or status.

With some humility I'd like to believe those were qualities he passed on to me.

CHAPTER SIXTY-THREE

I GREW UP IN CHICAGO'S SOUTH SHORE NEIGHBORHOOD, just south of Hyde Park, home to the University of Chicago. The Obama Presidential Library now rises nearby in Jackson Park, where I often played golf as a kid on the municipal course. Years later Michelle Obama would grow up only three blocks from my childhood home and attend the same grammar school.

Looking back, my childhood in Chicago felt close to idyllic. My parents built our house at 7447 South Constance Avenue, two blocks from South Shore High School. It wasn't a mansion, but it had something most of my friends didn't: a backyard with real grass. That small patch of turf was enough to convince my close high school buddy, Larry Ellison—yes, *that* Larry Ellison, founder of the tech giant Oracle and now floating between first or second wealthiest person in the world—to anoint me the "rich" kid. Larry grew up nearby in a classic Chicago three-flat, with not a blade of grass in sight. On the South Side of Chicago, all it took to look like a Rockefeller was a lawn mower.

In truth our house was modest—a two-bedroom with maybe twenty-five hundred square feet. But my dad believed a lawyer should always drive a new Cadillac, and with that car parked out front and a patch of lawn in back, Larry thought I was living at Downton Abbey. He still teases me about it to this day, which is ironic considering he now treats Monopoly as real life, scooping up properties and dropping hotels like it's his personal game board.

Our house sat at the edge of the residential neighborhood, across from a fast-food hot dog stand that gave me my first job—and my first taste of the restaurant business. It didn't exactly spark a lifelong passion. I worked part-time while also juggling a newspaper route, which meant dragging myself out in the brutal early-morning cold to deliver papers up icy back stairwells. The pay wasn't much, but the lessons learned stuck. In the back of my mind, I quietly vowed that if life ever offered me a ticket out of winter, I'd take it. Spoiler: I did.

At the time South Shore was a predominantly white, middle-class neighborhood, and its high school ranked among the top ten public schools in the country. My classmates—girls and boys—were bright, focused, and often several steps ahead of me. If anyone believed back then that boys held some academic edge, they hadn't spent much time in our classrooms. South Shore also had a significant Jewish population at the time, and in Jewish culture, women were always respected for their intellect and strength. That was certainly true of the girls I knew.

Much has been written about the changes in South Shore, including Michelle Obama's reflections on "white flight" in her memoir *Becoming*. In 1960, when I was fifteen, the neighborhood was 89.6 percent white; by 1970 it was 70 percent Black. During my high school years, I saw the first signs of that shift as Black students began enrolling. Frankly, it wasn't something my friends or family discussed much. My parents didn't sell our home until 1969, well into the transition and long after I had moved out.

Years later, around 2005, I took Esther and our daughters, Nicole and Dana, back to South Constance to see the old house. We knocked, and the woman who answered told us she had bought it from my parents. She welcomed us in. What struck me most was how small the place felt. As a kid, it had seemed so much bigger—proof, I suppose, that childhood has a way of enlarging everything around you: spaces, experiences, even the people who fill them.

Over the years I've come to realize that being a South Sider isn't just about geography—it's an identity that stays with you for life. It's more than rooting for the White Sox and disliking the Cubs. It's a kind of quiet toughness, a pride in where you come from, and a deep appreciation for grit, loyalty, and authenticity. It shapes how you see the world—and how you move through it.

My father loved to cook, especially grilling outdoors whenever Chicago's famously unpredictable weather cooperated. His father had been a butcher by trade, so our meals were often what today would be called high protein: a steady rotation of steaks, chops, and roasts.

As for my early love of Chicago's iconic hot dogs, Polish sausage, and Italian beef, I'm not sure whether that came from my father, but it definitely ran in our family. Sunday nights were often reserved for Chinese food, sometimes in Chinatown, or my personal favorite: barbecued ribs at the Tropical Hut, better known as "T-Hut," in nearby Hyde Park. They're still my favorite indulgence. These days, though, I tend to make them myself, not slathered in sauce but prepared with a Tuscan rub of rosemary, sage, and fennel pollen.

In high school we'd drive to the Near North Side for deep-dish pizza at the legendary Pizzeria Due. At the time the farthest thing from my mind was that one day I'd take a classic Chicago dish like Chicken Vesuvio—with its crispy potatoes, rosemary, and garlic—and turn it into a pizza. Even more unlikely? That I'd eventually open a California Pizza Kitchen just up the street on Ohio Avenue.

My father wasn't content to limit our tastes to Chicago. His love for New Orleans cuisine, rooted in his wartime posting there, stayed with him. And he passed it on to us. He, my brother, and I would drive down to New Orleans and eat our way through its culinary landmarks: Antoine's, founded in 1840 and credited for inventing Oysters Rockefeller in 1899; Arnaud's, established in 1918; Galatoire's, serving French Creole cuisine on Bourbon Street since 1905; and Felix's Oyster Bar, first opened in the '40s. And of course, beignets and chicory coffee at Café du Monde, a New Orleans institution since 1862.

Our fishing trips to Florida always started with plans to reach the Keys but never made it past Miami. We always got happily sidetracked by the food. Dinners at Joe's Stone Crab, a Miami Beach icon since 1913 (and still a favorite of mine, along with its Las Vegas and Chicago outposts); milkshakes at the counter of the Fontainebleau Hotel; and overstuffed sandwiches at Wolfie's Delicatessen, a beloved fixture since 1943.

We may not have caught many fish, but we always came home full—if not from the sea, then certainly from the table. Looking back now, with the perspective of my own family, I can see what I didn't fully grasp then: Those trips were never really about fishing. They were about a father making time, creating memories, and forging a lasting bond with his sons—one delicious stop at a time.

And perhaps just as important, they planted the earliest seeds of a passion for food, for flavor, for the way meals could bring people together—a passion that would one day take root in a restaurant called California Pizza Kitchen.

My dad's law partner, his younger brother, Harold, was a striking figure: silver-haired, smooth talking, and endlessly charismatic. As a young lawyer, Uncle Harold had the rare privilege of working in the law office of Clarence Darrow, the legendary trial attorney renowned for defending the underdog and shaping American legal history. Darrow's stirring defense in the Scopes "Monkey Trial" even inspired Spencer Tracy's character in the Academy Award–winning film *Inherit the Wind.*

Later in his career, Harold served as president of the Chicago Criminal Defense Lawyers Association. Sadly, he passed away from cancer while I was still in law school. But before his death, he left an indelible mark on me, fostering my fascination with criminal law and setting me on the path that would carry me first to the Department of Justice as a federal prosecutor and eventually to the other side of the courtroom as a defense side attorney.

My dad, meanwhile, never lost his love of the navy. After the war, he stayed active in the naval reserves and rose to commander of his local VFW Post. What strikes me is how little my family spoke about their wartime experiences. Like so many of their generation, they carried the memories silently, shouldering the weight without complaint.

What he did pass down came in quieter ways. Years later, while researching his naval records, I came across a form that asked about his hobbies. His response stopped me cold and brought tears: "Boating, fishing, hunting, and golf." Reading that was chilling. I truly am my father's son!

My father remained a lifelong sailor, and we kept a boat moored at

Burnham Harbor just outside downtown Chicago, in the shadow of the Field Museum, the Shedd Aquarium, and the Adler Planetarium. In my mid-teen years, Dad became commodore of the yacht club, and I spent summers operating the club tender, ferrying boat members and their guests to and from their boat and later buzzing around in my own little speedboat.

My friends often joined me on Lake Michigan, including Larry Ellison—who got his very first taste of sailing aboard our thirty-foot sloop, the *Ann*, named after my mom. The *Ann* was hardly glamorous. Tubby, slow, more workhorse than racer, she planted a seed. Even then Larry had a need for speed.

First came *Sayonara*, a dominant maxi-class yacht that he shipped to Chicago in 1998 to win the Chicago to Mackinac Race and later sailed through and won the cyclone-ravaged Sydney to Hobart Race. From there the biggest stage of all: Oracle Team USA captured the America's Cup in the most dramatic comeback the race has ever seen—this time racing not sloops but sleek wing-sailed, hydrofoiling marvels. They weren't sailboats so much as something out of a sci-fi movie—machines that seemed to hover and fly, defying gravity as much as they defied tradition. Not a bad trajectory—from the *Ann* to the *America's Cup*.

Larry, a semester ahead of me in high school, was a fellow member of our fraternity, Tau Omega Mu ("Tommies"). He went "downstate" to the University of Illinois at Champaign-Urbana, where he joined Tau Epsilon Phi ("TEP"). When I enrolled there a semester later, Larry convinced me to join TEP as well.

Over the years Esther and I have been lucky to ride the wave of Larry's generosity. We've cheered at America's Cup races in New Zealand and Bermuda, sailed the world with his family and friends, and celebrated on the Hawaiian island of Lanai. (He now owns 98 percent of the island.) We've been captivated by the cherry blossoms in bloom in Woodside and sat courtside for top-tier tennis at Indian Wells. From growing up together in South Side Chicago to building Oracle and fueling groundbreaking medical research, what Larry's accomplished is nothing short of incredible.

What inspires me most isn't the wealth—though, admittedly, it does lend a certain credibility he didn't have when we were just a couple of South Side kids. It's Larry himself. Time with him is never ordinary. When he's holding court—expounding on whatever's captured his imagination, whether it's ancient history, his photographic recall of World War II (and everything else), the future of medicine, artificial intelligence, or geopolitics—I hang on every word.

He's not funny in the traditional, joke-telling sense. He doesn't tell jokes. But there's a humor that comes from the sheer scale of his vision and the audacity of how he sees the world. The way he connects dots, leaps from idea to idea, and says the most audacious things with absolute conviction. He's brilliant, and yes, funny. Not because he's trying to be but because no one else thinks, or talks, quite like he does.

Or perhaps there is someone who does. His best friend, Elon Musk—who, in a kind of cosmic rivalry, trades places with Larry as the richest person in the world. I've never met Musk, but when I see him on TV, there's something familiar—maybe the cadence of his voice, or simply the sheer scope of his vision. Like Larry, he has that restless drive to imagine what's next—and then make it real.

Perhaps both Larry and Elon were shaped by a line Jack Kennedy once quoted from George Bernard Shaw: "Some people see things as they are and say why. I dream things that never were and say why not." It may be the clearest summary of how they think and how they push the world forward—whether the rest of us are ready or not.

One anecdote that captures Larry perfectly was an hour-long interview he gave to Maria Bartiromo on Fox. It was thoughtful and revealing and, for anyone paying attention, a glimpse into the Larry I've been lucky to know throughout my entire life. Near the end she asked, "I hear you took out a four-billion-dollar loan." Larry corrected her: "It wasn't a four-billion-dollar loan—it was a four-billion-dollar line of credit. And there's a big difference." Then came the natural follow-up: "Why would you need a four-billion-dollar line of credit?" Larry's response? "In case I go shopping and find something I like." She pressed. "Like what?" He didn't hesitate: "The Lakers."

One more Larry story—too good to leave out. Years ago we were anchored off Capri aboard *Katana*, Larry's 243-foot megayacht. Moored nearby was Paul Allen's 200-foot yacht. *Meduse* was a beauty, a classic Feadship, cruising at twelve knots. But *Katana* was something else entirely—waterjets, twin five-thousand-horsepower diesels, and an eighteen-thousand-horsepower jet turbine. It could hit thirty-two knots, which, on a yacht that size, felt like liftoff.

We were mid-game on the aft deck, where Larry had installed a half court, shooting hoops, just like when we were kids, when *Meduse* began a leisurely dinner cruise. I could see the wheels turning in Larry's head as he paged the captain: "Nigel, we're going for a cruise. Fire up the turbine."

Minutes later, *Katana* tore past *Meduse*, sending up an eight-foot wake. As we turned hard, the swell rolled straight into *Meduse*'s aft deck—where Paul and his guests were calmly enjoying dinner. Plates—and probably tempers—went flying. Yes, it was a little childish. Would he do it today? Maybe not. But let's just say his boats have only gotten bigger and faster, throwing even bigger wakes.

Sometime later *Vanity Fair* was preparing a profile of Larry, and Oracle PR connected the reporter with me for background on his younger days. At the end of the interview, the journalist asked if I had anything colorful to add. I called Larry: "Should I tell him the Paul Allen story?" Without hesitation Larry said, "Absolutely." Naturally, the article opened with that story.

But before I move on, there's something more important. Beyond the headlines, the yachts, and the other trappings, Larry is—at his core—deeply philanthropic. He's donated hundreds of millions of dollars to transformative causes, including the Lawrence J. Ellison Institute at USC, and was among the first to sign the Giving Pledge with Gates, Buffett, and others committing to give away at least half his wealth. Knowing Larry, that pledge wasn't for show. It reflects something I've always seen in him: a belief in big ideas—and an even bigger desire to give back.

Now back to my family.

My father and uncle were both my dear friends and mentors. Sadly, both were taken too soon. My father had picked up smoking during the war, and by the time I was a boy, he was up to four packs a day. I remember visiting him at his office, where two or three cigarettes might be smoldering at once in various ashtrays.

When I was fourteen, a doctor bluntly told him he was killing himself. To his credit he quit cold turkey that very day. But the damage was done. While I was in law school, he was diagnosed with throat cancer and underwent a laryngectomy. Losing his voice was devastating, especially for a trial lawyer. The cancer later returned, and he passed away when I was just twenty-six. Still, he lived long enough to see my early successes in law, and I know how proud he was. I had also seen the grind of law frustrate him at times, which makes me think he would have been proud that I ultimately found success in business—building something of my own.

I never smoked. In fact my aversion to smoking made it an easy decision for us to make CPK the first national restaurant chain to ban smoking in 1991. My brother, for reasons I still don't fully understand, did smoke. Tragically, it was his undoing as well. He died of lung cancer at sixty-two, the same age as our father.

I wasn't as close to my mother. Severe asthma kept her from joining my father, brother, and me on our excursions. I had asthma, too, though not as bad. When I was nine, she and I spent a year alone in Tucson, Arizona, hoping the dry desert air would bring her relief. In 1954 Tucson was still a small desert town. We lived at the El Corral Motel, which had a kitchenette, and I went to school alongside barefoot Native American kids. That year gave me a lifelong love of the desert, especially the towering saguaro cacti.

My mother wasn't much of a cook, but she had a few specialties—her chocolate-swirl icebox cake log and twice-baked potatoes. More often, my brother and I survived on Swanson TV dinners, a staple I don't look back on fondly. In hindsight those aluminum trays filled with some indistinguishable gravy may have planted an early seed of my own interest in cooking, or at least my determination to avoid that kind of monotony.

What I remember most about my mother was warmth. She was loving, caring, and sensitive—always close with her friends, spending countless hours playing mah-jongg and canasta. In later years she took to bingo, and I marveled at her ability to juggle dozens of cards with laser focus.

When I was fourteen, she took my brother and me on an unforgettable road trip down Route 66 from Chicago to Los Angeles in her coral-colored Ford convertible. We stopped in Las Vegas, stood in awe at the Grand Canyon, and capped it off with a visit to Disneyland just four years after it opened. For two kids it was pure magic.

I remember visiting the original Hamburger Hamlet on the Sunset Strip and thinking, "Wow, that's a lot to pay for a hamburger." But something about it stuck. Years later, when we set out to create CPK, we modeled it in part on the Hamlet as a welcoming, family-friendly place that could be visited often and become part of the community fabric.

On that same trip, we spent time with my mother's brother Harold; his wife, Jean; and their three boys (Howie, Larry, and Robby). They had just moved from Chicago, and years later, when I was weighing a move to California, the knowledge that I had family there tipped the scales.

We turned the trip into a seven-thousand-mile cross-country adventure, looping back along the northern route. We were awed by Yellowstone's raw beauty, the eerie Badlands, and the chiseled grandeur of Mount Rushmore. It was a monumental experience—so much so that I repeated the route after my first year of college, this time behind the wheel of my mom's turquoise Chevy Nova.

My companions were two of my fraternity brothers: Alan Charles (who went on to become a distinguished professor and respected periodontist in Los Angeles) and Ken Adelman (who later made history as deputy ambassador to the UN and director of the US Arms Control and Disarmament Agency [ACDA]). Ken even accompanied President Reagan to the landmark Reykjavík summit with Gorbachev and later chronicled it in his remarkable book *Reagan at Reykjavik: Forty-Eight Hours That Ended the Cold War*.

Perhaps the highlight—other than Yellowstone, the Badlands, and Mount Rushmore—was our stop in Las Vegas. If memory serves me correctly, despite being underage, we may have managed a drink or two and pulled the handles on a few slot machines, all in the spirit of youthful adventure.

For all his political achievements, Ken's real stroke of genius was backing an old friend. He made a savvy early investment in CPK. Betting on pizza paid off. The returns funded a home remodel, which he commemorated with a custom CPK logo tile in the bathroom—a cheeky nod to the pizza that paid for it. History may remember him for helping end the Cold War. I'll always remember him for backing us when it counted.

Another tale from my friendship with Ken is just too good not to share. At the time of our travels, Ken was at Grinnell College, where he befriended Nordahl "Nord" Brue, a blond Iowa farm boy I met a few times. Nord was smart, charming, interested in politics, and if I recall correctly, president of the Young Republicans Club. I always assumed that he was destined for political office.

Years later, when Ken was running the US ACDA, he invited me to lunch at the Army and Navy Club and mentioned that Nord would be joining us. Naturally, I assumed that my old prediction had come true.

I arrived early and found another man waiting. He sported balding, light-brown hair—not the Nordic farm boy I remembered. He looked at me and said, "Rick?" I answered, "Nord?" We laughed and caught up before Ken arrived. As it turned out, Nord didn't go into politics. He became a lawyer and eventually the founder of Bruegger's Bagels, a clever play on his name.

We both laughed at the irony: An Iowa farm boy starting a bagel chain and a Jewish kid from Chicago starting a pizza chain? Life has a way of flipping expectations on their heads.

CHAPTER SIXTY-FOUR

BOATING AND GOLF WERE CLOSE TO HOME, BUT IT was my father who instilled in me a love of fishing. I still see him packing his little Johnson three-horsepower outboard motor into the trunk as we headed to the Fox River Chain of Lakes, casting for bass and crappie, while eating the corned beef sandwiches and potato salad he'd packed for us. Those early trips weren't about the fish. They were about time together.

As I grew, fishing widened my world. My father, brother, and I boarded float planes in Canada, sparking my later passion for flying, and chased sailfish in Florida and trout in the Ozarks. On one trip our guide was Forrest L. Wood, later the founder of Ranger Boats. After we capsized and lost my tackle box, Forrest went back, dove for it, and mailed it to me. That simple act told me everything I needed to know about his character.

Through law school, fishing became both work and play. While classmates clerked in law firms, I sold tackle, guns, and golf clubs in a sporting goods store.

Fishing was always more about the company than the catch. At Waterfall Lodge in Alaska with Steve Garvey, his father, and Larry, the highlight wasn't the monster halibut Steve's dad caught. It was Steve dismantling a cocky guest at the Ping-Pong table who hadn't factored in the hand-eye coordination of a ten-time MLB All-Star.

In Canada, Larry loved the fishing, but even more the shore lunches: walleye frying over an open fire, beans bubbling at the edge, guides keeping half an eye out for bears. And Larry, being Larry, was always suggesting new recipes to the guides who were simply carrying out a one-hundred-year-old tradition.

The true gift was sharing it with the people I loved: British Columbia for salmon with Garry Peters and wild steelhead with Mick Humphries; in Idaho with Marshall Geller at his award-winning Lodge at Palisades Creek; marlin in Cabo and bonefish in the Bahamas with Ian; and Wollaston Lake Lodge with Larry's stepson, Peter Gillette, Nick Coussoulis, the Rudins, and later, Jack Carr.

Jack—Navy SEAL turned number one *New York Times* bestselling author of *The Terminal List* and, as of now, seven top-selling sequels—became one of the most meaningful friendships of my later life.

We met fortuitously—another act of fate that's brought such good fortune into my later life. At the time he was the operations officer at the SEAL Base in Coronado—essentially the military equivalent of a company's chief operating officer. My friend Ric Kayne had recently met him on a charity pheasant hunt and invited him to a small luncheon that I was also attending.

Sitting across from Jack, I mentioned that I was getting back into firearms and hunting after a forty-year hiatus. I'd just bought my first long-distance target rifle but had never fired it. With the graciousness that defines him, Jack said, "When you get a chance, drive down to the SEAL Base. I'll show you around BUD/S, then take you out to my buddy's range and teach you how to shoot. When can you do that?"

I glanced at my watch and deadpanned, "Looks like it's too late for this afternoon."

Two weeks later I took him up on it. Jack gave me the full tour, then drove us an hour into the mountains to a deserted airstrip. There I was, getting rifle instruction from a Navy SEAL sniper. Lying in the dust beside me, he coached me through each shot, his calm voice slowing me down.

"Settle in. Breathe in . . . let it out slow. At the bottom of the breath, let it break." It was more than a shooting lesson—it was a glimpse into a world defined by precision and control.

Months later, with Jack at a Navy SEAL charity event in Half Moon Bay, California, I was seated beside a young SEAL in uniform. When I asked if he knew Jack previously, he said, "No, sir, I'd never met Commander Carr, but *everyone* knows who he is. He got all the lucky assignments."

I understood what "lucky" meant—it meant the toughest missions: Najaf and Ramadi—fighting door-to-door in brutal combat.

Jack remains somewhat an enigma to me—one of the kindest and most humble people I've ever met—with an insatiable curiosity. A devoted husband to his wife, Faith, and father of three, including a middle child with special needs, Jack retired after twenty years of service to provide for his family. Everyone he meets is struck by his quiet integrity and warmth.

Yet this same gentleman is a hardened, battle-tested war hero. Later, when I met his friend Matt Bissonette—a SEAL Team Six operator and hero of the Osama bin Laden raid, who chronicled the mission in *No Easy Day*, under the pseudonym Mark Owen—Jack's reputation was sealed. Matt put it simply: "I've never worked for a better officer—and he can be one badass." (Only recently has Matt gone public with his identity and image, which has long been concealed for obvious security concerns.)

I'm proud to have played an indirect role in helping Matt with a major health issue. During the bin Laden raid, when the first helicopter crashed in the courtyard, Matt's neck was broken. The navy offered only pain medication and no further treatment. By a stroke of fate, shortly after I met Jack, I introduced him to my brilliant neurosurgeon and friend, Dr. Robert Bray Jr.—a former air force major, surgeon, and world-renowned spine specialist. After Dr. Bray resolved a lingering neck problem for Jack, he, in turn, introduced Matt to "Rob" Bray. Rob stepped in without hesitation, performing the surgery that finally fixed Matt's injury—gratuitously and with great skill.

Today I have the privilege of serving alongside Jack and Matt—along with other distinguished members—on the honorary board of directors of Dr. Bray's nonprofit, Valor for Life. The organization with no-cost surgical spine care and treatment for post-traumatic stress disorder. The driving force behind this work is Dr. Bray himself. His willingness to donate his time, expertise, and the full resources of his state-of-the-art facilities is nothing short of remarkable. He brings to this mission not just surgical brilliance but heart—and the impact on these veterans' lives is immeasurable.

I'd be remiss, however, not to note—clearly on a far less important level—that Rob Bray has been expertly untangling my own spine problems for years.

Those early events led to a lasting friendship. A few years later, I returned the favor of the rifle instruction by taking Jack to Africa for an unforgettable plains game hunt to celebrate my seventieth birthday. Around the same time, I reconnected with Jon "JD" Dubin—my longtime friend and former Chicago prosecutor turned FBI SWAT team leader, and together—encouraged by Larry Ellison—we co-founded Pineapple Brothers on Lanai (pineapplebrothers.com). Soon, we added another brother, Frank LeCrone, a close friend of Jack's, now ours as well.

The island faced a quiet crisis: Axis deer, gifted to King Kamehameha in the nineteenth century, had multiplied unchecked, stripping vegetation and threatening the watershed. Hunting was part of the culture, but it needed management, not eradication. Pineapple Brothers became that balance: conservation, culture, and adventure coexisting. Lucky sportsmen (or sportswomen) can enjoy a one-of-a-kind experience, staying at one of Larry's two luxurious Four Seasons resorts—often with their families—while taking part in guided hunts across one of the most breathtaking settings in the world—all the while helping to preserve the island's delicate ecosystem.

For me though, it was also about the "Brothers"—JD, who once led FBI raids as the first man through the door; Jack, who served seven combat deployments, first as a SEAL sniper and later as a lieutenant commander and team leader; and Frank LeCrone, whom I've come to know as an astute businessman and a friend to all who meet him. Men who command respect among their peers.

In the end that's what Pineapple Brothers was about: friendship and trust. The name may say "Pineapple," but the best part has always been the "Brothers."

CHAPTER SIXTY-FIVE

FRANKLY, I DON'T RECALL MY FIRST COMMERCIAL flight—probably because it didn't happen until later in life. Growing up, we drove everywhere. Family trips usually meant fishing adventures with my father and brother or food pilgrimages to New Orleans. And of course, there was the unforgettable cross-country Route 66 adventure with my mother in her coral-colored Ford convertible. Flying simply wasn't part of our world.

My first memory of being airborne came on fishing trips to Lake of the Woods in Ontario, where we reached the lodge in rugged Beaver floatplanes. I was awed by the bush pilots, navigating unpredictable weather with steady, almost casual confidence.

The spark came later, thanks to my brother, Neal. On a visit to Chicago, he showed off his new pilot's license by flying us—quite nervously in my case—to lunch at the Playboy Club in Lake Geneva. I was impressed and more than a little jealous. Four months later, fueled as much by sibling rivalry as passion, I earned my private pilot certificate.

Once Larry and I launched our law practice, we bought a 1967 Beechcraft Bonanza V-tail, "the Rolls-Royce" of single-engine planes, fast and sleek but notorious as the "doctor and lawyer killer" for luring ambitious amateurs into trouble. I flew by the book and never forgot I had passengers—Larry and (later) Esther—trusting me with their lives.

Most flights were short hops to Vegas for clients, but flying soon became more than utility. After I met Esther—a Delta flight attendant based in New Orleans—my trips took on new flair. We met on October 28, 1974, just two days after her twenty-fifth birthday. That December, I mapped out a whirlwind: Fly solo to New Orleans to pick her up, enjoy the French Quarter, then on to Miami to see my client Bernie Rubin, and finally island-hop the Bahamas with Larry—Nassau, Abaco, Eleuthera. Unforgettable.

I eventually earned my instrument rating, but when CPK later acquired a corporate jet, I happily rode in the back. I loved flying, but I left the cockpit to the pros.

CHAPTER SIXTY-SIX

WILLIAM SHAKESPEARE FAMOUSLY WROTE IN *Henry VI, Part 2,* "The first thing we do, let's kill all the lawyers." Considering Larry's and my backgrounds, that feels a bit harsh—though I'll admit, I've come to understand the sentiment. We were lucky to escape the profession with our boots on. And I can't begin to count the number of lawyers over the years who've pulled me aside to say—only half joking—how jealous they were that we got out and made it big in the restaurant world.

Not all lawyers are created equal. Some stand out not only for their skill but for their character. One of them came into our lives during a tough chapter for CPK and has remained my close friend ever since.

We were managing the fallout from the recession when CPK became a target for a class action wage-and-hour lawsuit in San Diego. We had started with a respected Los Angeles firm, but after losing a critical motion, it became clear that we needed local firepower. I called Steve McCracken, general counsel of Callaway Golf, and asked who the best lawyer in San Diego was. Steve didn't hesitate: "Bob Brewer."

That was how we found Robert "Bob" Brewer, lead partner at Jones Day's San Diego office. His résumé was formidable: army airborne ranger in Vietnam, respected prosecutor in the US Attorney's Office in Los Angeles, and—more recently—inductee into the Army Ranger Hall of Fame.

The case itself was brutal, draining us in time and cost. At mediation the judge looked at Larry and me and said, "I think you're 100 percent right—on the law and on the facts. But you know what that means: You've got a 90 percent chance of winning before a jury." He wasn't wrong. We settled—for millions. To us it was a travesty of justice.

But the bright spot was Bob. He brought a steady hand, unshakable integrity, and quiet strength when we needed it most. Later, he returned to public service as US attorney for the Southern District of California, overseeing a vast region that included San Diego and the US–Mexico border.

And I can't mention Bob without also recognizing his wife, Irma Gonzalez. She made history as the first Latina to serve on the federal bench in San Diego, later becoming chief judge. Together, they embody public service at its best.

The case may have left us bitter, but meeting Bob Brewer was its silver lining. His friendship remains one of the most meaningful gifts to come out of that difficult chapter.

And to bring the story back to a lighter note: Bob later invited me, as Jones Day's guest, to the Masters Tournament in Augusta, Georgia—an experience that sits high on any golf fan's bucket list. Fifteen years later we still reconnect every spring during the tournament, always harkening back to that unforgettable trip.

Those moments with Bob reminded me of something I learned long before we ever opened our first restaurant: Relationships—real ones—are what carry you through. In law, in business, in life, it's the people you trust and respect who become your true compass.

CHAPTER SIXTY-SEVEN

WHILE I'VE BEEN SHARING STORIES ABOUT FISHING, hunting, flying, food, and friendships, golf has been something else entirely—not just a hobby but a meaningful part of my professional life as well.

I'm naturally left-handed, and I started playing at eleven, with my uncle's lefty clubs—until I realized, as in baseball, I was better swinging right-handed. By thirteen I'd switched, later captained my high school team, and even tried out for freshman squad at the University of Illinois. Technically, I think I made the team, though I may have ranked just above the mascot. It didn't take long to accept reality: Competitive golf wasn't in the cards. I shelved my clubs until long after law school, when the game found its way back into my life—this time in a big way.

I first crossed paths with Ely Callaway in the late '70s, soon after he'd founded Callaway Vineyards. Actually, he met Esther first—his philosophy was to hire attractive women as salespeople, and he tried (unsuccessfully) to charm her onto his team. Later, I did some minor legal work for him, for which he sent me a case of wine. Fair market value: about $100.

Years later, after selling the winery and launching Callaway Golf, Ely and I reconnected at the Vintage Club in the Palm Springs area. In 1994, not long after the company went public, he asked me to join the board. To me Ely wasn't just a visionary who revolutionized the game with the Big Bertha driver; he became a mentor and friend.

Serving on the Callaway board during Ely's leadership was a remarkable education and sometimes a source of perks. One story stands out. I was chair of the Compensation Committee when Ely presented a generous new proposal for himself and his team. I glanced at the numbers, then looked up, and said, deadpan, "Ely, I can't even look at these. There's something that's really been bothering me."

He looked surprised. "What's that, Rick?"

"Ely, every time someone hears I'm on the Callaway board, they assume I get my clubs for free. When I tell them I don't, they're stunned, and it makes Callaway look cheap."

Ely paused, then flashed that familiar gleam. "OK, Rick. Starting now, all independent directors get their clubs for free."

"Perfect," I replied. "And this compensation package? Totally reasonable."

And with that I haven't paid for a golf club since 1994—or a golf ball since the late '90s, when Callaway entered the ball business.

There were other perks too: Callaway Pro-Ams at Pebble Beach, a round at Spyglass Hill with Annika Sörenstam on the stormiest day I've ever played, and three appearances at AT&T Pro-Am—the crown jewel.

I've played with plenty of pros, but one experience stands out heads and tails: the day I played at Sherwood Country Club with my greatest sports hero, Arnold Palmer. (Sorry, Garvey!) Imagine the King himself leaning over my ball and saying, "Want me to read that putt for you, Rick?" Surreal! The capper came later, when he turned with that easy grin and asked, "Mind if I join you guys for a beer?" Not the drink that bears his name—half tea, half lemonade—but the real thing. A cold beer with Arnie. For me nothing topped that.

There was also the CPK connection that came full circle. At dinner with Swedish pro Niclas Fasth and his wife, Niclas asked what I did for a living. I told him I was co-founder of a restaurant chain. (Since Larry wasn't there, maybe I just said founder.) He asked which one. I said, "California Pizza Kitchen." Blank looks. Then I added, "We do things like Barbecue Chicken Pizza." Suddenly, they lit up. "You mean *CPK*! We go there all the time. We never knew it was called California Pizza Kitchen!"

After all that agonizing over the perfect name, what really traveled was the acronym. Which, truth be told, was the plan all along. CPK was the magic shorthand—and it worked.

But nothing prepared me for the events of 2001.

In April the phone rang. It was Ely's longtime assistant, Diane Duvall. Her voice carried an urgency I'd never heard before: "Ely wants to see you—immediately." I told her I was leaving with my family for Hawaii in two days. She paused, then called back: "Ely will send a jet for you tomorrow." That had never happened before. Until then I'd always just driven. Clearly, this was no casual meeting.

The next morning Ely met me at Palomar Airport, proudly behind the wheel of a Callaway Range Rover, his son Reeves's high-performance creation, as rare and distinctive as the man driving it. Over lunch at the Four Seasons, Ely, at eighty-one, looked sharp as ever. But his tone was serious.

I was then chairing the board's Management and Succession Planning Committee. Ely told me he planned to retire later that year and proposed Ron Drapeau, the manufacturing VP, as CEO. Then he fixed me with those piercing eyes and asked, "Would you do me the honor of succeeding me as chairman?"

Stunned and honored, I accepted immediately.

I left for Hawaii the next day, exhilarated. With tensions mounting at CPK, this felt like a new beginning—a way to step back from the drama and be active in another business I loved.

Then just before our return flight came the call I'll never forget. Steve McCracken, Callaway's counsel and friend, told me Ely had undergone gallbladder surgery. Doctors had discovered pancreatic cancer. I never saw or spoke to Ely again.

The board accelerated the plan. On May 15, 2001, they named Ron Drapeau president and CEO. Ely passed away on July 5.

By August the board convened to name a new chairman. I arrived, expecting Ely's wish—that I succeed him—to be honored. Instead, the ground shifted beneath me. Drapeau summoned me into his office and said flatly, "I know what Ely wanted, but I don't want you as chairman. You're too visible. I want to be chairman."

The words landed like a gut punch. Ely had looked me in the eye and entrusted me with the mantle. Drapeau knew it. And still, with pure hubris, he'd dismissed Ely's wish as if it had meant nothing.

At the time the Callaway board was impressive. Vernon Jordan, Ely's longtime friend, was a towering presence, both literally and figuratively. A confidant to presidents and a power broker in Washington, he was as famous for his counsel at the highest levels of government as he was infamous for helping Bill Clinton arrange Monica Lewinsky's move out of town. But the board also included powerhouses such as Tony Kobayashi, the seasoned Japanese businessman who chaired Fuji Xerox; Bill Baker, a hard-nosed entrepreneur from Orange County; and Ron Beard, the seasoned former chairman of Gibson, Dunn & Crutcher.

That night at the Four Seasons, over a quiet dinner with Ron Beard, Vernon Jordan strode up to our table, ready to make his move. He dropped the hammer: "You're lying about Ely asking you to be chairman. It's not going to happen."

I was floored. Vernon had been Ely's friend for decades, but in that moment, truth and loyalty gave way to raw politics—the kind of hardball, backroom maneuvering he was famous for. His tone wasn't debate; it was decree. He told us outright: He had Tony Kobayashi's vote, and he was backing Drapeau.

The math was clear. I had Baker and Beard. With my own vote, that made three. Jordan, Kobayashi, and Drapeau made three more. Deadlock.

From the moment Ely honored me as his successor, I had envisioned a seamless transition—an anointing with his blessing. Instead, it had turned into a knife fight. I wasn't about to fracture the board or drag Ron and Bill into open warfare. The next day I cast my vote—for Drapeau.

To paper over the betrayal, the board dreamed up a so-called solution: an "executive committee" with me as chairman. A token gesture. They even rewrote the press release to announce *Callaway Golf Elects Ron Drapeau Chairman of the Board; Rick Rosenfield Will Chair New Executive Committee.*

It read like parody. Who declares a chairman in one breath and in the next doles out a consolation prize? Everyone in that room knew what it was—crumbs. It did nothing to assuage me. I had been entrusted with Ely's legacy, and in the span of weeks, that promise was buried under backroom deals and ambition.

As for Drapeau, in that moment I saw him clearly, not as Ely's heir but as an opportunist, seizing his chance. He didn't inherit the mantle. He stole it.

I left that boardroom gutted, humiliated, and ready to walk away.

And then came John.

I had first met John Imlay of Atlanta by chance—a last-minute golf trip to Scotland when a mutual friend, Howard Smith, invited me to fill a slot. That one invitation sparked one of the most meaningful friendships of my life.

John was a technology pioneer, noted philanthropist, and partner in the Atlanta Falcons. In both American and Scottish golf circles, he was a legend—respected, generous, and connected to the game's most storied clubs: Muirfield, Troon, Prestwick, and the Royal and Ancient at St. Andrews. His estate, Westerdunes, looked out over the fairways of North Berwick, and over the years, I was fortunate to be his guest there many times.

After Ely's passing, I flew to Scotland and poured out my doubts. I was disillusioned, ready to quit the Callaway board, and unwilling to endure more politics. John listened quietly, his eyes steady, and then spoke with calm certainty: "You owe it to Ely to protect what he built."

That was it—no speeches, no drama. Just one sentence. But it carried more weight than all the boardroom maneuvering I'd just endured. Those words pulled me back from the brink. They reminded me that loyalty runs deeper than politics. And they kept me in the game, even when it meant sitting through the quietest, most frustrating years of my tenure.

"You owe it to Ely to protect what he built."

Those words echoed in my head long after that night at Westerdunes. They steadied me, even as I swallowed my pride and stayed on. I promised myself I'd give Drapeau a fair chance. So I went to the board meetings, sat quietly, and let the clock run. Just watching. Marking time. Waiting for the inevitable.

From the start I never believed Ron Drapeau had earned Ely's mantle. He wore the titles of CEO and chairman, but he lacked Ely's vision, his charisma, his instinct for the game. And truth be told, he pissed me off.

Still, I kept my head down, watching the cracks spread, waiting for the day the whole structure would give way.

The warning signs came early. In November 2001, just weeks after 9/11, Callaway hosted its top customers at the Pebble Beach Pro-Am—a moment that called for inspiration, reassurance, and joy. Instead, at the opening cocktails, Drapeau took the microphone and delivered a dirge. He spoke of how terrible the times were for the golf industry, how steep the challenges were, how grim the future looked. He was bleak and joyless, like a mortician presiding over a wake. The room froze. I was stunned.

The next morning my phone rang. It was Bruce Parker—Ely's first salesman, the marketing genius who'd helped build Callaway into a powerhouse. Bruce had been my early link into Callaway, and we had become close friends. He asked if I could meet him for breakfast, urgently.

When I arrived, Jim Thompson, president of Golfsmith, one of Callaway's biggest customers, was sitting with him.

Thompson didn't hold back: "What is this guy doing? We need Callaway to lead. We need a cheerleader—not a gravedigger."

Bruce nodded grimly. He was hearing the same from other customers.

Fellow board member Ron Beard and I carried those concerns straight to Drapeau. We told him in no uncertain terms that his message was alarming people at exactly the wrong moment.

Drapeau listened, nodded, and assured us he'd do better at the closing dinner.

I waited, hopeful. The setting couldn't have been more perfect—an elegant dining room overlooking Pebble's iconic fairways, guests relaxed, glasses raised. Then Drapeau took the mic again. And once again he sank the room into silence with the same bleak, tone-deaf speech.

Beard and I locked eyes across the table—stunned. We didn't need to say a word. We both knew.

This wasn't going to end well.

There was nothing I could do but bide my time. Three long years later, in August 2004, the inevitable happened. Drapeau resigned.

When the news broke, I thought back to John's words on that windswept night in Scotland. What he had offered wasn't just advice—it was prophecy. My role wasn't to win a power struggle or prove a point. It was to honor Ely, to safeguard what he had built, and to wait for time to deliver its own verdict.

Years later, at a social event, Vernon Jordan pulled Larry aside. "Tell Rick I'm sorry. He was right."

When Larry relayed the message, it didn't feel like vindication. It felt hollow. The bitterness came rushing back.

"No, Vernon," I thought. "It wasn't me who was right. It was Ely. Apologize to him." Too little. Too late.

Still, I stayed. Out of loyalty to Ely, I remained on the board until 2017 (twenty-three years in total).

Callaway Golf had its highs and lows, but Ely's philosophy always guided me. In his 2025 memoir, *The Unconquerable Game: My Life in Golf & Business*, he put it plainly: "The purpose of a board was not to run the company, but simply to choose the chief executive and to give him or her free rein to run the company as they see fit. Today, boards screw things up by harassing the executive and making his job six times harder than it needs to be."

Ely made his views clear to me early on. I agreed—with the caveat that a board must still meet its legal governance obligations. I'd like to think my conduct reflected his vision, which is part of why he honored me by asking me to succeed him as chairman.

I was fortunate to serve alongside an extraordinary group: Ron Beard of Gibson, Dunn & Crutcher; John Cushman of Cushman & Wakefield; Sam Armacost of Bank of America (and Augusta National member); Tony Thornley of Qualcomm; Bayo Ogunlesi of Credit Suisse First Boston; John Lundgren of Stanley Black & Decker; and most recently Linda Segre, a former golf pro and EVP of Diamond Foods. I was often in awe of them—but confident they respected me too. Like Ely, I had built a brand from scratch, and that perspective shaped my contributions.

After Ely's passing, the company struggled through a string of CEOs before finding exactly the right leader: Oliver G. "Chip" Brewer, whom we recruited from Adams Golf in 2012. He's been at the helm ever since, a steady hand and the best steward we could have hoped for.

I played a small role, but one of my contributions became something none of us could have imagined. Shortly before his passing, in his memoir, Ely reflected on the future with new innovations coming down the pike, specifically mentioning a trip Steve McCracken and I took to Watford, England, to scout a quirky new golf concept called Topgolf. At the time it was nothing more than a range with targets—a golf version of Skee-Ball—with microchipped balls and scoring screens. No food. No nightlife. But I told Ely I thought it had potential.

Callaway invested modestly at first. Then Topgolf exploded, evolving into full-scale entertainment venues and eventually eclipsing Callaway itself in scale. In 2020 Callaway acquired Topgolf outright for $2.6 billion, rebranding as Topgolf Callaway Brands.

That one hunch—just a passing instinct at the time—became part of Callaway's future in a way none of us could have predicted. I like to think it would have brought that familiar gleam to Ely's eye.

I retired from the board in 2017 as the longest-serving director in the company's history. And when I finally stepped down, it wasn't easy. But Chip and the board honored me by naming me director emeritus. That meant something then. It still does.

Yet with golf—as with fishing—the greatest moments were never about the score. They circled around the friendships. At Riviera there were the regular rounds with Ralph Rudin, Michael Smith and Howard Smith, Gary Lieberthal, and Peter Neuwirth—highlighted by Ralph's unforgettable eagle at the notoriously tough second hole, and my own at the famous short tenth. And then there was the day I brought my friend Thomas Keller as my guest. Word spread quickly through the clubhouse, and even at "Riv," long known as a celebrity hangout, heads turned.

In Scotland I played alternate shot with my host, John Imlay, and Dr. Bobby Kaufmann, when John leaned over just before I teed off on Muirfield's bunker-lined thirteenth hole and whispered, "Just don't leave me in a bunker." Thankfully, I didn't.

At the Vintage Club, camaraderie came with friends, including Dennis Beck, Tony Esernia, Norman Schultz, and Mickey Targoff—along with two wonderful friends we lost—Tony Terlato and Dr. Tom Lombardo.

At Stone Eagle, Nick Coussoulis routinely shot under his age—an achievement that never stopped amazing me. And through Ric Kayne, I had the privilege of playing his spectacular course in New Zealand, Tara Iti, which may be the most beautiful track I've ever walked and astonishingly instantly ranked among the world's best—almost unheard of for a new course.

Since then Ric has added two more world-ranked layouts—quite the feat.

At Hillcrest I played often with Gary Freedman and leaned on the steady guidance of my teaching pro, Ron Skayhan. I often teamed up in tournaments with my friend Steve Garvey and his son—and my godson—Ryan. Ryan's three-hundred-yard drives were awe-inspiring, but my favorite moment came in a member-guest tournament, when Steve saved par by muscling a driver out of a steep greenside bunker lip on a par three, leaving our opponents astounded.

That brings me to another cherished connection: my goddaughter, Olivia Garvey, who honored me by asking me to sing recently during her wedding ceremony. Singing has been a lifelong passion, dating back to my professional training as a teenager. Over the years, other than in the shower, I've saved my voice mostly for personal occasions—weddings, bar and bat mitzvahs, or the occasional karaoke night (where my family insists, I keep it to one song). My greatest thrill came in Sicily, when I sang at my daughter Dana's wedding—though holding back tears nearly cost me the high notes. Next up, I'm bracing myself for a Garvey family reprise at my godson Sean's wedding in Chicago. At least this time, I'll be smart enough to pack tissues along with the sheet music.

Beyond golf and fishing, I'd be remiss not to thank Nick Coussoulis for welcoming me into his eight-member duck-hunting club at the Salton Sea near Palm Springs. Hunting there with Nick, Marty Davis, and golf legend Dave Stockton (once the game's most feared putter and now every bit as deadly in a duck blind)—where the biggest concern was sunburn—was a world away from my childhood days with my father, shivering on the frozen banks of Southern Illinois rivers. The chance to also share those hunts and the camaraderie of the outdoors with my dear friends

Chris Cox, David Lehman, Andrew Kline, and Michael Walsh, and with American war heroes Navy SEAL Lieutenant Commander Jack Carr and Marine Special Operator Billy Birdzell, was a gift I will treasure for life.

CHAPTER SIXTY-EIGHT

COMING FULL CIRCLE, I REALIZE THAT ALL MY PASTIMES— fishing, golf, hunting, even cooking—aside from flying—were passed down by my father. Over time I saw how much I had become his son. It wasn't just about the activities—it was about connection.

The most meaningful bonds in my life were forged in those simple spaces: casting a line with my son, walking a golf course with friends, hunting in the field, or sharing a meal with people I loved. What mattered wasn't the fish or the scorecard; it was the conversations, the silence, the laughter, the easy companionship. Those moments endured long after the rest faded.

With my daughters, Nicole and Dana, the bond wasn't built around sports but through travel and everyday life. And always—at the center of it all—was Esther. She didn't just share the journeys—she made them. Together, we explored France, Hawaii, Italy, and beyond. Dana's wedding to Ryan Jackson-Healy in Sicily, a moving tribute to Esther's heritage, remains one of the most beautiful milestones in our family's story.

But one memory stands apart, etched in my mind for very different reasons.

In December 2004 Esther and I set out for Phuket with our daughters. We spent our days exploring beaches and nearby islands. On our last morning, Esther had planned a full itinerary: canoeing through sea caves, then a jungle trek with elephants, and finally a Thai cooking class. As usual, the girls were running late. That small delay forced us to skip the canoe trip and head straight to the mountains.

Around 9:00 a.m., as Esther and I rode together on an elephant, something strange happened. Without warning the elephant veered off the trail and marched down the mountainside, away from the others. When it finally stopped, we looked up to see our daughters far above us. The mahout said nothing.

What we didn't know—what no one knew—was that at that exact moment, the Indian Ocean tsunami was slamming into Phuket.

Later, we learned that a French family, scheduled for the same canoe trip we had missed, had been swept into the sea. Miraculously, they'd survived. Back at the hotel, the scale of the devastation became clear. The news was harrowing, but what struck me most was the quiet courage of the Thai people. Despite their own losses, they showed up for their guests—with grace, calm, and compassion.

The next morning at the airport, I witnessed a scene I'll never forget: travelers wrapped in hotel towels, boarding planes with no luggage or passports. Photos of missing loved ones taped to the walls. Families wheeled through the terminal in stunned silence.

I didn't sleep for weeks. The images wouldn't leave me. That day seared into me life's fragility and the truth that sometimes survival is nothing more than chance.

What I've learned is this: Life can turn in an instant. Sometimes with joy, sometimes with tragedy, sometimes with the sheer luck of being spared. What endures are not the businesses built, the titles held, or even the crises survived but the people who walk beside you through it all.

For me that has always been Esther (the love of my life), Ian (now a devoted father to two boys, Largo and Laird), Nicole and Dana (principled, brilliant, strong women who make us proud every day), and the friends who became chosen family.

Looking back, I see that the memories—whether in Phuket, Sicily, or a fishing lodge in Canada—were never the point. They were the backdrop. The real story was always the people.

That's what grounded me then. That's what still does.

If there's one thing I hope you carry from my story, it's this: The true measure of a life isn't in the successes or its struggles. It's in the love and laughter you share along the way.

AFTERWORD

WHEN RICK TOLD ME HE WAS WRITING THIS BOOK, I wasn't surprised. He was always the writer. Always the storyteller. Even in the middle of building a business at full speed, he had a way of seeing the larger narrative taking shape—understanding how individual moments fit into something bigger.

What did surprise me, as I read these pages, was just how precisely he captured what we lived through.

The events. The decisions. The tension. The moments of doubt and conviction. The way partnership actually works—not in theory but under pressure. Again and again I found myself thinking, "Yes, that's exactly how it happened. Not just what we did but how it felt to do it."

Rick captures especially well something that's difficult to explain from the outside: the unique synergy we shared. From the beginning our partnership was never a simple division of labor. Ideas built on ideas. The push and pull made the work stronger. We used to say—only half jokingly—that one plus one didn't equal two. It equaled three. Something larger emerged when we worked together than either of us could have created alone.

What makes this all the more remarkable is that Rick didn't rely on notes or a diary to tell this story. There were none. We were too busy moving forward—solving problems, taking risks, building something we believed in. Rick relied instead on memory and instinct. But that, too, makes sense. He always had a way of holding the story in his head, even while living it.

From the decision to leave the law to the risks we took together to the culture we tried—sometimes imperfectly—to build, this book reflects the truth of that journey. It doesn't smooth the edges or rewrite history. It tells it straight.

I'm grateful Rick chose to tell this story, and I'm proud of how he told it. What we built together was real, complicated, and meaningful—and this book captures it with honesty and clarity.

—LARRY FLAX
Co-founder, California Pizza Kitchen

ACKNOWLEDGMENTS

THIS BOOK TELLS MY STORY, BUT IT EXISTS BECAUSE OF the people who stood beside me—often quietly—through decades of risk, reinvention, and growth.

First and always, my deepest gratitude is to Esther, my partner in every sense of the word. From the earliest days of California Pizza Kitchen, she was not only my wife but a steady force of judgment, warmth, and perspective. CPK would not exist without her, and neither would this book.

To Larry Flax—my co-founder, law partner, and friend—our journey from federal prosecutors to restaurateurs was improbable, intense, and unforgettable. We challenged each other constantly, trusted each other implicitly, and built something far bigger than either of us imagined. Whatever success followed began with that partnership.

On the writing side, I owe special thanks to Julie Cantrell, whose editorial guidance, discipline, and encouragement helped turn memory into narrative—and to everyone who pushed me to be more honest, clearer, and braver on the page.

Also, special thanks to Lisa Pennington. She served Larry and me as our executive assistant with extraordinary loyalty and professionalism and has continued, seamlessly and selflessly, to support each successive CEO. Few have contributed more consistently—or more quietly—to the continuity and culture of CPK.

I am grateful as well to the board members and advisers who challenged our thinking, supported bold decisions, and, at times, forced difficult but necessary change. The lessons—both positive and painful—shaped not only CPK, but me.

To the original twenty-two investors who believed in two former prosecutors with a radical idea—and to the thousands who followed before and after we went public—thank you for sharing our vision.

California Pizza Kitchen was built by people—talented, committed individuals who believed in a vision long before it was proven. I owe an enormous debt to the long-tenured leaders and team members who formed the backbone of the company through its growth and global expansion. Many of you appear in these pages; many worked just as hard behind the scenes. Your contributions mattered deeply.

It is with humility—and some inevitable risk—that I name a number of those who stand out in my memory. There were thousands of devoted ROCKstars who carried this brand forward. Perfect completeness is impossible. But gratitude deserves specificity.

From the early days: John Kaufman, Philip Gay, Don Fitzgerald, Tom Beck, John Shambra, Rick DeMarco, Louis Graffeo, Tim Acquino, Trace Lankford, Geri Wise, Doug Middleton, Fred Morgan, John Blake, Barry Gilmartin, Joel Mayer, Denise Diamond, Dawn Watson, Anna Perkins, Tony Shizuru, Gabe Sinohuiz, and Debra Kohklin.

Vice presidents: Brian McCarthy, Fred Morgan, Rico Cuomo, Kenny Hom, Clint Coleman, Carlos Delgado, Tim Gleeson, Bob Dowling, Peter Gillette, Rudy Sugueti, Don Watson, Eric Stenta, Brad Gramlich, Edie Ames, Chris Ames, Jim Rich, and Sue Collyns, our CFO, COO and EVP.

Directors: Bill Blodgett, Leslie Williams, Melissa Myers, Pat Ellis, Phil Mastrionni, Brian Fowkes, Rocio Arroyo, Jim Austin, Matt Druliner, Luis Zuniga, Doug Hanna, Mark Fenton, Marcie Book, Peter Pirozzi, Mark Poplawski, Bill Snodgrass, Mark Dion, Eric Stewart, Ken Borsuk, April Carr, Tim Elkins, Eddie Spencer, Dave Dwyer, Doug Djordjevic, Art Arcevedo, Tom Delsecki, Jim Weiland, Kevin Jarvis, Bill Widmer, Chris Huynh, Doug Doyle, Jesse Legasppy, Brian Lester, Doug Boyer, Jesse Arriola, Amy Rodman (Hom), Kevin Gadberry, Nancy Mote, Ray Chouinard, Bill Long, and Chris Hedges.

Culinary Team: Gary Beauregard, Brian Sullivan, Paul Pszybylski, Roy Alamillo, Juan Borrayo, Celestino Flores, Marvin Alvarado, Celestino Lara Flores, Ricky Hernandez, and Ray Chouinard.

My thanks also extend to the chefs, managers, servers, restaurant support teams, and staff across the CPK system who brought energy, pride, and heart to the restaurants every day. You were the face of the brand long before it became a brand.

There is another group whose belief in us deserves special recognition—those who supported our later ventures, Bottlefish and ROCA Pizza. Entrepreneurship carries risk, and not every vision reaches its intended destination. Esther and I remain deeply grateful to those who stood with us in those chapters, offering confidence, partnership, and friendship even though the outcome did not unfold as we had hoped. In honoring your privacy, we won't list your names, but be assured that your faith in us was never taken lightly, and it remains deeply appreciated.

In memory of Ed LaDou, whose early culinary contributions—including the creation of Barbecue Chicken Pizza—left a lasting mark on our story.

And in memory of the original ROCKstar, Julie Carruthers, whose spirit and leadership helped define the culture we were so proud to build.

To Ohad Yosef, executive chef at our later ventures, who poured out his heart, talent, and passion every single day.

Finally, to my children—Nicole, Ian, and Dana—thank you for your patience, perspective, and love. You grew up alongside this company, shared in its chaos and triumphs, and kept me grounded when the stakes felt overwhelming. Any success was meaningful only because of you.

This book reflects a lifetime of experiences, but in many ways, it belongs to all of you.

ABOUT THE AUTHOR

RICK ROSENFIELD is a former federal prosecutor and defense attorney. He is the co-founder of California Pizza Kitchen, the restaurant brand that helped redefine how America eats pizza and reshaped modern casual dining.

Before entering the restaurant business, Rosenfield began his legal career at the US Department of Justice in Washington, DC, where he worked on cases before the US Supreme Court and the US Courts of Appeals. He later served as an assistant US attorney in Los Angeles, prosecuting major criminal cases, including organized crime matters, before transitioning into private practice representing high-profile clients.

In 1985, Rosenfield and his partner, Larry Flax, made the unconventional decision to leave the law field and open the first California Pizza Kitchen in Beverly Hills. What began as a single restaurant grew into a global brand while maintaining a distinctive culinary vision and culture.

Rosenfield lives in Palm Beach, Florida, with his wife, Esther. They have three children and two grandchildren.

CONNECT WITH RICK AND JOIN THE CONVERSATION ON LINKEDIN

in /RICKROSENFIELD